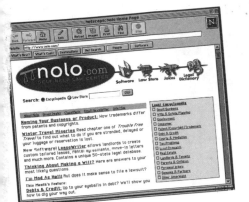

4TH NATIONAL EDITION

Sexual Harassment on the Job

✓ **WHAT IT IS &**
✓ **HOW TO STOP IT**

BY ATTORNEYS WILLIAM PETROCELLI & BARBARA KATE REPA

nolo

KEEPING UP-TO-DATE

To keep its books up-to-date, Nolo issues new printings and new editions periodically. New printings reflect minor legal changes and technical corrections. New editions contain major legal changes, major text additions or major reorganizations. To find out if a later printing or edition of any Nolo book is available, call Nolo at 510-549-1976 or check our website at www.nolo.com.

To stay current, follow the "Update" service at our website at www.nolo.com. In another effort to help you use Nolo's latest materials, we offer a 35% discount off the purchase of the new edition of your Nolo book when you turn in the cover of an earlier edition. (See the "Special Upgrade Offer" in the back of the book.) This book was last revised in: **January 1999**

FOURTH EDITION	JANUARY 1999
Editors	RALPH WARNER
	MARCIA STEWART
Book Design	JACKIE MANCUSO
Cover Design	TONI IHARA
Index	SAYRE VAN YOUNG
Production	AMY IHARA
Proofreading	SHERYL ROSE
Printing	BERTELSMANN INDUSTRY SERVICES, INC.

Petrocelli, William.
    Sexual harassment on the job : what it is & how to stop it / by
William Petrocelli and Barbara Kate Repa -- 4th national ed.
        p. cm.
    Includes index.
    ISBN 0-87337-484-3
    1. Sexual harassment of women--Law and legislation--United States-
-Popular works. I. Repa, Barbara Kate. II. Title.
KF3467.Z9P47 1998
344.7301'4133--dc21   98-24164
                                              CIP

For information on bulk purchases or corporate premium sales, please contact the Special Sales department. For academic sales or textbook adoptions, ask for Academic Sales. Call 800-955-4775 or write to Nolo at 950 Parker St., Berkeley, CA, 94710.

Acknowledgments

Many people worked hard and fast to help make this book possible. We owe special thanks to:

Lisa Guerin, for her unflinching and good-humored assistance in research and writing during the first edition,

Our editors, Jake Warner and Marcia Stewart, whose ever-ready pens, ever-probing minds and energy kept us going,

Jackie Mancuso and Michelle Duvall for a highly elegant book design,

Stan Jacobsen, for ferreting out names and numbers—and supplying a bottomless batch of lemon drops, and

Beth Laurence, who single-cursoredly updated Chapter 7 for the third edition.

And our thanks to the many others who contributed their time and special expertise, including:

Beth Behner of the Anchorage Equal Rights Commission, Trisha Brinkman of Brinkman & Associates, Attorney John Erickson, Psychotherapist Elizabeth Evans, Ron Glover of Digital Equipment Corporation, Barbara Jerich of Honeywell, inc., Sharon Kinsella of 9to5, Attorney John McGuinn, Attorney Margaret Murray, Sharon Nelson of Women Employed Institute, Attorney Wayne Outten, Sandy Pope of the Coalition of Labor Union Women, Attorney Kenneth Pratt, Vera Repa, Rita Risser of Employment Law Specialists, Jane Walstedt of the Women's Bureau of the U.S. Department of Labor, Brian L.P. Zevnik of the Alexander Hamilton Institute, Inc.

Contents

4

WORKPLACE POLICIES AND PROGRAMS

5

A LOOK AT THE LEGAL REMEDIES

6

THE EEOC AND THE U.S. CIVIL RIGHTS ACT

7

STATE FAIR EMPLOYMENT PRACTICES LAWS

8 COMMON LAW TORT ACTIONS

9 LAWYERS AND LEGAL RESEARCH

APPENDIX

INDEX

Foreword

STRIKING A NERVE

Sexual harassment on the job took a dramatic leap into public awareness in October 1991, when Professor Anita Hill's charges against Judge Clarence Thomas became known after his nomination to the United States Supreme Court. When the U.S. Senate—98% of it men—appeared ready to confirm Thomas without airing the charges, an outpouring of protest from American women stopped the proceeding in its tracks and forced a public hearing. The ensuing days of revelations and testimony, charges and countercharges, played in front of a massive television audience that seemed mesmerized. And the spectacle was even more dramatic because the charges were leveled at the man who had been responsible for enforcing the laws against sexual harassment.

Suddenly, sexual harassment was featured on every talk show and debated in every workplace in America. Within a few days, the number of sexual harassment complaints filed with government agencies quadrupled. Well over one-half of the working women in America, according to public opinion polls, said they had been sexually harassed at some time during their careers. Female reporters, commentators and witnesses on both sides of the hearing began discussing the sexual harassment that they had suffered. A great many working women who had suffered silently from sexual harassment began to speak out. It was one of those rare moments in American history when a simmering major issue boiled to the surface of public consciousness.

The laws against sexual harassment are today an established part of American law. In recent cases in which the U.S. Supreme Court has addressed the issue of sexual harassment on the job, it has given a strong endorsement to the laws prohibiting it and to the need to protect all workers from an intimidating, hostile or offensive working environment.

A SNAPSHOT OF A MOVING PICTURE

This book explains what sexual harassment is and what you can do about it. We've attempted to explain the laws that prohibit sexual harassment on the job and to show you what you can do to assert your rights under those laws.

Today, in theory at least, laws protect against most workplace harassment. But don't expect your rights to be easily vindicated. In practice, sexual harassment laws are fraught with problems of interpretation, enforcement and inadequacy. Many of these problems are the result of an underfunded legal apparatus overstretched to cope with a growing problem. Other problems reflect serious rear-guard efforts to slow the thrust of social change.

Sexual harassment is a new area of law full of rough edges, anomalies and uncertainties. It yields less to logic and orderly development than it does to political pressure and counterpressure. The law against sexual harassment looks nothing at all like it did five years ago—and it will look entirely different five years, or even one year, from now.

What we are giving you is a snapshot of a moving picture.

TAKING CHARGE OF THE FUTURE

After talking with many women about sexual harassment, several things became clear: Women simply want to be left alone in the workplace to do their jobs. Women don't want to use the law to gain an advantage, to get revenge or to put themselves in positions of power. In virtually every case in which a woman has turned to the courts for help, she has done so in desperation after other efforts to solve the problem have failed.

We have premised this book on the assumption that working women want to use all available resources to persuade their employers and co-workers to end sexual harassment. Much of what we discuss is preventive—things a woman can do on her own, or together with other women and sympathetic men, to change their workplaces.

We realize that men are sometimes harassed as well. But the problem is intricately linked to the larger problem of sexism in America and the unresolved power relationships between the genders. This has proven to be one of the more intractable problems of human history.

One hopeful thought: Sexual harassment on the job is deliberate, learned behavior; it can be unlearned. The relearning process may be difficult in many cases and efforts at change often are slow to yield results. But it's something that can—and should—be done.

We hope this book helps.

■ ■ ■

1

Background, Causes and Effects

A. DEFINING SEXUAL HARASSMENT

In legal terms, sexual harassment is any unwelcome sexual advance or conduct on the job that creates an intimidating, hostile or offensive working environment.

That's a shorthand version of the definition used by the federal government and most states. But it's not necessary to couch the problem in legalisms. Simply put, sexual harassment is any offensive conduct related to an employee's gender that a reasonable woman or man should not have to endure.

1. The range of behavior

Critics of sexual harassment laws always focus on cases that they consider to be the most trivial, while those who have suffered harassment usually are talking about something far more serious.

While it is essential to distinguish the severity of the offensive behavior, it is still important to remember that sexual harassment can take a wide variety of forms. An employee who has been led to believe she must sleep with her boss to keep her job has been sexually harassed, as has one whose co-workers regularly tell offensive, sex-related jokes and plaster their walls with pictures of nude women. An employee who is pinched or fondled against her will by a co-worker has been sexually harassed, as has one whose colleagues leer at her, block her path or act like they're going to grab her.

An employee who is constantly belittled and referred to by sexist or demeaning names has been sexually harassed, as has one who is subjected to repeated lewd or pornographic remarks. Sexual harassment occurs when a supervisor acts as if the women working under him owe him sexual favors, and it also occurs when a co-worker attacks or intimidates a woman because he doesn't think she should be doing what he considers Man's Work.

Although it is usually men who sexually harass women on the job, such harassment can be inflicted by women against men, by women against women, and by men against men. Hostility based on gender is the test, rather than the gender of those involved.

The forms that sexual harassment can take are as varied as a perverse imagination can create. They range from offensive sexual innuendoes to physical encounters, from misogynist humor to rape. The offending behavior occasionally derives from an excess of sexual desire by the harasser, but most often it is motivated by fear, power or hate.

Most cases of sexual harassment are never reported, because the harassed employees are either too degraded, too uncertain of their rights and options or too fearful of retaliation to do anything about it. However, thousands of harassment claims have been filed through government agencies and company complaint procedures—and there is no evidence that any of them were faked or brought for revenge or spite.

While relatively few cases have gone all the way through a court hearing, those that have reveal a wide variety of harassing activity:

- Female office workers at AT&T Technologies in North Carolina who were "rated" by male employees as they passed the men's desks, followed by lascivious comments about their hips and breasts. (*Wall v. AT&T Tech.*, 754 F. Supp. 1084 (M.D.N.C. 1990).)

- Women who were subjected to a dress code by their supervisor, established by him specifically so he could admire their legs. (*Dias v. Sky Chefs*, 919 F. 2d 1370 (9th Cir. 1990).)

- An administrative sales assistant whose co-worker repeatedly requested that she wear revealing clothing—and commented frequently on her figure. (*Hrabak v. Marquip, Inc.*, 798 F. Supp. 550 (W.D. Wis. 1992).)

- A *Penthouse* model whose employer coerced her into having sex with the company's financial advisor. (*Thoreson v. Penthouse Int'l, Ltd.*, 563 N.Y.S. 2d 968 (N.Y. Sup. Ct. 1990).)

- Two male employees whose supervisor threatened to fire them if they refused to participate in various sexual antics including strip poker and striptease performances at the worksite after hours. (*Showalter v. Allison Reed Group, Inc.*, 767 F. Supp. 1205 (D.R.I. 1991).)

- A student at the New York City police academy who had to fight off the assault of a male student by hitting him with a box of ammunition and who had her breasts fondled from behind by her instructor as she tried to fire her gun. (*Watts v. New York City Police Depot*, 724 F. Supp. 99 (S.D.N.Y. 1989).)

- Two female workers for a construction firm in Iowa whose male colleagues repeatedly "mooned" them, flashed obscene photos, urinated in their water bottles, cornered them between trucks and reached out the windows of their trucks to rub the women's breasts and thighs. (*Hall v. Gus Constr. Co.*, 842 F.2d 1010 (1988).)

These examples only scratch the surface. Put almost any five working women in a room, and chances are three or more of them will have harassment stories—some as serious as the ones just listed.

2. Common misconceptions

One common misconception about sexual harassment is that the laws prohibiting it restrict normal socializing between men and women at work. The truth is that sexual harassment consists of unwelcome conduct of a sexual nature—and it in no way affects ordinary social contact between employees.

The sexual harassment laws do not apply to trivial slights. As the U.S. Supreme Court held in a recent case, "common sense and an appropriate sensitivity to social context" will determine whether a particular act constitutes sexual harassment. To illustrate the point, the Court gave the vivid example of a professional football player who would have no claim for harassment "if the coach smacks him on the buttocks as he heads onto the field." This is so, the Court opined, "even if the same behavior would reasonably be experienced as abusive by the coach's secretary (male or female) back at the office" (*Oncale v. Sundowner Services, Inc.*, No. 96-568; 3/4/98).

The oft-repeated fear of many people—mostly men—that sexual harassment laws prevent them from complimenting a woman or asking her out for a date is simply misplaced. Nothing in the law prevents dating, as long as it is done in a reasonable manner that respects a co-worker's dignity and wishes. Office romances are not unlawful, as long as both employees involved welcome the relationship. (See Chapter 3, Section C.1.)

Another misconception, at the opposite end of the spectrum, is the notion that anything goes in the workplace as long as there is no physical contact with another employee. That, too, is wrong. Sexual harassment can result from any verbal or physical conduct of a sexual nature. Many types of sexual harassment involve no touching, but they are nevertheless offensive or intimidating to the employee—as well as being clearly illegal.

> "The shocking and pathetic response of the U.S. Senate to charges of sexual harassment against Judge Clarence Thomas triggered the most spontaneous and massive outpouring of women's rage I have witnessed in my lifetime. Clearly the boys on Capitol Hill just don't get it. And just as clearly, millions and millions of American women have had it."
>
> —*Eleanor Smeal, President of the Fund for the Feminist Majority, in an October 1991 appeal to members*

B. THE CAUSES OF SEXUAL HARASSMENT

Sexual harassment usually results from a misuse of power—not from sexual attraction. Far too many cases of sexual harassment involve meanness, anger and abuse of power to blame it all on a dating ritual gone awry or to dismiss it as an adult version of schoolboy pranks.

Not all sexual harassment is directed against women, but women certainly endure the vast majority of it. It is important, then, to look at some of the underlying causes of this sad phenomenon.

1. Violence and self-perceptions

The relationship between the sexes in modern America includes a great deal of violence against women. One out of every ten American women are raped or sexually assaulted during their lives, while more than half of all women living with men have experienced a battering or similar incident of domestic violence.

This volatile mixture of sex and violence is also played out in the workplace. Susan Faludi, author of *Backlash: The Undeclared War Against American Women*, suggests that one explanation for male hostility can be found in surveys that track male attitudes about the proper role of a man in society:

> *For twenty years [pollsters] have asked subjects to define masculinity. And for twenty years, the leading definition, ahead by a huge margin, has never changed. It isn't being a leader, athlete, lothario, decision maker, or even just being "born male." It is simply this: being a "good provider for his family."*

> *If establishing masculinity depends most of all on succeeding as the prime breadwinner, then it is hard to imagine a force more directly threatening to fragile American manhood than the feminist drive for economic equality.*

2. The economics of women's work

Focusing on the economics of men's work and women's work exposes sexual harassment as something that has a perverse logic from the harasser's point of view: It is one way that many men express their resentment and try to reassert control when they view women as their economic competitors.

Despite the impediments women face to obtaining jobs, the number of working women has steadily increased. In 1860, only 15% of American women were in the paid labor force. By 1947, their number reached 32% and jumped to nearly 60% by 1994.

Women's entry into the workforce has been prompted by necessity, since many families cannot make ends meet if the wife and husband don't both work at full-time jobs. There is also a large and growing number of families in which a woman is the sole means of support. Between 1980 and 1990, the number of female-headed families in the United States increased by 27%. According to the AFL-CIO Working Women's Department, by 1997, two out of every five working women were the sole head of their households. Within that group, more than one-quarter had dependent children.

DISPELLING THE MYTHS

Myth: Some women ask to be sexually harassed.

Reality: Being subjected to sexual harassment is a painful and difficult experience. Defenses such as "she wore provocative clothes" and "she enjoyed it" are neither acceptable nor accurate.

■

Myth: If a woman really wanted to discourage sexual harassment, she could.

Reality: Often, the harasser is in a position to punish the woman by withholding a promotion, or giving a bad evaluation. In this society, men often rationalize their behavior by claiming that a woman's "no" actually means "yes."

■

Myth: Most charges of sexual harassment are false.

Reality: Women have little to gain from filing false charges. It is exceedingly difficult to file sexual harassment charges and confronting the harasser can be both physically and financially draining.

■

Myth: Sexual harassment is inevitable when men and women are working together.

Reality: While interaction between the sexes might be inevitable, uninvited sexual overtures are not.

■

Myth: If you ignore sexual harassment, it will go away.

Reality: Only 29% of the women recently surveyed who said they tried to ignore the behavior said that it "made things better." Over 61% said that telling the person to stop made things better.

—Adapted from *Combating Sexual Harassment: A Federal Worker's Guide*, a pamphlet published by Federally Employed Women, Inc.

As more women have tried to obtain wage-paying jobs, they have had to fight continuously for fair treatment. In 1990, the median annual earnings for a full-time female employee in the United States was $19,816 per year—only 71% of the median earnings of a full-time male employee. By 1997, that figure was 75%, according to the AFL-CIO. Despite that modest advance, the problem of unequal pay seems to be creating a greater sense of greater economic insecurity among women. Just over 52% of working women now report that they contribute half or more of their household's income, and a fair level of compensation for their work looms as an issue of survival for their families.

Society's segregation of jobs into Man's and Woman's Work means most women work for low pay. The leading occupations for women in 1994 were still the traditional ones: secretaries, cashiers, account clerks, nurses and nurses' aides, schoolteachers, waitresses and sales clerks—all of them relatively low paying. A disproportionately large number of women work in part-time jobs, as domestic workers, or in piecework jobs where the pay is extremely low and the benefits non-existent.

And for women, education is no still way up. According to Women Employed Institute, a Chicago-based clearinghouse offering workplace counseling and training, even when women invest time and money in their educations, economic discrimination follows the same distressing but familiar pattern. The group took women's educational portrait in the workplace in 1992, which revealed that:

- female high school graduates earned 29% less than male high school graduates

- women college graduates earned 27% less than male college graduates

- women with doctorate degrees earned 21% less than males with doctorate degrees, and

- women with high school degrees earned only $2,017 a year more than males with less than a ninth grade education.

3. Discrimination as a form of workplace control

If sex discrimination forces women into lower-paying jobs, sexual harassment helps keep them there. This may not be the intention of the harasser in every instance, but it is often the effect.

Seen in this context, male workers who harass a woman on the job are doing more than annoying her. They are reminding her of her vulnerability, creating tensions that make her job more difficult and making her hesitant to seek higher paying jobs where she may perceive the tension as even greater. In short, sexual harassment creates a climate of intimidation and repression. A woman who is the target of sexual harassment often goes through the same process of victimization as one who has suffered rape, battering or other gender-related crimes—frequently blaming herself and doubting her own self-worth.

There is no Typical Harassed Woman. Women of all ages, backgrounds, races and experience are harassed on the job. Women in traditional Woman's Work, such as waitresses and secretaries, are often given menial, degrading tasks. They are called "Honey," "Sweetie" and other demeaning names. And they are led to believe that a certain amount of male domination and sexism is normal. All of this reinforces the idea that women workers are of little value in the workplace. Women who try to break into traditionally all-male work, such as construction jobs, medicine or investment banking, often suffer even more intense harassment clearly aimed at getting them to leave. (See Section C.3.)

Thus sexual harassment often accomplishes informally what laws against sex discrimination theoretically prohibit: gender-based requirements for a job. A woman subjected to sexual harassment endures pressure, degradation or hostility that her male co-workers don't have to endure—making it just that much harder to compete for the job and for advancement.

Catharine MacKinnon, author of the 1979 book *Sexual Harassment of Working Women*, was the first legal scholar to draw attention to the connection between sex discrimination and sexual harassment:

> ... [W]omen tend to be in low-ranking positions, dependent upon the approval and goodwill of male superordinates for hiring, retention and advancement. Being at the mercy of male superiors adds direct economic clout to male sexual demands.... It also deprives women of material security and independence which could help make resistance to unreasonable job pressures practical....

...[S]exual harassment of women can occur largely because women occupy inferior job positions and job roles; at the same time, sexual harassment works to keep women in such positions.

"The trouble with being in the rat race is that even if you win, you're still a rat."

—Lily Tomlin, American Actress

BIG FIRMS, LITTLE CHANGES IN HARASSMENT

According to a recent survey of 768 lawyers affiliated with firms, female attorneys are becoming somewhat more assured in the workplace—flummoxing their male co-workers. And the problem of sexual harassment still looms large.

Over 51% of the women attorneys surveyed said that they had been harassed. Of those instances of harassment:

- 39% involved suggestive looks and gestures

- 29% involved being touched, pinched, cornered or leaned over, and

- 19% involved unwanted pressure for sex or dates.

Only 6% of the male attorneys reported that they had been sexually harassed.

About 15% of the women lawyers reported the harassment to firm management in 1993—up from 8% in 1989. But one-third of those responding said they would not report being harassed, and another one-third said they were not sure what they would do.

Source: *The National Law Journal,* December 20, 1993

C. THE EFFECTS OF SEXUAL HARASSMENT

Sexual harassment on the job can have very serious consequences both for the harassed individual as well as for other working women who experience it second-hand.

The consequences to the individual employee can be many and serious. In some situations, a harassed woman risks losing her job or the chance for a promotion if she refuses to give in to the sexual demands of someone in authority. In other situations, the unwelcome sexual conduct of co-workers makes the working conditions hostile and unpleasant—putting indirect pressure on her to leave the job. In some cases, the employee is so traumatized by the harassment that she suffers serious emotional and physical consequences—and very often, becomes unable to perform her job properly.

The consequences to working women as a group are no less serious. Sexual harassment has a cumulative, demoralizing effect that discourages women from asserting themselves within the workplace, while among men it reinforces stereotypes of women employees as sex objects. Severe or pervasive sexual harassment in certain types of businesses creates a hostile or intimidating environment that causes women to leave their jobs and look elsewhere for work or discourages them from seeking those jobs in the first place.

The effect on the morale of all employees can also be serious. Both men and women in a workplace can find their work disrupted by sexual harassment even if they are not directly involved. Sexual harassment can have a demoralizing effect on everyone within range of it, and it often creates a lose-lose situation in terms of company productivity. The U.S. Equal Employment Opportunities Commission (EEOC) recognizes this in its statement: "The victim does not have to be the person harassed but could be anyone affected by the offensive conduct."

1. Job-connected injuries

Sexual harassment causes direct economic injury to many workers. These are injuries directly related to his or her status as an employee and wage earner, and they include lost wages, lost promotions and other job benefits as well as loss of the job itself.

And where a sexual harassment case makes it to court, job-connected injuries play a special role. The U.S. Supreme Court characterizes these injuries as "tangible employment actions." When a supervisor's sexual harassment results in this type of injury to an employee, courts are more likely to hold the company responsible for the supervisor's actions. (See Subsection b, below.)

a. Loss of job

Sometimes the connection between sexual harassment and the injuries it causes is simple and direct: A woman is fired for refusing to go along with the sexual demands of her employer. Usually the management uses some other pretext for firing her, but the reasons are often quite transparent.

> *Example: A federal court found that a female bartender was fired because she refused her supervisor's plea to rub against his sexual organ, even though the employer argued she was fired for her use of "unladylike" language. Ironically, the court also found the employer's use of the term "unladylike" to be direct evidence of discrimination, since there was ample testimony that he tolerated vulgar language in the workplace—as long as it was men doing the talking.* (EEOC v. FLC & Bros. Rebel, Inc., *663 F. Supp. 864 (W.D. Va. 1987).)*

> *Example: A California federal court found that a waitress was given unfair job assignments and finally fired after she refused to go along with the manager's fondling, kissing and obscene humor. The court gave no credence to the manager's claim that she was fired because she failed to follow work rules.* (Priest v. Rotary, *634 F. Supp. 571 (N.D. Cal. 1986).)*

Sometimes the firing technically occurs because of some other event, but it is still clearly related to sexual harassment. For example, if a company downgrades an employee's job and assignments because of a harassment incident and then fires her for complaining about the demotion, her injury is legally caused by sexual harassment.

> *Example: An employee of a Texas real estate development company was forced up against a wall by her supervisor while one of the salesmen slipped a camera under her dress and took a picture. She objected to this and other harassing incidents. When she came to work one morning, someone else was sitting at her desk without any explanation. She complained to her boss, and the ensuing argument led to her firing. A federal court found that although the argument was the incident that precipitated the firing, the entire set of events arose out of a sexual harassment situation.* (Ross v. Double Diamond, Inc., *672 F. Supp. 261 (N.D. Tex. 1987).)*

If an employee is temporarily unable to work as a result of the harassment and the management uses that as an excuse to fire her, this is also sexual harassment.

Example: A Philadelphia policewoman was subjected to sexual slurs and pornography, crank phone calls and dangerous pranks by her male co-workers, causing her to become emotionally upset and unable to work. The police department fired her for going beyond her allotted sick leave, but a federal court found that the firing was directly related to the sexual harassment. (Andrews v. City of Philadelphia, 895 F. 2d 1469 (3d Cir. 1990).)

b. Loss of wages and other benefits

An employee who is demoted or denied a promotion or raise because of resisting sexual advances from a supervisor or objecting to obscene humor and other sexual activity in the office suffers a serious loss.

But even if an employee doesn't suffer an immediate economic loss, a denial of a promotion or other adverse change in her job status can both harm her standing within the company and jeopardize future pay increases.

A loss of wages usually entails a loss of other job benefits as well, such as pension contributions, medical benefits, overtime pay, bonuses, sick pay, shift differential pay, vacation pay and participation in any company profit-sharing plan.

c. Forced reassignment

Sometimes a company responds to an employee's complaint of sexual harassment by transferring her to a different department and leaving her harasser unpunished. This forced reassignment is another form of job-connected injury, and it may be compounded if combined with a loss of pay or benefits or reduced opportunities for advancement.

d. Constructive discharge

Sometimes the sexual harassment is so severe that the employee quits. If her situation was intolerable and she was justified in quitting, sexual harassment caused her to be constructively discharged—that is, forced to leave. This is the same as an illegal firing.

Example: A female truck driver for the Celanese Corporation in South Carolina received frequent threats as well as blatant sexual solicitations from her co-workers. These co-workers also told her that they had established a "club" to determine which one of them would be the first to have sex with her. She complained to management but got nowhere. She finally quit her job to seek medical attention after one employee burst out of the restroom and exposed himself to her. A federal court hearing the case ruled that the woman employee had been constructively discharged—and was entitled to the same legal relief as if she had been fired. (Llewellyn v. Celanese Corp., 693 F. Supp. 369 (W.D.N.Y. 1988).)

e. Retaliation for reporting sexual harassment

Employees are frequently fired or penalized for reporting sexual harassment or otherwise trying to stop it. This is called retaliation. In such cases, the injury is legally considered to be a direct result of the sexual harassment.

Example: A California office worker found the phrase "How about a little head?" flashed across her computer terminal from an unknown source within the company. She reported it to her supervisor, who was a woman, and the two women reported the incident to higher management. In response to their complaint the company embarked upon a campaign of downgrading their jobs and benefits until both women were forced to resign.

The court held that the injuries suffered by the two women were in retaliation for their reporting the sexual harassment incident. The legal consequences of these acts of retaliation were the same as if the injuries had resulted from the sexual harassment. (Monge v. Superior Court, 176 Cal. App. 3d 503 (1986).)

In serious, egregious sexual harassment cases, retaliation is often a major issue. Some company managers do not want to hear about sexual harassment when it arises within the company. They often retaliate against those pressing the issue as they would against other whistleblowers reporting other illegal activity. Frequently, this retaliation is an attempt to cover up the managers' own involvement in the harassment, either by condoning it or actively engaging in acts of harassment themselves.

Acts of retaliation take on a life of their own, making a bad situation just that much worse. In legal terms, they are just as unlawful as the original sexual harassment acts themselves. And they frequently expand the group of people who suffer from the harassment. Many of the sexual harassment cases that reach the courts involve claims by men and women who were retaliated against by their companies because they tried to speak up on behalf of co-workers who were the targets of the original acts of harassment.

2. Personal injuries

A sexually harassed worker often suffers personal injuries in addition to the job-connected losses just described. In many sexual harassment cases, these injuries—ranging from stress-related illnesses to serious physical and emotional problems—are the most serious and costly results.

a. Stress-related problems

A recent study by the Working Women's Institute showed that 96% of the women who were sexually harassed experienced emotional stress. Between 35% and 45% of these women also suffer physical and work performance stress that can affect the way they do their jobs.

The American Psychiatric Association recognizes stress-related problems resulting from sexual harassment as a specific, diagnosable medical ailment. It can produce symptoms such as distractions from tasks, dread of work or an inability to work at all.

Although many sexual harassment cases lead to cases of stress that are diagnosed medically, the U.S. Supreme Court has made clear that an employee does not have to be this seriously injured to bring a case against sexual harassment under the U.S. Civil Rights Act. In a recent case, the Court reasoned that the purpose of the Civil Rights Act is to give employees a way of getting help from the EEOC and the courts before a situation gets completely out of hand and not have to wait until their injuries are so severe. (*Harris v. Forklift Sys., Inc.*, 510 U.S. 17 (1993).)

b. Other physical and mental injuries

Sexual harassment also causes a great many other types of physical, mental and emotional injuries. Some of these injuries are stress-related, but others are caused by physical pranks or violent acts directed at the harassed worker.

A sampling of cases that have gone through the courts illustrates the types of injuries that can occur.

- A California woman who was repeatedly harassed by the company vice president, was diagnosed with an "adjustment disorder"—and suffered accompanying symptoms of anxiety, depression, headaches, dizziness, vomiting, diarrhea, weight loss, sleep disturbances, teeth grinding and a facial twitch. (*Bihun v. AT&T Information Sys., Inc.*, 16 Cal. Rptr. 2d 787 (Cal. App. 1993).)

- A truck driver who was subjected to constant solicitations and threats from her co-workers developed a seizure disorder similar to epilepsy. (*Llewellyn v. Celanese Corp.*, 693 F. Supp. 369 (W.D.N.Y. 1988).)

- A folder operator in a printshop who was constantly propositioned and touched by her supervisor suffered a high level of anxiety and stress, withdrawal symptoms and sleeping and eating disorders. (*Maturo v. Nat'l Graphics Inc.*, 722 F. Supp. 916 (D. Conn. 1989).)

- A federal employee whose supervisor made defamatory remarks about her sexuality and then continued to follow and telephone her put her in such fear of sexual abuse that she suffered a miscarriage. (*Otto v. Heckler*, 781 F. 2d 754 (9th Cir. 1986).)

- A Philadelphia policewoman suffered severe burns when she put on a shirt from her locker that her co-workers had laced with a lime substance. (*Andrews v. City of Philadelphia*, 895 F.2d 1469 (3d Cir. 1990).)

- Two women drivers suffered carbon monoxide poisoning when male mechanics ignored their complaints about leakage of that gas into the truck's cabin. (*Hall v. Gus Constr. Co.*, 842 F.2d 1010 (8th Cir. 1988).)

These personal injuries can be severe and long-lasting—and the recovery can be difficult and expensive.

3. Injuries to women as a group

In addition to the injuries suffered by the harassed employee, sexual harassment can also have pernicious consequences for other working women who may not be in the immediate line of fire. An atmosphere of sexual harassment tends to segregate the workplace and to limit the job options for working women.

Sexual harassment often has its harshest consequences where women are trying to break into previously all male occupations—firefighters, bankers, surgeons, welders, doctors, lawyers.

a. Limited job options

A recent study of 100 women working in a factory revealed that female machinists, a job traditionally held by men, were harassed far more often than assembly line workers, a job where women had worked for years, although both fields had roughly the same number of male co-workers. And harassment isn't confined to factory jobs. A high level of sexual harassment occurs in every non-traditional job category that women enter. In fact, women bankers and surgeons report the highest levels of harassment.

The simple explanation is that the more male-dominated the job, the more likely it is that men will be threatened when they see women moving into their workshoes. That threat is likely to be compounded during tough economic times when people worry about losing their jobs.

And women in non-traditional jobs are most often subjected to the most violent and egregious harassment. These acts of harassment would be highly improper and illegal in any situation, but they are particularly harmful in situations where women are trying to break into jobs from which they have been excluded.

On the plight of women factory workers in the early 1900s: "Wherever they worked, women were sexually harassed by male workers, foremen and bosses. Learning to 'put up' with this abuse was one of the first lessons on the job... It was common practice at the factories for male employers to demand sexual favors from women workers in exchange for a job, a raise, or a better position."

—From A History of Women in America by C. Hymowitz & M. Weissman (1978)

b. Stereotyped workers

When sexual harassment occurs in jobs that are predominantly male, it reinforces patterns of discrimination and makes those patterns that much harder to break. In jobs where women workers are a rarity, a woman worker is very likely to be judged in stereotypical, sexual terms. This creates a burden that the male employees do not have, because women employees in such a situation must be constantly vigilant as to how their actions may be interpreted or misinterpreted. One court recently recognized this underlying historical struggle in the battle between the sexes:

> *Women must constantly monitor their behavior to determine whether they are eliciting sexual attention; they must conform their behavior to the existence of the sexual stereotyping either by becoming sexy and responsive to the men who flirt with them or by becoming rigid, standoffish and distant so as to make it clear that they are not interested in the status of sex object. (Robinson v. Jacksonville Shipyards, Inc., 760 F. Supp. 1486 (M.D. Fla. 1991).)*

The debilitating effects of such pressure are enormous. A woman working in an environment that has been traditionally closed to her group has a difficult enough time trying to adjust to a new situation and prove her worth to skeptical old-timers on the job. If sexual harassment is added to the situation, it often increases the pressure to the level where the job environment is no longer endurable.

At the same time that the tolerance of sexual harassment is demoralizing to a female employee, it reinforces stereotypical attitudes of male co-workers and management and makes them less open to the idea of female employees in their particular workplaces.

Sexual stereotyping creates a no-win situation for a woman who is sexually harassed. If, for example, a male co-worker squeezes her buttocks, she can either complain about it or do nothing. She loses either way. If she says nothing, she reinforces the idea that women really like such activity or, at the very least, accept their role as sex objects. If she objects, she reinforces the idea that women are complainers. In either case she is not likely to fit the mental image of what management is looking for when considering employees for advancement.

WHAT'S DOWN, DOC?

A 1991 survey of 200 doctors by the Massachusetts chapter of the American Medical Women's Association revealed that:

- 27% said they had been sexually harassed during a one-year period ending in 1990.

- More than half said they had received unwanted sexual attention during that time.

- 2/3 of those surveyed said they had received offensive comments about their gender.

- Half of the general surgeons and 37% of the interns said they had been harassed.

D. SEXUAL HARASSMENT LAWS: A CHECKERED HISTORY

Today's laws against sexual harassment are a collection of pieces that don't quite fit: a labyrinth of legal dead ends and pitfalls that have assumed their present form because of historical rather than logical reasons. Even if you're not a history buff, it's worth taking a brief look at how the laws against sexual harassment have evolved.

Prior to the 1980s, there were no federal or state laws prohibiting sexual harassment on the job and few instances in which it was prevented or punished. A woman who was beaten, seriously molested or raped in the workplace might file an assault and battery lawsuit, for example, but that happened only rarely. The term sexual harassment was unheard of—and sadly, the problems that women experienced in their jobs were almost invisible to the male legislators who wrote the laws.

Nothing was done about sexual harassment on the job, or the broader problem of sex discrimination, until the refueled women's movement began pushing the issues in the 1970s. "Pushing" is not really the right word: It was more like running the high hurdles.

1. Making sex discrimination illegal

Sexual discrimination in employment became illegal in the United States when the Civil Rights Act of 1964 was adopted. That Act established the Equal Employment Opportunities Commission (EEOC), which later issued important regulations and guidelines on sexual harassment. But there is a mountain of irony in this, because the virtually all-male Congress had no real intention of passing a law against sex discrimination or sexual harassment.

As originally introduced in Congress, the Civil Rights Act of 1964 only prohibited discrimination in employment based on race, color, religion or national origin. Discrimination on the basis of gender was not included. It was attached to the bill at the last moment, when conservative Southern opponents of the measure introduced an amendment prohibiting discrimination on the basis of sex. They thought that adding sexual equality was so obviously preposterous that it would scuttle the entire bill when it came to a final vote.

The very idea of prohibiting sex-based discrimination engendered mirth on the floor of the Congress and on the editorial pages of major newspapers: Men, it was laughingly argued, could now sue to become Playboy bunnies. The Lyndon Johnson administration, however, wanted the bill passed badly enough that it decided not to oppose the amendment. So the Civil Rights Act, including the ban on sex discrimination, was voted into law. Only one of the proponents of the erstwhile bill-killing amendment on sexual equality actually voted for the final bill that included it.

With that less-than-ringing endorsement, discrimination in employment on the basis of sex became illegal. But for several years, the law was all but a dead letter. The first head of the EEOC—the agency charged with enforcing the statute—considered the sex discrimination provisions of the law a joke, saying that it was "conceived out of wedlock." The EEOC took no action against sexual discrimination in employment until several years later when it started to feel pressure from the women's movement. Finally, the agency realized it had to begin enforcing the law as it was written.

2. Equating harassment with discrimination

After convincing the EEOC to begin enforcing the law against sex discrimination, women faced another problem: how to stop sexual harassment in the workplace.

The term "sexual harassment" wasn't mentioned anywhere in the Civil Rights Act, nor was it found in the fair employment practices statutes enacted in most of the states within a few years of the U.S. Civil Rights Act. But many women cogently argued that sexual harassment was a form of sex discrimination—and that laws prohibiting discrimination should outlaw harassment as well.

Nevertheless, most courts considering the issue early on refused to pin down whether sexual harassment was prohibited by the Civil Rights Act. They characterized harassment cases as some sort of personal dispute between the woman employee and her harasser that was not covered by the law. For example, when Adrienne Tompkins, an employee at New Jersey's Public Service Electric and Gas Company, was physically detained, assaulted and then fired by her boss for refusing to have sex with him, a federal court judge ruled in 1976 that the Civil Rights Act was not intended to prevent a "physical attack motivated by sexual desire on the part of a supervisor" just because it "happened to occur in a corporate corridor rather than a back alley." (*Tompkins v. Public Serv. Elec. & Gas Co.*, 422 F. Supp. 553 (D.N.J. 1976).)

Women's groups kept pressing the issue, however, urging the EEOC to rule that sexual harassment is a form of sex discrimination. Harassment, they argued, makes it impossible for women to work in certain types of situations, and so it discriminates against them as much as a Men Only employment policy. Finally, in 1980, the EEOC under the leadership of Eleanor Holmes Norton issued regulations defining sexual harassment and stating that it was a form of sex discrimination prohibited by the Civil Rights Act. It wasn't until 1986 that the U.S. Supreme Court acknowledged that progress, holding that sexual harassment on the job was a form of sex discrimination—and illegal. (*Meritor Sav. Bank v. Vinson*, 477 U.S. 57 (1986).)

3. Putting teeth in sexual harassment laws

After 1980, when EEOC regulations finally made sexual harassment on the job illegal, several states followed suit and enacted their own laws and regulations making sexual harassment illegal. But whether state fair employment practices (FEP) statutes provide decent protection for a sexually harassed employee depends upon where she works. Employees in a few states are pretty well protected, but those in other states are afforded little or no protection under state FEP laws.

> "They just don't get it. Those men just don't understand how injurious, how demeaning and how frightening sexual harassment really is. So it took a massive eruption of outrage from women across America—and across party lines—to shock those senators into delaying the vote on Thomas so the charges could be investigated."
>
> *—Molly Yard, President of the National Organization for Women, in an October 10, 1991 plea to members to help finance campaigns of women for Congress*

a. State laws

All of the state fair employment practices (FEP) laws that were enacted after the U.S. Civil Rights Act have theoretically outlawed sexual harassment on the job, but in terms of enforcement they have ranged from the strong to the useless. Some states, like Alabama and Arkansas, have no statute at all. Others, like Georgia, set up an enforcement agency but enacted a law that applies only to public employees. Most states, however, have done somewhat better, naming an enforcement agency or specifying that the courts have the power to reinstate a sexually harassed worker who is fired or forced out of her job, as well as being able to award the worker any lost wages.

On the key issue of compensation for personal injuries, some states, like New York and Massachusetts, have relatively good programs that allow an employee to recover full compensation. Unfortunately, many state FEP laws do not allow compensatory damages for any personal injuries. (See Chapters 5 and 7 for a detailed discussion of state FEP laws.)

b. Common law tort cases

Since 1980, attorneys for employees who suffered severe emotional or physical injuries have taken legal actions for personal harm—called torts—such as rape, assault and battery and intentional infliction of emotional distress, and adapted them to fit the specifics of a sexual harassment situation. In a number of these lawsuits, sexually harassed employees recovered large money awards.

But common law tort cases have not been a perfect solution, either. They are generally available only where the injuries are quite severe, and they are limited further by the practicalities of time and money required to pursue them. Moreover, some states have greatly hampered the use of common law tort lawsuits by restrictive interpretations of the state FEP law, workers' compensation law or the tort laws themselves. (See Chapters 5 and 8 for a full description of these legal theories and how they apply to a sexual harassment situation.)

As with state FEP statutes, the evolution of common law tort suits in the last decade has provided a good legal remedy for some sexually harassed women, but many are without adequate legal protection.

c.   The EEOC and the Civil Rights Act

Even though the U.S. Equal Employment Opportunities Commission (EEOC) has been dealing with sexual harassment complaints since 1980, its enforcement powers have been limited and its record uneven. (See Chapter 6.)

For example, the EEOC can investigate harassment claims, subpoena witnesses, settle cases and, if necessary, take the matter to court. But funding limits and heavy caseloads have resulted in the EEOC taking well over a year for most investigations, rather than the six months prescribed in the law. And even when it has decided an employee's case has merit, the EEOC has had the resources to file a lawsuit in only a small percentage of the cases.

An even bigger problem throughout the 1980s was that even if a harassment case was proved in court, the only money a woman could recover under the Civil Rights Act was for lost wages. The statute did not allow for what would be the most effective remedy: compensatory damages for physical, emotional and other personal injuries. And even though the EEOC eventually issued extensive guidelines amplifying its rules against sexual harassment, its moral bark continued to be far stronger than its enforcement bite.

d.   Amendments to the Civil Rights Act

In 1990, women's groups and others pushed a bill through Congress that would have allowed an employee to sue for compensatory damages for personal injuries in a sexual harassment case. President Bush vetoed that bill.

In late 1991, in the wake of the Clarence Thomas–Anita Hill hearings, the issue came up again before Congress. The Bush administration still opposed allowing employees to sue for damages—and it was set to scrap the bill again. But at the last minute, feeling the political heat, it agreed to a compromise version of the bill that allowed an employee to sue for damages but put a strict limit on the total amount of damages that an employee could recover in any case—$50,000 to $300,000 based on the number of employees in the company.

Women's groups and their supporters in Congress were quick to point out the unfairness of it: No other group is subject to such severe limits on the amount of damages that can be recovered in a personal injury action. But since the alternative was to stay with the status quo—with no right to recover money damages at all—they reluctantly supported the bill. It was then enacted into law.

In 1993, the U.S. Supreme Court gave a strong re-endorsement of the laws against sexual harassment and set out some valuable parameters. In *Harris v. Forklift Sys., Inc.*, 510 U.S. 17 (1993), the Court ruled that a woman who suffered repeated gender-based insults and unwanted sexual innuendoes from the mouth of the company president could press a claim for sexual harassment even without proof that she was psychologically harmed in a medical sense.

The company had pressed for a rule that would have limited sexual harassment cases under the U.S. Civil Rights Act to cases where the employee suffered severe injuries, undermining the law's purpose of correcting such situations in the workplace before they cause serious injuries to the workers. The Court hailed back to a standard of reasonableness. It held that while the "mere utterance of an… epithet which engenders offensive feelings in an employee" is not sufficient basis for a sexual harassment claim, the law "comes into play before the harassing conduct leads to a nervous breakdown." Proof of severe or pervasive discriminatory and harassing conduct is enough for an employee to invoke the protection of federal law.

4. Expanding the concept

The 1990s have witnessed state and federal courts grappling with the issues raised in the many sexual harassment cases that have passed through them. Although the law is still not totally clear, certain patterns are now apparent. Two developments in particular have changed the terrain of sexual harassment on the job.

a. Common sense is the key

Recent U.S. Supreme Court decisions on sexual harassment have focused more and more on reasonableness and common sense as the determining factors.

For example, in *Harris v. Forklift Systems, Inc.* (114 S.Ct. 367 (1993)), the Court held that the "mere utterance" of an offensive statement would normally not constitute a violation of the law nor would a statement that the other person does not "subjectively perceive" as abusive. But on the other hand, the Court recognized that harassing conduct does not have to be so severe as to affect an employee's psychological well-being before it becomes illegal. The Court noted it will not require an employee to wait until she has a nervous breakdown before taking the employer to court. According to the Court, employees can pursue their cases when abusive behavior "will detract from employees' job performance, discourage employees from remaining on the job, or keep them from advancing in their careers."

Cases since then have added even more credence to the reasonableness standard, with courts looking at the totality of the workplace environment rather than any rigid rules to decide whether harassment occurred.

b. Same sex harassment is prohibited

Perhaps the biggest leap forward in recent years was the U.S. Supreme Court's recent decision in *Oncale v. Sundowner Offshore Services* (No. 96-568; 3/4/98). In that case, the Court expanded the concept of who is protected under the sexual harassment laws and gave those laws a broader underpinning.

The *Oncale* case involved a straight male who worked on an oil rig and who claimed he was sexually harassed by his supervisors and other members of the crew, all of whom were ostensibly heterosexual as well. The harassment was relatively severe, including allegations of threats and physical assault.

But what made the case so significant was that it clearly answered the question of how and whether gender and sexual orientation play in sexual harassment. The Court was undeterred by the fact that the harassers and harassed worker were of the same gender. It was also unswayed by the fact that the acts of harassment—although sexual in content—were apparently not motivated by sexual desire. The Court instead focused on the conduct and found it to be illegal sexual harassment.

Although maintaining that it had not expanded the law, it seems clear that the Supreme Court did just that. If the Court could find in this situation—as it did unanimously—something that it could characterize as "discrimination because of sex," it seems likely that it would do so in cases in which the sexual component is closer to the forefront in the harasser's motivation. In the future, a person who is harassed because he or she is a gay man or a lesbian is very likely to be covered.

This was a big step forward for the Supreme Court. In ruling that the law's prohibition against sexual harassment "must extend to sexual harassment of any kind that meets the statutory requirements," the Court came close to placing sexual harassment on a legal footing of its own. Earlier cases suggested that the prohibition

---

HARASSMENT UP, SALES DOWN

Results of a recent survey of sales personnel, as reported in *Sales & Marketing Management* magazine, September 1995.

Percentage who feel they have been sexually harassed:

      Men—9%   Women—63%

Percentage who were sexually harassed by a customer, but ignored it for fear of losing a sale:

      Men—4%   Women—30%

Percentage who feel that sexual harassment is more likely to occur in sales than in other professions:

      Men—20%   Women—33%

Percentage who feel that sexual harassment is most likely to occur:

• In the office	Men—3%	Women—27%
• While on the road for business	Men—45%	Women—74%
• During a company-sponsored event for clients	Men—4%	Women—15%

Percentage who work at companies that offer sexual harassment prevention training: 39%

against sexual harassment was simply a necessary extension of the law against sexual discrimination—a way of preventing a person from accomplishing indirectly, through violent or threatening conduct, what he or she was prohibited from doing directly by discriminating. The opinion in *Oncale* simply recognizes that abusive sexual conduct should not be allowed in the workplace whatever the relationships between those involved. (See Chapter 3, Section A.)

E. ENDING SEXUAL HARASSMENT: THE ALTERNATIVES

An employee faced with a sexual harassment situation today has a variety of alternatives for dealing with the situation. No one of them is entirely satisfactory, and several of them are complex and overlapping.

If you face a sexual harassment situation that is serious enough that it could end up in a legal battle—or if you are interested in a basic legal definition of sexual harassment—take a good look at the legal issues of sexual harassment discussed in Chapter 2.

One way to look at the solutions for ending harassment discussed in this book is as a series of alternatives: In a few cases, only one approach may work. In most cases, you have clear choices as to how to proceed.

But these alternatives can also be viewed as a series of escalating steps. If the sexual harassment isn't ended by using one option, you can switch to other, increasingly formal strategies until you find an effective method.

Here are some alternatives for dealing with sexual harassment.

1. Confronting the harasser

Often the best strategy for the employee sounds the most simple: Confront the harasser and persuade him to stop. This is not appropriate or sensible in every case, particularly when you have suffered injuries or are in some danger. But many situations can be defused by a face-to-face conversation with the person who is creating the problem. (Strategies for confronting a sexual harasser are discussed in Chapter 3.)

2. Using a company complaint procedure

Some companies have good policies against sexual harassment and effective complaint procedures to handle them. You can file a complaint under the company procedure immediately, or you can use that procedure as the next step if your face-to-face meeting with the harasser produces no satisfactory result.

It is particularly important for a harassed employee to use the company's grievance procedure in light of the U.S. Supreme Court's recent opinion in *Burlington Industries v. Ellerth* (No. 97-569; 6/26/98).

In that case, the Court suggested that an employee who "unreasonably fails to take advantage" of a company complaint process will have a more difficult time winning a case.

(Chapter 4 discusses company sexual harassment policies and complaint procedures and gives guidance about how best to use them. The ideas in that chapter are helpful even if there is no immediate sexual harassment problem, because an employee or employee group can use such ideas to help convince management to adopt an effective policy.)

3. Using mediation or arbitration

Mediation or arbitration are increasingly popular ways to rectify the wrongs caused by sexual harassment on the job. Often lumped together under the handle Alternative Dispute Resolution, these procedures are less formal than court proceedings. In mediation and arbitration, the accused harasser, the employee claiming to be harassed, the employer and a neutral outside person meet to work out a solution. These methods are sometimes used to help negotiate the terms of an agreement to end a work relationship. But they are most effective where those involved want to find a way to work together. (See Chapter 9, Section A.)

4. Filing a complaint with a government agency

If the sexual harassment does not end after face-to-face meetings or through use of the company complaint procedure, consider filing a complaint under the U.S. Civil Rights Act with the U.S. Equal Employment Opportunities Commission (EEOC) or filing a complaint under a similar state law with a state or local fair employment practices (FEP) agency.

Filing a complaint with the EEOC or a state FEP agency is important for two reasons:

1. It sets in motion an investigation by the EEOC or the state FEP agency that may resolve the employee's sexual harassment complaint, and

2. It is a necessary prerequisite under the U.S. Civil Rights Act and under some state FEP statutes if an employee wants to file a lawsuit.

Sometimes an EEOC or a state FEP agency can resolve a sexual harassment dispute at no cost to the employee and with relatively little legal involvement on her part. Almost all of these agencies provide some sort of help in negotiating an amicable settlement with the company. A few state FEP agencies also provide an administrative hearing panel that can compensate you for your personal injuries, although the EEOC and most other state agencies do not have this important additional power.

(Chapter 5 compares the EEOC and the state FEP agencies. The procedure for filing a complaint with the EEOC is described in Chapter 6 and similar state-by-state information about the various FEP agencies is included in Chapter 7.)

5. Filing a lawsuit under the Civil Rights Act or FEP laws

If all investigation and settlement attempts fail to produce satisfactory results, your next step may be to file a lawsuit for damages under the U.S. Civil Rights Act or under one of the state FEP statutes.

Even if you intend right from the beginning to file such a lawsuit, you sometimes must first file a claim with a government agency. For example, an employee pursuing a claim under the U.S. Civil Rights Act must first file a claim with the EEOC, and a similar procedure is required under some state FEP laws. At some point, that agency will issue you a document referred to as a right-to-sue letter that allows you to take your case to court.

What you can hope to win in such a lawsuit varies considerably from state to state. Generally, the right to obtain money damages under the U.S. Civil Rights Act is better than the rights available under the laws of about half of the states, because the FEP laws in such states don't allow money damages for personal injuries caused by the sexual harassment. By contrast, the Civil Rights Act allows the employee to recover some damages—out-of-pocket losses plus $50,000 to $300,000 in damages depending upon the number of employees in the company. However, about half of the states allow you to recover greater money damages than you could get under the U.S. Civil Rights Act.

(See Chapter 5 for a further comparison of federal and state statutes. See also Chapter 6 for a discussion of the EEOC and the Civil Rights Act and Chapter 7 for a state-by-state look at FEP statutes.)

6. Filing a common law tort suit

If the sexual harassment has resulted in severe injuries, consult an attorney. You may then decide to skip all of the above steps and instead file a lawsuit for damages based on any one of several common law tort theories such as the intentional infliction of emotional harm or wrongful discharge. Generally, common law torts are best suited for harassed employees who have been seriously injured, because you must prove the conduct was truly outrageous—and such actions are costly in time and in money.

Torts are significantly different from state to state. Not every sexual harassment case will fit within a common law tort theory. However, in the appropriate case where a tort is proved successfully, a judge or jury is free to award large sums in damages.

(See Chapter 8 for a detailed discussion of tort actions most often filed in sexual harassment cases.)

When filing a tort action, you will almost always need to hire a lawyer for help. (See Chapter 9, Section B.) ■

2

The Legal View

T his chapter focuses on the basic issues of sexual harassment as defined by law and interpreted by the EEOC and the courts. It will give you the working knowledge you need to prove your case of sexual harassment.

Of course, most sexual harassment disputes do not end up as courtroom battles. The widespread use of the term "sexual harassment" sometimes creates confusion as to when the law has been violated. In popular terms sexual harassment has been used to describe conduct that ranges from annoying, obnoxious behavior up to situations that are nearly indistinguishable from rape. But not all boorish behavior is illegal. It is important, therefore, to define carefully those types of situations that constitute sexual harassment in a legal sense.

Many women deal each day with harassment that is not severe enough to warrant a lawsuit—and many more feel the need to approach the problem from a different direction. If you are more interested in workplace strategies for stopping harassment than in whether what's happening to you meets the legal definition of harassment, skip to the next chapter.

Chapter 3 discusses sexual harassment from a more personal perspective—looking at the practical problems it can create and stressing what a woman can do on her own to deal with the situation.

Certain basic legal issues are involved in most sexual harassment, and this chapter focuses on four of them:

- Was the conduct sexual in nature?

- Was the conduct unreasonable?

- Was the conduct severe or pervasive in the workplace?

- Was the conduct unwelcome?

These are the factors that a government investigating agency or a court will look at to determine whether you have been sexually harassed. All four factors are usually present in every case—and it is important to keep in mind that they usually relate to one another.

But proving that sexual harassment has occurred is just part of the problem; the other part is to determine who is legally liable for it. The harasser will be found liable in most instances, but that finding is usually not enough to rectify the situation. A more important issue is to determine when a company will be held liable for sexual harassment committed by its supervisors and other employees.

Under the law now emerging, a company will generally be held liable for the actions of its employees when its own management:

- is involved in the harassment

- has knowledge of the harassment, or

- is held liable under the legal doctrine of vicarious liability.

A. CONDUCT OF A SEXUAL NATURE

Conduct of a sexual nature that may be legally considered to be sexual harassment includes:

1. Sexual advances, propositions or attempts to get sexual favors from an employee. These are the situations that most people probably think of first when they hear about sexual harassment on the job. (See Section A.1.)

2. Outright hostility toward employees of a particular gender. This type of hostility most often occurs against women in jobs that have not been traditionally open to them. The U.S. Supreme Court has indicated, however, that this type of hostility can give rise to a claim of sexual harassment even when the situation involves men harassing other men. The key is "whether members of one sex are exposed to disadvantageous conditions of employment to which members of the other sex are not exposed."

3. Lewd, sexual, or pornographic pictures, language and jokes permeating the workplace, creating an environment—or a "sexually poisoned workplace"—that is offensive to many female employees or in some instances, male employees. The sexual commentary and lewd humor in such cases may or may not be directed at the particular employee, but she may nevertheless find the sexually charged atmosphere to be intimidating and offensive—and that it puts her at a distinct disadvantage with respect to her male co-workers. (See Section A.3.)

Because it may be essential to you in evaluating whether the problems you are encountering in the workplace qualify as illegal sexual harassment, each type of sexual conduct will be discussed in more detail below.

QUID PRO QUO OR HOSTILE ENVIRONMENT

The terms "quid pro quo" and "hostile environment" have often been used in the cases and literature about sexual harassment.

Quid pro quo describes a situation in which an employee is confronted with sexual demands to keep her job or obtain a promotion. As the Latin term quid pro quo suggests, you have to do "this" to get "that." In more familiar vernacular, this is called a sex-for-jobs situation.

Hostile environment is frequently used to describe other types of cases in which the threat—or the trade-off—is not as blunt. This typically involves sexually offensive conduct that permeates the workplace, making it difficult or unpleasant for an employee to do her job.

However, the line between the two types of harassment has become very blurry. A couple of recent U.S. Supreme Court decisions have undercut the importance of the distinction.

This is simply a concession to reality. If, for example, a supervisor threatens to punish an employee for not yielding to sexual demands and then fails to follow through on the threat, it is unclear which category applies. At first, courts started analyzing an incomplete quid pro quo situation like this as really a hostile environment. This makes sense, because a sex-for-jobs threat—whether or not it is acted upon—certainly creates an intimidating workplace for the employees involved.

The Supreme Court has now gone one step further. In the recent case of *Burlington Industries, Inc. v. Ellerth* (No. 97-569; 6/26/98), the Court analyzed the problem this way: In a true quid pro quo situation, one act alone that smacks of sex-for-jobs violates the sexual harassment laws. With an unfilled quid pro quo threat, however, you must look at additional evidence to determine the severity or pervasiveness of the threat. If the threat is real, the courts will treat the situation as illegal sexual harassment.

In other words, quid pro quo and hostile environment cases should from this point forward be treated the same.

1. Sexual advances or demands

Unwelcome sexual advances and propositions are one of the most common forms of sexual harassment. Whether a particular sexual advance is illegal sexual harassment usually depends on who is making the advance and how he or she is doing it.

a.   By supervisors or others in authority

Here the focus is on who is making the sexual advance. Sexual advances from a supervisor or other person in authority will be scrutinized far more closely than those of other co-workers because of the strong possibility of intimidation and abuse of power. Supervisors are in unique positions of power in the workplace. It is usually presumed that the employer has knowledge of any sexual harassment committed by supervisors, and so the employer is very likely to be responsible for their actions.

Sexual advances by supervisors frequently involve the classic sex-for-jobs situation. The EEOC regulations state that sexual advances under these circumstances are unlawful if they are "explicitly or implicitly a term or condition of an individual's employment." In other words, if a woman must put up with these demands as part of her job, they may qualify as harassment.

> *Example: A sales manager invites a saleswoman on his staff to dinner. While eating dessert, he says softly: "Let's go up to my apartment after dinner, have a drink and get comfortable. If you want, we can discuss the performance reports and the salary recommendations that I have to make next week."*

> *Although the sales manager makes no explicit reference to sex, it is strongly implied. By mentioning "getting comfortable" and "salary recommendation" in the same conversation, he creates a strong link between the two. This would very likely be considered sexual harassment.*

In a supervisor-subordinate relationship, very little conduct of a sexual nature is needed to support a finding of harassment. Even a relatively polite request for a date by an employer or supervisor can be the basis of a sexual harassment charge if it appears to be connected to future work assignments, promotions or raises.

An unwanted sexual advance can qualify as sexual harassment even if the person in authority makes a favorable employment decision on behalf of the employee. If an employee submits to an unwelcome sexual advance because of a promise from a supervisor, the supervisor is guilty of sexual harassment—whether he or she delivers on the promise or not. It's the act or threat of using sexual conduct as the basis for making employment-related decisions that gives rise to the sexual harassment charge.

The same rules apply to anyone with real or apparent power over the employee who threatens to use such power as the basis for making an employment decision—even if the person in authority is not in the employee's immediate chain of command.

> *Example: A secretary has a raise application pending. A senior staff member of the personnel department invites her several times to go out for dinner and dancing, but she refuses him. Finally he tells her: "I've got a lot of recommendations on my desk for raises, and it usually takes me quite a while to get around to processing someone's raise if she isn't a little more friendly." His conduct qualifies as sexual harassment.*

b. By co-workers

Unwelcome sexual advances or demands from a co-worker can also be the kind of conduct giving rise to a sexual harassment charge. However, since these cases do not involve a supervisor or someone in authority, the threat to the employee is not as direct. These cases require a greater look at all the surrounding circumstances.

There is another important practical difference between a situation involving a co-worker and one involving a supervisor or someone in authority. As mentioned, with a supervisor or someone in authority, the company is presumed to know what's going on and therefore to be legally responsible for the situation. However, this presumption of knowledge does not apply to co-workers.

PROVING YOUR CASE

To hold the employer—as opposed to the individual—responsible for sexual demands by a co-worker, you must usually prove that the company knew about the harassing acts and did nothing effective to stop them. It is important, therefore, to tell the co-worker that his advances are unwelcome and, if he persists anyway, to tell someone in authority. (See Chapter 3, Sections E and F.)

Sometimes an employer's reaction makes the sexual harassment situation worse and may result in the company being liable when it might not otherwise have been.

> *Example: An office worker in California received an anonymous, unwanted sexual solicitation from a co-worker on her office computer screen and reported it to her woman supervisor. The company responded to the complaints from the two women by demoting both of them, cutting back on their privileges and eventually forcing them to leave. Whether the company would have been held responsible for the original solicitation by the co-worker is unclear, but the act of retaliating against the two women employees made the company clearly liable for what later happened.* (Monge v. Superior Court, 176 Cal. App. 3d 503 (1986).)

If the sexual solicitation comes from a co-worker and management is not involved, directly or indirectly, the focus is on the nature of the sexual advance. The emphasis is less on the "who" and more on the "how." Many facts are important in determining whether a co-worker has crossed the line from friendly bantering into sexual harassment: the frequency of the solicitation, the nature of the proposition, the language used, the physical gestures and proximity and the behavior of the co-worker. There is no hard and fast rule as to how much is too much.

> *Example: Arthur approaches Clara, a co-worker, at her desk in the office. In polite, non-threatening language he asks, "Would you like to try that new Chinese restaurant Saturday night?"*
>
> *That alone would not be sexual harassment. It could either be argued that such a request is not conduct of a sexual nature or that a reasonable woman would not find it offensive. Either way, the result is the same: There is no sexual harassment.*

But if a polite request for a date is made in sexually explicit terms or in a highly suggestive tone, it could give rise to a sexual harassment claim unless the employee had previously indicated that such an overture was welcome.

Example: Arthur asks Clara for a dinner date, but in this instance he leans over her desk, winks at her and makes suggestive movements with his tongue.

Not only is his conduct explicitly sexual, but a reasonable woman would also be more likely to find it offensive. With these two factors strongly present, this conduct is likely to be considered sexual harassment.

The strength of the employee's initial response is often the key to showing that the sexual advance is unwelcome. If she firmly rejects a co-worker's initial request for a date and makes it clear that no further solicitation is welcome, any subsequent advances by him, whether in polite language or not, might constitute sexual harassment. "No" should definitely be taken to mean "no."

Example: Arthur asks Clara for a dinner date in polite language. She says no— and she makes it clear that she is not open to dating him. He persists in coming by her desk every workday for the next month and asks her if she's changed her mind and will go out with him, and each time she firmly tells him no. Arthur's request has crossed over the line from polite to harassing.

c.　By customers and others

An employer can be legally responsible for sexual harassment if it creates or allows a situation where an employee will be sexually harassed by customers, salespeople, visitors or even passersby. This can happen where the employer puts an employee in a situation where it knows or should know that unwelcome sexual advances are likely to occur—for example, when a company requires an employee to dress in provocative clothing where customers or passersby are likely to make sexual advances to her.

The legal status of the harasser within the company is not as important as the nature of the harassment itself. In a recent pronouncement on the subject, the EEOC has stated: "The harasser can be the victim's employer, an agent of the employer, a supervisor in another area, a co-worker, or a non-employee."

A very serious situation occurs when the employer tries to force an employee to have sex with a client or someone else it wants to please.

Example: A Penthouse model successfully sued the magazine and Robert Guccione, the publisher, for $4,000,000 in damages under the New York Human Rights Law based on Guccione's coercive efforts to make her have sex with the company's financial advisor and others. The court viewed that situation as the equivalent of one in which the employer attempted to get sexual favors for himself. (Thoreson v. Penthouse Int'l, Inc., 563 N.Y.S.2d 968 (N.Y. Sup. Ct. 1990).)

d. Showing preferences

A sexual harassment claim may also arise when sexual advances are made to two or more women with differing results. For example, if the office Lothario denies a promotion to Ms. A because she won't sleep with him and then gives the same promotion to Ms. B because she will, both women have experienced the kind of unwelcome sexual conduct that amounts to sexual harassment. Ms. A would obviously have a sexual harassment claim based upon the improper denial of her promotion by a person in authority in a sex-for-jobs situation. Ms. B would also have a claim if his sexual advances were unwelcome and she submitted only out of fear of losing the promotion.

But what if a supervisor has a consensual affair with one of his employees and gives her promotions and raises in preference to other employees? This type of favoritism, combined with abusive behavior toward other employees, can be a form of sexual harassment. While the supervisor is looking for someone willing to say "yes," he is frequently harassing the women who say "no."

Example: A male supervisor made the rounds of the office, propositioning several of the female employees. He then boasted that he was giving one woman a promotion because "she knew how to make him feel good." Although he had never specifically promised anyone else a promotion in exchange for sex, the court nevertheless held that his preferential treatment for his new girlfriend was part of an overall discriminatory treatment of women employees. (Toscano v. Nimmo, 570 F.Supp. 1197 (D. Del. 1983).)

Sometimes it is not the preferential treatment that amounts to sexual harassment so much as the retaliation against those who complained about it.

> *Example: In a crackdown on harassment in a government workplace, the court found that the U.S. Securities and Exchange Commission had created a hostile environment for women who complained about male supervisors giving preferential treatment to women with whom they were having affairs.* (Broderick v. Ruder, *685 F.Supp. 1269 (D.D.C. 1988).)*

PROVING YOUR CASE

If you feel you have been passed over in favor of your employer's paramour, carefully examine your working environment. If the employer's favoritism arises out of sexual conduct in the workplace, creates an atmosphere of intimidation or sets a different standard for female employees, it may also qualify as sexual harassment. Here, the strongest proof may be evidence that other women workers feel the same way you do.

---

2. Hostility related to gender

Hostile acts related to an employee's gender are another type of prohibited conduct of a sexual nature, even though they may not involve sexual overtures at all.

Sometimes, the hostility comes as a reaction from a rejected lover. But many cases of sexual harassment are based on outright hostility by a male supervisor or co-worker toward a particular woman employee or toward women employees in general. Other times a male supervisor may be hostile toward a particular woman employee right from the outset and indulge his hostility in ways that he wouldn't think of doing if she were a man.

In many situations, the hostility stems from men's opposition to women in previously all-male jobs—and it manifests itself against any woman worker who happens to come upon the scene. But this is not limited to situations in which men abuse their power in the workplace with respect to women. Women also can sexually harass men, men can sexually harass other men and women can harass other women. (See Section A.4, below.)

Some employers have argued that sexual harassment is not involved if a co-worker treats a woman employee with hostility. Sexual harassment, they argue, requires some evidence of sexual overtures to the female employee who registered the complaint. Fortunately, the courts have firmly rejected this argument, finding instead that sexual harassment can exist without sexual misconduct.

Example: A Washington, DC court found that a supervisor who blocked the doorway and forcefully twisted a woman employee's arm had sexually harassed her. She conceded that he wasn't after sexual favors, but the court ruled in her favor anyway, reasoning that her supervisor wouldn't have treated a man in that manner. (McKinney v. Dole, 765 F.2d 1129 (D.C. Cir. 1985).)

Hostile conduct is often a thinly disguised effort to force a woman employee out of the workforce.

Example: A supervisor at a bakery plant stated that he didn't think a woman should be foreman and then boasted that he would make it "rough enough for her to leave." He then went on a campaign of yelling at her, ridiculing her and giving her impossible tasks to do. Although he didn't demand sexual favors, the court ruled in the woman's favor anyway, holding that "threatening, bellicose, demeaning, hostile or offensive conduct by a supervisor in the workplace because of the sex of the victim" was enough to state a claim for sexual harassment. (Bell v. Crackin Good Bakers, Inc., 777 F.2d 1497 (11th Cir. 1985).)

It is sometimes easier to visualize cases involving overt hostility as sexual discrimination cases rather than sexual harassment. If a supervisor subjects his female employees to ridicule and abuse because he would prefer to have men working for him, he is treating them differently than he treats male employees and, therefore, discriminating against them. Fortunately, the conceptual difference between a sexual discrimination case and a sexual harassment case is not important, because both are subject to the same legal prohibitions. In fact, the laws against sexual harassment are largely derived from the laws against sexual discrimination.

3. Pornographic and vulgar behavior

There is a growing recognition by the EEOC and the courts that pornographic material and vulgar behavior in the workplace can create an offensive working environment or a "sexually poisoned" workplace—particularly for women employees.

Here, the offensiveness is not always directed at a specific individual; it usually derives from the cumulative effect of a lot of offensive and demeaning acts that may seem relatively innocuous when viewed in isolation.

Often the main injurious effect of this type of sexual conduct is to create a working atmosphere that is hostile to working women as a group. The sexually poisoned workplace creates a situation where discrimination against women commonly flourishes.

> *Example: A court recently concluded that a proliferation of pornographic magazines, vulgar employee comments about the magazines, sexually oriented pictures in a company sponsored film and slide presentation and offensive sexual commentary during the film all contributed to a hostile working environment, because it creates "an atmosphere in which women are viewed as men's sexual playthings rather than as their equal co-workers." (Barbetta v. Chemlawn Serv. Corp., 669 F.Supp. 569 (W.D.N.Y. 1987).)*

Lewd and vulgar behavior is often sexist and woman-hating as well, making the potential discriminatory effect on women's careers even more clear—and often revealing a very clear double standard for male and female employees.

> *Example: A woman employee in a Florida shipyard complained that the walls displayed pictures of a woman's pubic area with a meat spatula, a nude woman wearing high heels and holding a whip, and a dartboard with a drawing of a woman's breast and nipple as the bull's eye. There were no pornographic pictures of men pinned up. The court noted that: "Pornography on an employer's wall or desk communicates a message about the way [the employer] views women, a view strikingly at odds with the way women wish to be viewed in the workplace." (Robinson v. Jacksonville Shipyards, Inc., 760 F.Supp. 1486 (M.D.Fla. 1991).)*

> **PROVING YOUR CASE**
>
> Although more courts are recognizing that lewd and vulgar behavior in the workplace is a form of sexual conduct that can amount to harassment, these are often difficult cases for an employee to win. The harassed employee must be prepared to show that the conduct is severe or pervasive throughout the workplace: isolated instances, unless they are particularly offensive, will not be enough. (See Section C.)
>
> To help clear this hurdle, look carefully at the entire working environment to see if an offensive atmosphere can be linked to other, more specific harm. For example, if an anti-woman joke makes the rounds of the office, it may seem to have no immediate ill effect. But if the same joke is repeated by someone who is about to recommend employees for promotion, it is an important indication of a possible bias against women employees. It is crucial in these cases to look for that connection.

4. Gays, lesbians and same gender behavior

For several years, the EEOC has taken the position that a harassed person "does not have to be of the opposite sex" from the harasser to prove a claim of sexual harassment.

The U.S. Supreme Court recently appeared to endorse that stance in the case of *Oncale v. Sundowner Services, Inc.* (No. 96-568; 3/4/98). But because the case did not squarely address the issues of same gender harassment, we may need to await additional case decisions to divine the parameters of the rules that apply. (See Chapter 3, Section A.)

a. Gays and lesbians

Although the Civil Rights Act does not directly prohibit discrimination against lesbians and gays, the courts appear likely to prohibit discrimination against lesbians and gays when it takes the form of sexual harassment. Sexual harassment of other employees by lesbians and gays is also prohibited by the Act. The recent *Oncale* case opens up these possibilities.

A gay man who is harassed by other men in the workplace would appear to have a case as strong—if not stronger—than Joseph Oncale. The harassers in that case made sexual threats and attacks against Oncale, all the while taunting that he was a homosexual. There is nothing in the Supreme Court's decision to suggest that Oncale would have a weaker case if he were, in fact, gay.

The reverse is also true. If an employee is harassed by supervisors or co-workers who are overtly homosexual, the situation would be indistinguishable from the actions alleged in the Oncale case. The actions by the ostensibly heterosexual supervisors and co-workers in that case could easily be categorized as a form of homosexual rape.

The rules that apply to men in these types of situations almost certainly apply to women as well. Lesbians being harassed by other women are likely to be covered under the protections of the Civil Rights Act as well as straight women harassed by lesbians. Lesbians who are harassed by men will in many cases have a double-pronged claim if they can show that their harassers engage in sexually abusive behavior against women in general and lesbians in particular.

b. Same gender behavior

The Supreme Court's recent rule in the *Oncale* case is easy enough to state: Sex discrimination consisting of same sex harassment is actionable under Title VII of the Civil Rights Act. But the opinion is skimpy on reasoning, so it sheds little light for those grappling for more guidance.

The Court held that Oncale had alleged enough facts in his complaint that he should be allowed to take his case to trial. What Joseph Oncale alleged was this: His supervisors and co-workers on the oil rig in the Gulf of Mexico where he worked had taunted him, accused him of homosexuality, used homophobic slurs, threatened him with rape, exposed themselves and forcibly subjected him to humiliating, sex-related actions. Both Oncale and his tormentors claimed to be heterosexual, so the issue of harassment of gay workers was not directly before the Court. Nevertheless, the Supreme Court found that the allegations were sufficient to allow the case to go forward.

This Supreme Court decision focused on protecting an employee from abusive behavior by supervisors and co-workers. But in deciding the case, the Court stated that the critical question is "whether members of one sex are exposed to disadvantageous terms or conditions of employment to which members of the other sex are not exposed." It is likely that the Court had to frame the issue that way to create the necessary legal link between the harassment and the anti-discrimination prohibition of the Civil Rights Act.

But that reasoning left a number of questions unanswered. Was the Court suggesting that Joseph Oncale was discriminated against because he is a man? What would have happened to a woman in that situation? Could any woman reading these allegations possibly believe that she would fare any better if she were left alone on this offshore animal house with these ostensibly heterosexual guys? Can the oil drilling company defend this case when it gets back to the lower court by showing that its crew would treat women just as badly in this situation as it did Joseph Oncale?

It is probably best to follow the Supreme Court's lead and not look at that issue too closely. If the sexually related behavior is abusive enough, the Court seems to have suggested that it qualifies as illegal discrimination.

B. CONDUCT THAT IS UNREASONABLE

The second legal factor required to find conduct to be sexual harassment is unreasonableness. The law only prohibits unreasonable sexual conduct in the workplace. Some harassing conduct is obviously unreasonable. For example, if a supervisor makes sexual demands on an employee as a condition of getting a raise or a promotion—a sex-for-jobs demand—this is clearly unreasonable. It is also always unreasonable for an employer to physically assault or attack employees.

Reasonableness typically becomes important only when the conduct may be ambiguous or subject to misinterpretation. Courts want to make sure that the employee bringing the case is not complaining about conduct that other people wouldn't find offensive. As the EEOC Compliance Manual, the handbook for personnel investigating harassment, states, somewhat pompously, the law should not "serve as a vehicle for vindicating the petty slights suffered by the hypersensitive."

THE COMING OF AGE OF THE REASONABLE WOMAN

In assessing whether conduct is unreasonable, courts have traditionally used an objective test—asking whether a reasonable person would find it offensive.

But in sexual harassment cases, some courts have opined that the reasonable person test seems particularly inadequate. These courts make note of the realization that there is often a big difference in how men and women view the same facts. As one court put it: "A male supervisor might believe, for example, that it is legitimate for him to tell a female subordinate that she has a 'great figure' or 'nice legs.' The female subordinate, however, may find such comments offensive." (*Lipsett v. University of P.R.*, 864 F.2d 881 (1st Cir. 1988).) (See Chapter 3, Section B.1 for a further discussion of gender differences in perception.)

The EEOC Compliance Manual suggests that the conduct might be judged from the viewpoint of the female employee: "The reasonable person standard should consider the victim's perspective and not stereotyped notions of acceptable behavior."

A few cases have been more explicit, including one in which the court noted:

Women who are victims of mild forms of sexual harassment may understandably worry whether a harasser's conduct is merely a prelude to violent sexual assault. Men, who are rarely victims of sexual assault, may view sexual conduct in a vacuum without a full appreciation of the social setting or the underlying threat of violence that a woman may perceive. (*Ellison v. Brady*, 924 F.2d 872 (9th Cir. 1991).)

But such courtly observations have not been universally hailed as advancements. Some people have criticized the proffered reasonable woman standard as being coddling and demeaning to women workers. When the U.S. Supreme Court considered the issue of sexual harassment in more recent cases, it remained mum on the reasonable woman standard.

The current standard is difficult to target. It may evolve that the unreasonableness of the sexual conduct will be judged by some androgynous "reasonable person" standard. Or it may be judged by the attitude of a reasonable person of the gender of the person being harassed. There is some evidence that the attitude of most males toward sexual harassment in the workplace is starting to change. The truly optimistic might argue that by the time the Supreme Court rules on the issue, the attitudes of both men and women as to what is unreasonable behavior might not be that far apart.

How a woman employee responds to a situation may, within certain limits, determine what conduct is reasonable or unreasonable within her own workplace.

To a certain extent, a woman employee makes her own rules as to what is—and is not—acceptable workplace behavior. Once a woman reasonably defines the boundaries of what is personally offensive to her, it will often be considered sexual harassment for a co-worker to cross such boundaries.

Example: A married woman works as a stockbroker. She shares a desk with another broker. He never asks her out, but he frequently prefaces remarks to her with the phrase, "If you weren't married…" and mentions how he can't find a woman he likes as much as her.

It's not clear whether a reasonable woman would find the comments offensive. However, if this particular employee tells her co-worker that she is bothered by his remarks and asks him to stop, she in effect creates a standard of conduct that applies to their relationship.

Of course, a woman employee can't impose unrealistic or unworkable standards on her co-workers. But there are grey areas in determining what kind of conduct is reasonable and what is not. By speaking up and explaining what conduct she finds offensive, a woman has some control over the standards that will apply in her own work environment. (See Chapter 3, Section E for a discussion on confronting your harasser.)

On the women who comprise management at *Playboy:* I think the true situation becomes more clear if you imagine Jews working for a magazine in which Jews are nude and Christians are clothed.

—Gloria Steinem

PROVING YOUR CASE

If you have been harassed by unreasonable conduct, the most important evidence you can present is that you let the harasser know that you found his conduct unreasonable—and that he persisted to violate the standard you set. Two kinds of documentation will be most persuasive in such a case. One is evidence that you told the harasser he was behaving unreasonably—a dated entry in your journal, a copy of any letter you sent him asking him to desist. Also important would be dated documentation that he kept up the harassing behavior even after you notified him it was unacceptable—again, dated journal entries or your statements to co-workers or others.

C. CONDUCT THAT IS SEVERE OR PERVASIVE

The third factor to consider in evaluating sexual conduct is whether it is so severe or so pervasive throughout the workplace that it creates an intimidating, hostile or offensive working environment.

Although important, this factor is often assumed or left unstated in certain types of cases. For example, if a co-worker physically molests or endangers a woman employee, the situation is obviously severe.

However, the severe or pervasive factor is important in less obvious situations, such as those involving sexual advances by a co-worker other than a supervisor. Here, it is usually necessary to weigh all of the circumstances to determine whether the particular conduct was severe in and of itself or so pervasive as to create a hostile or intimidating environment.

1. EEOC guidelines

The EEOC Compliance Manual sets out guidelines for investigators to follow in determining whether any sexual conduct is severe or pervasive. According to the EEOC, investigators should consider:

- whether the conduct was verbal or physical, or both

- how frequently it was repeated

- whether the conduct was hostile and patently offensive
- whether the alleged harasser was a co-worker or a supervisor
- whether others joined in perpetuating the harassment, and
- whether the harassment was directed at more than one individual.

The Compliance Manual explains how conduct should be evaluated using these factors. According to the EEOC, unless there is a single, "quite severe" incident, the investigator should go through a weighing process to determine whether the conduct gives rise to a sexual harassment claim. No weighing process is necessary in a sex-for-jobs situation, however, because the EEOC says that "a single sexual advance may constitute harassment if it is linked to the granting or denial of employment benefits." In other words, a sex-for-jobs situation is always considered severe without anything further.

Cases involving intrusive types of touching or fondling are also usually considered severe even if the offensive behavior only occurs once. This is true whether or not it involves a supervisor.

In general, the EEOC considers physical actions by a co-worker to be much more serious than words, because "even a single unwelcome physical advance can seriously poison the victim's working environment."

And the EEOC Compliance Manual takes the position that "the more severe the harassment, the less need to show a repetitive series of incidents. This is particularly true when the harassment is physical."

2. The totality of the circumstances

In the case of persistent sexual advances from co-workers or a sexually poisoned workplace, it is usually important that the harassed employee build his or her case fact by fact, with an eye toward showing the totality of the working environment.

The abusive behavior must be substantial to support a claim of sexual harassment. The U.S. Supreme Court has stated this requirement in a number of ways. According to the Court, the lower courts should be looking at all the circumstances—including "the frequency of the discriminatory conduct; its severity; whether it is physically threatening or humiliating, or a mere offensive utterance;

and whether it unreasonably interferes with an employee's work performance" (*Harris v. Forklift Systems, Inc.,* 510 S.Ct. 17, 21-22 (1993)).

In another recent case, the Court set out the dictate to weed out cases that only involve "innocuous differences in the ways men and women routinely interact with members of the same sex and of the opposite sex" (*Oncale v. Sundowner Services, Inc.,* No. 96-568; 3/4/98).

No one fact may be decisive, but the sum total of them all might be. Here is how one court looked at it: "A play cannot be understood on the basis of some of its scenes but only on its entire performance; similarly, a discrimination analysis must concentrate not on individual incidents but on the overall scenario." (*Robinson v. Jacksonville Shipyards, Inc.,* 760 F.Supp. 1486 (M.D.Fla. 1991).)

The case from which that quote was taken is a good example of how the cumulative effect of offensive behavior worsens the work environment. At the trial of the case, Lois Robinson testified that there were groups of pornographic pictures displayed at nearly 40 sites throughout the Jacksonville Shipyard where she worked—and that she found them to be offensive.

But she also took the case one step further, directly connecting the pornographic photos to her working conditions. She testified that several male co-workers made suggestive remarks to her when they neared the pornographic photos. One told her: "I'd like to get in bed with that." Another said: "Hey pussycat, come here and give me a whiff."

The connection between the pornographic workplace and Robinson's individual harassment went still further. When she objected to the pictures, her co-workers increased their sexual taunting. When she objected to a sexist joke in which sodomous rape was referred to by the term "boola-boola," her co-workers started calling her by that name. It was the cumulative effect of all this interrelated behavior that created a hostile and intimidating working environment.

Even behavior that a woman worker does not witness can still have a cumulative, pervasive effect in creating an abusive working environment.

> *Example: A woman works in an office where pornographic pictures are passed around by the male employees and where they persist in telling obscene, sexist jokes. She tells them that she is offended by their conduct. The next time she walks into the room one of her co-workers says, "Look out—here comes Snow White. Let's go in the other room so I can finish this story."*

Here, the joke that the woman's co-workers tell out of earshot just "among the boys" is relevant to her claim that she is working in a sexually poisoned workplace. The co-workers' condescending attempt to protect her from one particular joke makes little difference, because her sensitivity to that joke is not the real point. The main issue is the cumulative impact of pornographic and obscene behavior in the workplace, and her co-workers' furtive manner doesn't change the situation.

PROVING YOUR CASE

Courts that have ruled against women employees in sexually poisoned workplace cases have often done so because there was insufficient proof that the offensive sexual conduct was severe or pervasive. An employee bringing such a case must usually show that such conduct permeates the workplace to overcome the inertia of a less-than-sympathetic judge.

In presenting a case, be prepared to list as many sexual or hostile incidents as possible, including dates, places and witnesses. Look for witnesses who can testify as to other similar incidents. Search hard for connections that link the overall atmosphere (the prevalence of pornographic pictures) to specific hostile incidents (sexual taunting when you object). Focus on whether supervisors participated in creating or tolerating the sexually poisoned atmosphere.

"Your boss might call you a slut once or 10 times, but a court might not consider it harassment because it doesn't affect your ability to perform your job."

—*Laurel Bellows, President of the American Bar Association's Commission on Women in the Profession, 1997*

D. CONDUCT THAT IS UNWELCOME

The EEOC regulations prohibit "unwelcome sexual advances, requests for sexual favors and other verbal or physical conduct of a sexual nature." This is a subjective test. The sexual conduct must actually be unwelcome and offensive to the employee bringing the complaint.

At first glance, it would seem that this factor would be easy to fulfill in any situation: If the conduct wasn't personally offensive and unwelcome, why would the employee bother to complain about it? The problem is timing. The woman must show that the conduct was unwelcome and offensive to her at the time it occurred. Sometimes that can be difficult.

In a sex-for-jobs situation, the supervisor or employer will frequently claim that the employee welcomed the sexual advances at the time and that the relationship was purely consensual. Likewise, in the case of the sexually poisoned workplace, an employer will often argue that the employee was a willing participant in the rough humor and sexual pranks and that she didn't really seem offended by it. The issue of unwelcomeness can be a problem in any kind of situation where there is no clear evidence of the subjective attitude of the employee when the events occurred.

1. Voluntary but unwelcome

In the past, employers have argued that if a woman voluntarily submits to her employer's sexual advances, she has consented to them. The legal rule, however, is more favorable to the employee: She is only deemed to have welcomed the sexual advance or conduct if it can be shown that it is something she wanted to do at the time.

The best example is taken from the first case involving sexual harassment that the U.S. Supreme Court decided. In that case, Mechelle Vinson testified as to what happened shortly after she was hired by the Meritor Savings Bank:

> *[Her supervisor] invited her out to dinner and, during the course of the meal, suggested that they go to a motel to have sexual relations. At first she refused, but out of what she described as fear of losing her job she eventually agreed. According to [Vinson], Taylor [her supervisor] thereafter made repeated demands upon her for sexual favors, usually at the branch, both during and after business hours; she estimated that over the next several years she had intercourse with him some 40 or 50 times. In addition,...Taylor fondled her in front of other employees, followed her into the women's restroom when she went there alone, exposed himself to her and even forcibly raped her on several occasions.*

Almost unbelievably, the lower court judges thought that this was not sexual harassment because they characterized the relationship between Vinson and her supervisor, Taylor, as "a voluntary one." The U.S. Supreme Court, however, held the behavior was clearly harassment. (*Meritor Sav. Bank v. Vinson*, 477 U.S. 57 (1986.).

PROVING YOUR CASE

A woman who gives in voluntarily to sexual demands out of fear of losing her job does not forfeit her right to raise a claim of sexual harassment. The test is whether the employee welcomed the sexual advance or conduct—not whether she felt compelled under the circumstances to go along with it.

Your strongest evidence in such a case is any proof that you found the behavior repugnant and felt apprehensive about the stability of your job at the time.

---

2. The employee's appearance

The U.S. Supreme Court has stated that a court can consider evidence of the employee's "sexually provocative speech or dress" along with other facts in determining whether the employee really welcomed any sexual advances.

There is justified criticism of this rule. It's virtually impossible to know what the Supreme Court was talking about when it referred to provocative speech or dress: provocation, like beauty, is in the eye of the beholder. It is safe to assume, however, that a woman employee who dresses in a way that might stimulate a man's fantasies has to be particularly careful.

PROVING YOUR CASE

Courts' emphasis on a harassed woman's wardrobe places an unfair burden on women who choose to dress in certain ways. But, fair or not, women in that position should be particularly explicit in telling a co-worker that his sexual advances are unwelcome in offsetting his own misplaced mindset. (See Chapter 3, Section C.2 for a further discussion of work clothes.)

---

3. Coping strategies

Speaking out against harassment, while preferred, is not always possible. Frequently, an employee is fearful of what will happen if she does. A woman faced with harassing conduct in the workplace often adopts a coping strategy—behavior that sometimes gives the appearance that she is a willing participant but in fact may only be her way of dealing with an unpleasant situation.

According to one expert on coping strategies:

> [W]omen respond to sexually harassing behavior in a variety of reasonable ways. The coping strategy a woman selects depends on her personal style, the type of incident, and her expectation that the situation is susceptible to resolution.

> Typical coping methods include:
>
> - denying the impact of the event, blocking it out
>
> - avoiding the workplace or the harasser, for instance, by taking sick leave or otherwise being absent
>
> - telling the harasser to stop
>
> - engaging in joking or other banter in the language of the workplace in order to defuse the situation, and
>
> - threatening to make or actually making an informal or formal complaint. (Robinson v. Jacksonville Shipyards, Inc., 760 F.Supp. 1486 (M.D.Fla. 1991).)

PROVING YOUR CASE

If your coping strategy has been to go along with the language of the workplace, you can still pursue a claim for sexual harassment. But coping in this way, although understandable, can create a difficult proof problem: you act one way while the events are occurring and later make the claim that you felt quite the opposite.

Fortunately, even a woman who reasonably believes that she cannot tell her harasser to stop without jeopardizing her job or facing worse harassment usually has ways to establish that she did not welcome the sexual advances or conduct when they occurred.

> *Example: A young woman works in a stock brokerage, and a co-worker tries to sit close to her and put his arm around her at office social events or informal gatherings. One time another employee saw him trying to kiss her as the elevator door opened. She is afraid to tell him to stop because he has a bad temper and their supervisor is his best friend and tennis partner.*

Here, the woman's coping strategy is to go along with the sexual conduct, but she must somehow establish facts that will show that the situation is really unwelcome to her. Probably the best way to do that is to tell as many people as she can trust, such as other co-workers, friends outside the business and counselors that the relationship is not what it appears to be and that she is only putting up with it out of fear. She needs to develop contemporaneous, corroborating evidence of her true attitude toward his sexual advances, even if that proof is outside of company channels.

4. Breaking off a relationship

In some situations, it is especially important for a harassed woman to take affirmative steps to show that sexual conduct is unwelcome. This may be particularly true if there has been a close relationship between the woman and her harasser.

An employee does not forfeit her right to protection from sexual harassment if she was romantically involved with a co-worker, but she has to make it clear to him that any further sexual advances are unwelcome. The prudent thing in this situation may be to tell everyone, including management and other employees, that the relationship is over, so as to dispel any appearance that she still welcomes his advances.

> **"Men need to understand why a compliment that would delight a lover may disturb the woman in the next cubicle. Women could use help in telling men when they're being offensive without going ballistic."**
>
> —*Joanne Jacobs,* San Jose Mercury News, *1994*

5. The employee's limited consent

Employers frequently argue that an employee has welcomed certain sexual advances or conduct because she willingly participated in some similar type of activity. An employer might try to generalize from the mild to the severe—citing instances in which the woman told an off-color joke or participated in a relatively harmless sexual prank as evidence that she must have no objection to the sex-charged working environment as a whole. But often that working environment includes hard-core, misogynist pornography, dangerous pranks and demeaning sexual comments that go well beyond the type of conduct that she did not find offensive. In tolerating certain types of mild sexual conduct she does not forfeit her right to challenge other, more serious forms of sexual harassment.

Even if a woman is hired to do a highly sexualized job, she does not waive her right to object to other forms of sexual conduct that she finds offensive. A leading case on this point involved a woman hired as Pet of the Month by *Penthouse* magazine and whose job involved movie and personal appearances in highly sexualized settings. Despite the nature of her job, the magazine and its publisher were held liable for coercing her into having sex with business associates and others that the publisher wanted to please:

> *The offensiveness of defendants' conduct is not mitigated by the fact that plaintiff's job as a model and actress for Penthouse involved, in part, the commercial exploitation of her physical appearance. Sexual slavery was not a part of her job description…. Protections against sexual harassment are arguably more necessary in a workplace permeated by conceptions of women as sex objects. When there is a significant potential for discriminatory abuse of power by an employer, the need for an effective deterrent to enforce public policy and protect employees is even greater.* (Thoreson v. Penthouse Int'l, Ltd., 563 N.Y.S.2d 968 (N.Y. Sup. Ct. 1990).)

6. Other employees offended by the harassment

Every employee has a right to a working environment that is not intimidating, hostile or offensive. If one employee is being harassed and it is affecting the working environment, however, other employees may question whether they have the legal right to do something about it. The answer is probably yes. A number of courts have taken the position that if the harassment against women is affecting the working environment, the other employees—including men who are offended by the conduct—can take action against it.

E. WHEN THE EMPLOYER IS LIABLE

Most employees who are sexually harassed initially focus on getting the harasser to stop. But if the behavior continues and begins to affect working conditions, then focus often shifts to the employer. What is it doing to stop the harassment? How widespread is the problem?

The focus on the employer becomes even more important if a harassed worker sues. An employee who sues for damages, for example, almost always tries to collect them from the company. Suing the harasser is likely to be a fruitless endeavor because he or she will not likely have sufficient assets to pay off a court judgment or to offer a reasonable settlement.

An employer sued for harassment will usually argue that it cannot be held responsible for any wrongful behavior unless it knows about it. But this raises questions about how and when companies have knowledge. Should a company be held to know about a case of harassment when it is reported to a supervisor? To the supervisor's supervisor? To the company president? To the board of directors? To solve this problem, courts have developed a set of rules—usually lumped under the legal doctrine of agency—to determine when a company should be held responsible for the actions of its managers and other employees.

1. Knowledge or involvement of management

If upper management workers are the ones engaging in the sexual harassment, then the employer will almost certainly be held liable.

But high-level conduct that is itself not sexual harassment may have the same result. If upper management sets a tone that either condones or tolerates sexual harassment, many lower level managers will take that as a cue that they can get away with outrageous behavior. If a company has a pattern of ignoring sexual harassment complaints or refusing to act against harassers, it will likely be held liable. The same is true if the company punishes or retaliates against a person who files the complaint.

2. Vicarious liability

In cases where actual knowledge of employee misconduct is confined to the lower levels of the company, the courts have grappled with the question of when the company should be held responsible. Under certain circumstances, the courts will impose liability on a company under a legal doctrine known as vicarious liability.

In the recent case of *Burlington Industries, Inc. v. Ellerth* (No. 97-569; 6/26/98), the U.S. Supreme Court attempted to fashion a rule of vicarious liability appropriate for sexual harassment claims. The rule that the Court announced revolves around the concept of a "tangible employment action." An employer will be held to one standard if the harasser committed a tangible employment action against the employee and to another, less rigorous standard if no such action occurred.

a. If tangible employment action occurred

According to the Court, a tangible employment action is something that "constitutes a significant change in employment status, such as hiring, firing, failing to promote, reassignment with significantly different responsibilities, or a decision causing a significant change in benefits." Tangible employment actions are usually documented in official records such as memos and personnel files, giving higher-ups within the company a chance to find out what is going on.

A company will be held to a stricter standard in such instances, according to the Court, because these actions inflict "direct economic harm" and can only be done by a person "acting with the authority of the company."

b. If no tangible employment action occurred

When no such tangible employment action has been taken, the Court indicated that an employer is free to defend itself. This may mean that it is completely off the hook or that damages will be reduced. A good defense will include two elements:

- that the employer exercised reasonable care to prevent and correct promptly any sexually harassing behavior, and

- that the employee unreasonably failed to take advantage of any preventive or corrective opportunities provided by the employer or to avoid harm otherwise.

In practical terms, the evolving rules can be reduced to a few simple precepts:

- An employer will be liable almost automatically if the harasser takes any action that ultimately shows up in the company records, such as a discharge, demotion, or undesirable reassignment.

- An employer may be able to protect itself from liability in certain other situations if it has an effective anti-harassment policy and complaint procedure. (See Chapter 4.)

- A sexually harassed employee should file a complaint through any company complaint procedure that exists. The Court has for all practical purposes made this mandatory for any employee who wants to take additional action on the claim. But a warning to employers: An anti-harassment policy must be meaningful and distributed to those within the company. Otherwise, it carries no weight as a defense against harasssment claims. ■

3

First Steps to Stopping Harassment

Having read Chapter 2, you are now familiar with how the law attempts to define sexual harassment on the job. While that is essential knowledge in evaluating any uncomfortable workplace situation, we now ask you to briefly suspend that legal knowledge.

This chapter analyzes sexual harassment from a strictly personal perspective—how it feels, what you can do about it, why it is so difficult to combat. Unfortunately, a large part of the burden of stopping harassment still often lies with the woman who is being harassed. But this chapter provides help—strategies for how to speak up to your harasser, how to report harassment, how to make it stop.

Recent surveys of women who have been sexually harassed indicate that less than 7% of them file a formal legal complaint or seek legal help. Most women most of the time stop harassment by taking direct action against it in the workplace, rather than in a courtroom or through a wrangling administrative procedure.

A. HAVE YOU BEEN HARASSED?

Despite the language of the Civil Rights Act, EEOC regulations and many court opinions interpreting both, sexual harassment can be very difficult to define. In all but the more outrageous instances, whether particular conduct is sexual harassment often turns on the individual facts, the sensitivities of those involved and the sensibilities of those investigating it.

Years ago, when asked in a case to define pornography, the U.S. Supreme Court justices hedged, ruling that while they couldn't define pornography, they knew it when they saw it. Sexual harassment is much the same. While a woman is rarely able to fit her situation neatly into a formula or definition, she knows she's being sexually harassed when she feels it.

This gut-check is your best barometer in knowing whether you have been sexually harassed at work. But deciding whether to take action against it—and what action to take—is often a more problematic decision. Start by learning about your possible legal actions and other options. (See Chapters 5 and 7.) Then with the help of this chapter, focus on what you can do now.

B. WHY IT'S HARD TO SPEAK UP

The statistics about workplace harassment, although often repeated, still have the power to shock: Most women who have been sexually harassed on the job never speak up about it. Only a small minority take informal action against harassment using company procedures. And only a miniscule number ever make a formal legal complaint with the EEOC or state enforcement agency. Why this heavy blanket of silence in the face of such abusive behavior?

There is no simple answer.

A number of feelings often combine to keep women's lips sealed: guilt, shame, embarrassment, fear of being labeled a troublemaker, too sensitive, bossy or humorless. Upbringing or experience may make the subject of harassment seem too painful or laden with other taboos for some women to come forward. Young or inexperienced workers may even assume harassment is all in a day's work. And of course, many women keep silent because they distrust the procedures for handling their harassment complaints, or don't believe they'll be effective. And some women simply say it is demeaning to have to turn to authorities for personal protection at work.

SAME SEX HARASSMENT: AN EQUAL OPPORTUNITY OFFENSE

In 1991, Joseph Oncale was hired as a roustabout by Sundowner Offshore Services (SOS). But marooned on an oil rig offshore the Gulf of Mexico, his excitement about the new job soon paled. The eight-man crew included two supervisors—a crane operator named John Lyons, and Danny Pippen, a driller. The two men shot leers and jeers at Oncale. Then one day late in October, as the crew was transferring from one platform to another, Pippen grabbed and held Oncale while Lyons rubbed his penis on Oncale's head, threatening to rape him. The next morning, the two repeated the assault, assisted by Brandon Johnson, who worked on the rig as a floor hand. Later that day, as Oncale was showering, Lyons and Pippen sexually assaulted him with a bar of soap.

Oncale reported the attacks to the two people he thought might help—first, the SOS's safety compliance clerk, who shrugged off the complaint, noting: "Those two pick on me all the time, too." Oncale then informed another SOS official on the rig, who neither investigated nor intervened. And when Lyons learned that Oncale had told others about the assaults, he redoubled his threats to continue them.

Oncale tendered his pink slip to SOS soon afterward—and indicated his reasons for leaving: sexual harassment and verbal abuse. "I felt that if I didn't leave my job, that I would be raped or forced to have sex," he later explained in a deposition.

SOS demurred that the attacks were mere horseplay.

Oncale sued, alleging that the behavior was sexual harassment—a form of sex discrimination on the job prohibited by Title VII of the federal Civil Rights Act. But both the Louisiana district court and the court on appeal held that Title VII simply does not protect against same-sex harassment.

On appeal, the U.S. Supreme Court held in March of 1998 that sexual harassment between members of the same sex can be illegal. And it bolstered its opinion with an earthy sports metaphor emphasizing that context is everything: "A professional football player's working environment is not severely or pervasively abusive, for example, if the coach smacks him on the buttocks as he heads onto the field," the Court opined, "even if the same behavior would reasonably be experienced as abusive by the coach's secretary (male or female) back at the office." (Oncale v. Sundowner Services, Inc., No. 96-568; 3/4/98.)

This ruling should help give needed direction to lower courts that have given same sex harassment cases a checkered treatment in the past. In their swervy reasoning, many courts have highlighted basic misunderstandings of sexual harassment as unrequited lust rather than obnoxious, unwanted workplace behavior.

For example, a Wisconsin court recently concluded that boys will be boys in ruling that a male co-worker did not mean what he said when he made repeated requests for oral sex—and that the requests did not add up to sexual harassment. The court may have been swayed by the facts that the oral banter between the two Coca-Cola bottling plant workers seemed reciprocal—and that one of their exchanges ended in a parking lot brawl in which they were armed with a baseball bat and tire jack. Still, the court's bottom line was that taunts and jeers at work, man to man, are not sexual harassment since they are not directed toward one another because of gender. The court used the example that when one man tells another to kiss his ass, "it has nothing to do with sex." (*Johnson v. Hondo, Inc.,* No. 9603492; 8/28/97.)

A Tennessee court recently reached an opposite conclusion, finding that a male Goodwill Industry worker's lewd and obscene remarks to a male co-worker were illegal sexual harassment. In that case, the court made much of the fact that the harasser was gay and his remarks were allegedly prompted by sexual attraction. The harassed employee at Goodwill, the court reasoned, "had to put up with abuse and harassment that women there did not have to endure." (*Yeary v. Goodwill Industries,* No. 96-5145; 2/24/97.)

Other courts, most consistently in California, Massachusetts and Minnesota, have ruled that taunts and assaults in the workplace are illegal sexual harassment, regardless of the sexual orientations of the harassed and the harasser. Interestingly, conclusions in these states may be bolstered by their strong state anti-discrimination laws which protect against discrimination based on sexual orientation. Nearly a third of the states have similar laws. (See Chapter 2, Section A.4.)

These reasons, although powerful, don't explain all of the hesitancy.

The answers may lie more in what is often overlooked. Traditional cultural programming also helps explain the silence. Women have long been socialized to be the sexual gatekeepers, responsible for setting the bounds of closeness in their relationships with men. The foremost thought on the minds of many women who have been harassed is: *What have I done wrong?*

This, perhaps, helps get at the deeper explanation of the meaning of silence. Sexual harassment is not about sexual attractiveness or a testosterone-induced urge to get close. It's not about sex at all. Sexual harassment on the job is almost always an abuse of power designed to discourage women from continuing in the workforce or getting more desirable, better paying jobs. Sexual harassment is a male tactic to make a woman vulnerable in the workplace.

It often works.

Experience shows that women who feel vulnerable and violated often have little strength to fight back, especially when they know the system is stacked against them.

> **"It was horrendous. I would go home and think 'How can my husband love me?' They would make me feel like a slut. I would think 'Why are these people doing this to me?'"**
>
> *—A Milwaukee woman who won a lawsuit after male co-workers sexually harassed her for over five years, including posting pictures of animals in crude sex acts and regularly dropping their pants in front of her*

1. Men and women: different perceptions

But it's not just women's socialization to silence that stands in their way of reporting workplace harassment. The fact that some men seem willfully blind to what harassing behavior is can sometimes be a greater barrier. Pollsters seized on this phenomenon when workplace harassment first came to the fore in the 1980s.

According to one of the earliest studies, a telephone survey of 1,200 Los Angeles residents: 67% of the men said they would be complimented if propositioned by a female co-worker; only 17% of the women said a workplace proposition would be a compliment. And 63% of the women but only 15% of the men said they would be insulted by it. That was in 1980. When the research was repeated over a decade later, perceptions had changed. "Fewer men say they would be flattered by such overtures now," according to Barbara Gutek, researcher at the University of Arizona Business School. "I think it was an issue men hadn't thought about very much in 1980," she added. "The sensitization to sexual harassment in the workplace has made them aware there can be no strings attached."

ONE WOMAN'S STORY

I've never told anyone this before, not even my husband—and we've been married almost 50 years:

It was 1943 and I was 20 years old when I started teaching school—I had to get a special license from the state. It was prestigious then to be a schoolteacher. That was something to be very proud of.

I got nothing but compliments the first two years.

Then one night, the school's head football coach told me he thought we could do more at pep assemblies. "I'd like to talk to you about it," he said. "But I wouldn't be comfortable in your home." We got in his car and he drove about 45 minutes out of town, finally stopping at a bar. He kept urging me to have a rum and Coke, something to drink.

When we got in the car to leave, the wrestling began. He told me he was grieving because his wife was very sick. I'll never forget that he said: "I just want to feel your underwear"— and he put his hand up my skirt. I told him to drive me straight home. He said: "I don't think you understand what can happen here. I'll just make one phone call—and you'll never work again." I wept all the way home. I really believed this was something I might have to go along with to keep my job. It was a small town and he was a local boy. The school board, principal and superintendent all revered him like an absolute saint—maybe even more powerful, since he was a coach, after all.

He avoided me after that. But my boss called me in and said my contract wouldn't be renewed for the next term. I had a permanent license that said I could teach forever. But I couldn't get a job anywhere without good recommendations. I became terribly disillusioned. I thought, if he can do this to me, then anyone else can, too. I left teaching.

It would have never occurred to me to tell my parents or my friends what happened. I hate hearing myself say this, but I just wonder if my parents would have thought I had done something to cause it. As immigrants, they believed so strongly you could come to America and be treated fairly. I think women friends, too, would have thought I was a hussy somehow.

Now it seems so sad. I loved teaching. It was the thing that I felt I did best. I feel that I was cheated and in some ways, I hope I don't sound immodest, but I think the students were cheated, too. They needed a younger person about.

I don't feel pain. I feel anger. I know now, given that the world is a somewhat more enlightened place, that I would do something about that kind of behavior.

In another poll, men and women workers were asked how they would respond to sexual advances at work. Only 15% of the men said they would be offended; 75% said they would be flattered. In contrast, over 75% of the women said they would be offended by the advances.

WALK A MILE IN OUR PUMPS

Ellen Wells, testifying at the 1991 Senate hearings on the confirmation of Clarence Thomas to the U.S. Supreme Court, when questioned about why a woman wouldn't talk to other people about being harassed:

You blame yourself. Perhaps it's the perfume I have on. . . . I remember one sister [in Catholic school] telling us that you have to be careful with the kind of perfume that you wore because the title indicated the kind of emotions you would generate in a gentleman...

And so you try to change your behavior because you think it must be me. You ask yourself: What did I do? I must be the wrong party here. And then I think you perhaps start to get angry and frustrated. But there's always that sense of powerlessness.

And you're also ashamed. What can you tell your friends and family, because they ask you: What did you do?

And so you keep it in. You don't say anything. And if someone says to you: You should go forward, you have to think: How am I going to pay the phone bill if I do that? And yes, perhaps this job is secure, but maybe they'll post me in a corner with the Washington Post to read from. And that won't get me anywhere.

So you're quiet. And you're ashamed. And you sit there and you take it.

More subtle behavior is eyed differently, too. In another study, workers were asked to assess the actions of a man who suggestively eyed female co-workers up and down. At least 24% of the women in the survey characterized the behavior as harassment; only 8% of the men did. (Reported in *Harvard Business Review*, March/April, 1981.)

Many men say they find it easiest to relate to women flirtatiously. Add to this the fact that when many men entered the workplace, teasing women with various types of sexual remarks and innuendo were common on the job—and seemed to win them approval. They simply don't consider such behavior to be wrong.

These differing gender responses to sexual harassment, borne out by many of life's daily experiences, come as little surprise. It should be even less surprising that they directly contribute to women's reluctance to report acts of harassment in the workplace. After all, if the male workers don't perceive their conduct as harassing in the first place, it seems futile to complain about it through a male-established power structure.

Despite recent case decisions that signal that courts are treating sexual harassment as a gender-neutral issue, many sociologists and other communications experts dismally portend that the differences in how men and women perceive it won't go away soon. They remind us that since men's workplace behavior is so tied to traditional socially enforced patterns of behavior and often based on a deeper desire to keep women out of the workplace, change is sure to be slow and difficult.

"Something highly offensive to Minnie Pearl might be an inviting dare to Madonna."

—Jonathan A. Segal, a Baltimore lawyer who advises employers on how to avoid harassment lawsuits

YES, VIRGIL. MEN GET HARASSED, TOO

A few years after sexual harassment against women came out of workplace closets across America, a new whisper emerged: "I've been harassed, too. And I'm a man." At first, many people—particularly women—took a dim view of this development. Sexual harassment on the job, after all, had been newly diagnosed as a social ill stemming from an abuse of power, and men had long dominated the powerful positions in most workplaces. It was harder to sympathize with The Harassed Man than to see him as the poor lunk who failed to duck as the pendulum was swinging.

The popular press and the silver screen seemed titillated by the thought of the role reversal. Michael Crichton was inspired to pen yet another novel on the theme, *Disclosure.* Still, when the book surfaced inevitably in a film version, even the threat of a besuited Demi Moore pinning a hapless male underling against her mahogany desk seemed less scary than, say, being passed over for a promotion.

The reality is, of course, that abusive behavior in the workplace is not limited by stereotypes of Bad Boys and Good Girls. Sexual harassment on the job is not about sex; it's about unwanted, abusive behavior—usually repeated and often in the face of requests to cut it out. Women as well as men dish out the discriminatory behavior that is sexual harassment, and they'll do it to harass men they want to intimidate or humiliate or drive out of their workplaces.

Some believe it's worse than we fear, that nearly as many men as women are harassed on the job, but few of them are willing or able to speak up about it—as if that extra chromosome reared up and got caught in their collective throats.

The most recent statistics available show a steady increase in the percentage of claims that men have filed with the EEOC—up from 7.5% in 1991 to 11.6% in 1997. Many expect a greater increase given the U.S. Supreme Court's recent recognition of same sex harassment. (See Chapter 2, Section A.4.)

The exciting development is that gender may not matter in the eyes of the law. Many judges who have considered sexual harassment issues recently—including the U.S. Supreme Court in the 1997-98 term—have edged toward making it gender-neutral. For example, most have stopped taking up space in their decisions over whether incidents of alleged harassment should best be viewed from the eyes of a reasonable woman or a reasonable man.

For a growing number of courts these days, the vantage point is common sense, the guiding premise that most workers, men and women, simply want to come to work and do their jobs.

2. Much ado about the sterile workplace

While the spotlight's focus on sexual harassment is long overdue, it has also prompted a new feeling of timidity in many workplaces. Some men claim that the increasing awareness of workplace harassment and the increasing likelihood of actions against it will cause them to become increasingly stifled and uncertain. For example, some men fret about whether they can freely compliment women co-workers on their appearance or even on their work without running the risk of a lawsuit. They worry that if they tell a risque joke in what we quaintly used to call mixed company, they'll lose their footing on the corporate ladder.

Other men trumpet more dire predictions:

- "Women are going to lose their femininity. It used to be that when a fellow left for another job or a vacation, you could kiss a woman good-bye at the office. You can't do that anymore. It's sad," lamented one 38-year-old office worker in California recently.

- A college professor complained that because of his school's new policy against sexual harassment, he would no longer be able to perform his job effectively. His biggest fear: He could not discuss his female students' dissertations with them over lunch.

- Wisconsin minister James D. Eckblad recently expressed his regret over fallout from the growing number of legal actions against clergy members for sexual misconduct: "It becomes almost impossible to give a caring hug spontaneously when you're worried about somebody else accusing you of being a criminal," he said.

The impending peril of the sterile workplace is greatly exaggerated. And of course, there is a huge upside to such male agonizing: It should result in more would-be harassers reining in their obnoxious workplace behavior. Awareness, coupled with education about sexual harassment, can go a long way toward increasing equality and decreasing discomfort in the workplace.

But there is also a downside: Excessive male handwringing over what is and what is not acceptable behavior may once again be engineered to make women feel foolish and intimidated—to still their tongues about harassment.

Some men have even vowed never to hire another woman worker; the threat of being sued looms too large in their minds. It might only fuel their fires to learn that the courts now recognize the fact that men harass other men. By their prediction, then, people would be best off replaced by computers.

In the aftermath of this firestorm, what makes most sense is for all workers, women and men, to treat one another with respect and act reasonably—to curb our tendencies to be either boorish or thin-skinned. Perhaps it's as simple as adopting a new workplace maxim: Don't Be a Jerk at Work.

C. GRAY AREAS OF BEHAVIOR

In some situations, it can be truly difficult to know whether particular behavior by a male co-worker amounts to harassment. Here, we look at the most troublesome borderline behavior from a personal perspective. (Chapter 2 analyzes the legal considerations of some of this behavior.)

Many women have the greatest difficulty in assessing and knowing how to handle the less blatant examples of male behavior—touching a co-worker on the shoulder, pinning up some kinds of less graphic pictures, looking a woman up and down. To some women, these things may feel like harassment; to others, they're innocuous.

Even worse, within the gray areas are often more shades of gray: Whether some conduct is harassment may depend on who does it. One request for a date by a co-worker may be OK, but one such request by a manager a week before a performance review may be harassment. Whether telling an off-color joke qualifies as harassment depends on whether it's welcomed by the listener. And sometimes, it depends on how off-color the off-color joke is—and the context in which it's told.

For both women and men, there is a benefit in knowing when they are treading upon shaky ground.

A LITTLE GUIDANCE FOR MEN

For men who now wonder if they will be overly hampered by the sudden attention to Proper Workplace Behavior, there is little reason to be fearful. The super-cautious advice—don't say anything to women at work except name, rank and serial number—is surely overkill.

The better advice is to use common sense. There is plenty of room to be friendly and personable without behaving in a way that is likely to offend workers of either gender.

Some rough guides for evaluating your own workplace behavior:

- *Would you say or do it in front of your spouse or parents?*

- *Would you say or do it in front of a colleague of the same sex?*

- *How would you feel if your mother, wife, sister or daughter were subjected to the same words or behavior?*

- *How would you feel if another man said or did the same things to you?*

- *Does it need to be said or done at all?*

- *If you are truly concerned that your words or conduct may be offensive to a particular co-worker, there is one foolproof way to find out: Ask her.*

---

1. Office romances

Studies have shown that as many as 70% of all male and female workers have dated someone they met in the workplace. Those are far better odds than you have of meeting someone at a bar, party or other social gathering specifically engineered to be a meeting place.

Some people point to this likelihood of meeting a date or mate at work to justify the prevalence of harassment there. This badly confuses the issue. Sexual attraction is a natural outgrowth of people working together—and is in no way illegal. Sexual harassment is unwanted, non-mutual, unacceptable conduct.

It's that simple.

Some employers have adopted a strict policy that prohibits supervisors from dating people they supervise. While this may be understandable given the relatively low legal threshold for a supervisor's conduct to be considered harassment, it is as unnecessary as it is impossible to enforce. Far better to remember that since workplace harassment is almost always about an abuse of power—not about romance gone sour—the focus should be on preventing intimidation.

Still, becoming romantically involved with someone you work with—especially a person you supervise or report to—requires caution. If you date someone at your workplace, it may be best to keep your socializing to after-work hours. If the relationship ends while the two of you still work together, be sure there is as clear an understanding as possible about it. If you have any indication that a former paramour may turn antagonistic or hostile to you at work, try at least to let a friend or office confidante know about it.

IS IT HOT IN HERE?

A 1998 survey of nearly 3,000 human resources personnel attempted to take the pulse of office romance and to find out whether things have heated up recently. Pollsters posed a number of probing questions.

What has happened to the number of workplace romances at your organization in the past five years?

Increased:	12%
Stayed the same:	48%
Decreased:	12%
Don't know:	26%

In the past five years, which of the following have occurred as a result of romance between employees?

Complaints of favoritism from co-workers:	28%
Claims of sexual harassment:	24%
Decreased productivity by those involved:	24%
Complaints of retaliation after it ended:	17%
Decreased morale of co-workers:	16%

Does your organization have a written policy about workplace romance?

Yes:	13%
No, but there is an unwritten policy:	14%
No:	72%

What do your policies prohibit?

Romance between superiors and subordinates:	70%
Public displays of affection:	37%
Dating a person who works in the same department:	19%
Dating a customer or client:	13%
All dating among employees:	4%

Source: Society for Human Resource Management

2. Work clothes and behavior

Wrongful behavior—especially behavior that harms women—is often explained away by blaming the victim.

It's no wonder she was raped, working so late at the office when she knows what a rough neighborhood it is.

She should have expected to be ogled at the convention, she was the only woman there.

She practically asked to be harassed, the way she dressed for work.

The simple response is that no one has the right to abuse another person.

But the convenient explanation of blaming a woman for her own harassment at work is much alive and deep-rooted—and crosses gender lines. About 49% of the women and 53% of the men polled by *Time* magazine as recently as 1986 agreed with the following statement: Women who complain about sexual harassment have often asked for trouble by the way they dress or behave. Paradoxically, this attitude prevails strongly to this day, even though there is absolutely no evidence that harassers are put off by conservative attire.

Wear whatever you feel is appropriate to work. But know that the issue may be more important than it seems at first glance. Many people are bothered when their co-workers wear tight-fitting, provocative clothes. It makes them feel uncomfortable—as if a vague sexual aura has pervaded the workplace. Some men may even wrongly interpret sexy clothes such as a low-cut blouse or short skirt as an invitation to act inappropriately.

If the clothes you usually wear to work are provocatively styled, take an honest moment to ask yourself why. In some workplaces, women workers are motivated to dress in certain ways because of some subtle expectancy that they are supposed to look like sex objects. Double-check to be sure that you are not playing into this type of sexist game.

So the bottom line is in a sort of limbo: There's no need to become a fashion victim by sacrificing your imagination in clothes for a wardrobe of button-down shirts and bowties. At the same time in this age of heightened sensitivity as to Proper Workplace Conduct, a definite—albeit nebulous—standard indicates you should dress differently for work than you might for a night of nightclubbing.

THE LAW LOOKS AT YOUR HEMLINE

As offensive and irrelevant as it may seem, if you do decide to take formal action against your harasser, what you wear to work and how you act there will likely be examined by the person investigating your complaint or evaluated by a court.

"Is she going to continue to go to the office in a tiny miniskirt and say, '*He's* not supposed to think about sex?' That's not realistic."

—*Ruth Westheimer, aka Dr. Ruth*

3. Pin-ups

As long as "cheesecake" or "girlie" pictures have been around—nude and semi-nude, sexually provocative pictures of women—so has raged the debate over whether they are smut or art.

Some people are unbothered by them and will defend anyone's wish to see and display nude or pornographic pictures as a constitutional right. Others find them acceptable only in private. Not surprisingly, many women find all such displays demeaning in the workplace.

Displaying highly suggestive pin-ups that some employees find offensive is almost always harassment. A good example is the recent *Robinson* case, already famous in the annals of sexual harassment history. (*Robinson v. Jacksonville Shipyards, Inc.*, 760 F. Supp. 1486 (M.D. Fla. 1991).)

In that case, a female welder in a Florida shipyard complained that cartoons, magazines, calendars, graffiti, posters, plaques and drawings featuring partially clad or nude women, most in sexually suggestive or submissive poses, were displayed throughout the workplace. Just a few of the more obnoxious examples from the hundreds that made up visual assault in the shipyard included:

- a picture of a woman's pubic area with a meat spatula pressed on it
- a sketch of nude female torso with "USDA Choice" written on it
- a dartboard picturing a woman's breast with the nipple as the bull's eye
- a lifesize drawing of a nude woman on a workspace divider
- a drawing of a nude woman with fluid coming from her genital area, and
- graffiti painted prominently on the workplace walls including: "lick me you whore dog bitch," "pussy," "cunt" and "eat me."

The court found that while the displays would not interfere with some men's abilities to get their jobs done, they could understandably seem offensive and distracting to a reasonable woman worker. It ordered the shipyard to implement at once a detailed sexual harassment policy which included a comprehensive procedure for making, investigating and resolving sexual harassment and retaliation complaints. In addition, the company was ordered to train all female employees how to resist and prevent sexual harassment and to train all supervisors and managers how to handle harassment complaints.

And if, as some men protest, pin-ups are a constitutionally protected artform, one might wonder why only women are the only subject. Men do appear on pin-ups, too, but it is rare that they are displayed in workplaces. In fact, one foreman in the Florida case testified that he did not know of a vendor distributing a calendar of nude men, but if one did, he would "think the son of a bitch was queer."

> **"Pornography on an employer's wall or desk communicates a message about the way he views women, a view strikingly at odds with the way women wish to be viewed in the workplace."**
> *—From Robinson v. Jacksonville Shipyards,* 760 F. Supp. 1486 (1991)

WHEN THE ARTWORK ISN'T ART

If there are pictures or graffiti displayed in your workplace that you find offensive, there are a number of steps you can take.

- If the pin-ups are displayed in a public area that is not part of another person's workspace, take them down.

- If only one person has posted pictures you find offensive, take him aside and tell him so. Ask him to stop doing it.

- If your company has regular staff meetings, bring up the matter of the unwanted office decor there.

- If it is not possible to take down the offending pieces, and the person who posted them is uncooperative, take pictures of the workplace walls—and be sure to date the back. That may be compelling evidence in later negotiations, claims or lawsuits. (See Section F.)

---

4. Jokes

Humor, by its nature, walks a fine line between delighting and offending—and perceptions of it are intensely personal. While the prospect of a workplace devoid of humor is as bleak as a workplace devoid of paychecks, it's also true that humor can hurt.

Because jokes are often used both to reinforce and deflect strong feelings, many are built around racist, homophobic and sexist punchlines. Parrying back with a witty retort to jokes that you find offensive may occasionally feel good, but it runs the risk of reinforcing the behavior—and may even cause it to escalate.

Whether a joke told in the workplace crosses the line from good-humored to mean-spirited depends first on its content. If a joke is not obviously directed at a particular person or not obviously raunchy, it's more likely to be acceptable for the workplace. And whether a joke is acceptable for the workplace also depends on the audience and context.

Example:

Q: How do you make a blond laugh on Monday?

A: Tell her a joke on Friday.

As they wait alone for an elevator at the end of the week, Debby tells this joke to her boss Robin, with whom she has a fairly close relationship. Both women are blond. Both laugh. No harm done.

Suppose Ted uses the same joke to close his Friday night speech at the real estate developers symposium. Robin is one of only three women in the large audience—and the only one with blond hair. Robin is embarrassed as the titters and stares focus on her. Ted should have held his tongue. Robin should call him on his unfortunate behavior privately, after he has finished his speech.

If you often feel like the butt of an unwelcome joke, there are good ways to show your disapproval and, hopefully, put an end to having them uttered in your presence.

Simply don't laugh. Stronger stuff than it sounds. Consider that nothing makes a stand-up comic sit down more quickly than the din of silence. If the harasser's aim is to make you uncomfortable or to catch you off-guard, a bored, unresponsive look may quickly show him he's off his mark.

Leave the room. While not always a practical solution, this can also act as a strong antidote for many wannabe comedians. The truth is, you don't want to go on 24-hour surveillance of the office buffoon to make sure he doesn't tell the one about the guy who goes to the whorehouse. But you don't have to encourage him by being among his listening audience.

Firmly but politely tell the jokester that you don't appreciate the remark. The first two responses may work best for one-on-one encounters, but if many others are present, your silence or leaving may not be noticed or may even be turned against you to add to the levity.

ONE MERE OFFENSIVE UTTERANCE IS NOT ENOUGH

The U.S. Supreme Court recently gave some guidance on the murky issue of how abusive behavior must be to be deemed sexual harassment.

The case arose when Teresa Harris alleged she quit her job at Forklift Systems only after being harassed by company president Charles Hardy.

Harris says the insults and innuendoes began soon after she took the job as rental manager at Forklift. Hardy called her a "dumb ass woman"; he asked her to retrieve coins from deep within his front pants pocket; he dropped things on the ground and asked her to pick them up so he could comment on her cleavage. And he urged her to negotiate her raise at the Holiday Inn.

The court below found the boorish behavior was not harassment, since they did not harm Harris' psychological well-being or cause her to suffer injury. This echoed holdings from other courts. Many applied the twisted reasoning that a worker without a record of psychiatric visits was not a truly harassed worker. And opponents perversely used evidence of seeking such help against the worker—claiming it was obvious proof of not being up to snuff.

In finding that Harris may indeed have been harassed at Forklift, the Court tried to define how bad behavior must be before it crosses the bounds into illegal. It held that one untoward joke or innuendo is not enough—that "mere utterance of an epithet which engenders offensive feelings" is not solid ground upon which to base a harassment claim. But it also held, on the other end of the spectrum, that harassing conduct need not "lead to a nervous breakdown."

Those caught up in determining whether behavior is harassment should look at a number of factors—one no more important than the other—including:

- the frequency of the discriminatory conduct
- its severity
- whether it is physically threatening or humiliating, or a mere offensive utterance
- whether it unreasonably interferes with an employee's work performance, and
- whether it harms the employee's psychological well-being (*Harris v. Forklift Systems, Inc.*, 510 U.S. 21 (1993)).

- You may need to be more upfront. You might say: "I'm sorry, but rape is not at all funny to me." Here, your own timing can be crucial. Don't take the jokester to task in front of his boss or other employees; you're likely to antagonize him completely and cause the discomfort to escalate. Call him aside and tell him how you feel. If you are uncomfortable speaking to him alone, ask him to talk with you and with others who share your feelings.

- A repeat performance or two usually signals that more than good-natured fun is intended: You're being harassed.

- A complaint to your supervisor or through your company's complaint procedure is your next logical step. (See Chapter 4.)

- If the offensive behavior does not stop after that, you may decide to file a complaint with your state fair employment practices agency or the EEOC. (See Chapter 6, Section G, and Chapter 7, Section A.)

5. Innuendos

Sexual and sexist innuendos are usually less direct than jokes, but no less damaging. While at their mildest, they are merely the annoying trademark of the office oaf, they can also be uncomfortably suggestive or even intimidating.

Example: Harry, the newly hired vice president of a large architectural firm, spots a co-worker, Roya, at the office water cooler. She has a pencil in her hand. "Sure wish you'd help me with some dictation," he says.

Roya is annoyed by his remark and finds it demeaning. To stop this sexist behavior from becoming a way of life at the office, she should firmly and clearly tell him so.

Example: Harry and Roya are in Harry's office discussing the site of a planned project. "Sure wish you'd help me with some dictation," he says, picking up the microphone to his dictaphone and waving it suggestively in his lap.

The same sentence, but this one far more loaded with sexual innuendo, may justifiably feel like harassment to Roya. Not only should she be upfront about telling him she finds his behavior offensive, it would be wise for her to begin keeping a written record of his unwanted behavior in case he repeats or escalates it. (See Section F.)

There are also many variations of sexist innuendos—a slightly different breed of quip that focuses on some real or imagined difference between the sexes. Some such common quips:

Don't even try to talk to Leslie today. She's got a whopping case of PMS.

The only reason Toni got a good performance review is because she'd cry if she didn't.

Mary can't handle that union contract. She's not hard-nosed enough.

It would be a waste to give that promotion to Sarah. Her husband's rich, so she doesn't even need to work.

Such comments may feel demeaning or embarrassing. Taken at their worst, they reinforce the societal prejudice that women are less capable and less dependable workers because of their gender and all their hormonal swings and surges. Innuendos may also feel particularly hard to combat because women are often chided for "being too sensitive" or for not being able to "keep up with" the men in the office.

If any comment makes you feel uncomfortable, do not laugh or respond with a quip of your own. Take the speaker aside and tell him how you feel. He just might not have known that he was being offensive. If nothing else, he'll be put on notice.

If he persists—or his comments take on the distinct tone of putdowns—consider taking more formal action against him.

> **"The one important thing I have learned over the years is the difference between taking one's work seriously and taking one's self seriously. The first is imperative and the second is disastrous."**
> **—Margot Fonteyn, English dancer**

WHEN THE BOSS IS THE BAD GUY:
SEEKING STRENGTH IN NUMBERS

If you've been there or done that, you know that it can be difficult to speak up about being sexually harassed on the job. And the prospect looms more difficult when the harasser also acts as your boss. Unfortunately, harassing heads of workplaces are nothing new— but some commonalities among them have surfaced since the public spotlight was turned on their behavior in recent years.

Many supervisors are repeat offenders—serial harassers who work at making a number of workers' lives miserable at a number of different jobs. Their patterns may go unreported and undetected for years; no one wants to rat on the boss. But when one brave soul comes forward, others often come out of the woodwork.

Heed the case of Martin Greenstein, a partner and top income producer in one of America's biggest law firms, Baker & McKenzie. In 1991, Greenstein's short-term secretary Rena Weeks complained that he had acted atrociously on the job, berating her without cause and grabbing her breasts and buttocks. Once Weeks sued for sexual harassment, six women—all of them Greenstein's former co-workers in a branch office— came forward for the 1994 trial. These women testified he touched them, made inappropri- ate sexual remarks and pressured them for sex before they quit their posts. Most of them had told management about the sexual harassment and got no response—or a hollow promise that someone would give Greenstein a stern talking-to about his bad behavior.

A jury awarded Weeks over $7 million in damages. Although that amount was later reduced by about half, the verdict sent a wave of shock through corporate culture. In the shadow of the expensive penalty, many businesses realized that they had been lax in checking employee work references and histories and in failing to respond to complaints about harassing behavior on the job.

With a taste for the courtroom that only a law firm could palate, Baker & McKenzie in 1998 appealed the portion of the damages verdict the firm was made to pay. The court ruled, however, that the firm needed to pay for turning a blind eye to the complaints against Greenstein and failing to take any effective action to stop him.

A lone complainant also found strength in numbers in the case of another boss gone ballistic: Dan Wassong, CEO of Del Laboratories. Women hired as Wassong's secretaries typically recalled that while their boss was the model of gentlemanliness at first, that didn't last long. Among the boorish behavior he adopted: urinating while leaving the restroom door flung open, slapping her on the backside, making lewd remarks, leaving his fly open and openly scratching his genitals while parading about the office cubicles. He went through secretaries quickly, replacing each one who quit.

Finally, in 1991, Jonneigh Adrion, one in the secretarial series, complained to the EEOC about Wassong's behavior. She had tried other routes first. At first, Adrion complained to the company's personnel director, who told her that Wassong could further her career if only she stayed on the job and braved his bad behavior. She took her case to two male attorneys. One suggested she leave scratchmarks on Wassong next time he assaulted her; the other suggested that she hire a temporary secretary to distract Wassong's attention.

Finally, she went to the EEOC. The agency located about three dozen women who stepped up to recount similar tales of his abuse on the job. In 1995, the case settled before trial. In addition to awarding $1.2 million to the harassed former employees, Del Labs was required to send company execs to a sexual harassment training program. In a confusing twist of inaction, Wassong was allowed to keep his CEO post, membership on the Del Lab board and ownership of 35% of the company stock.

Workers at Baker & McKenzie and Del Labs report that today, years after the verdict was read and the settlement reached, their workplaces remain uncomfortable places in which they talk and walk gingerly around the topic of harassment. It's severe reaction to a severe verdict awarded to right a severe problem—an unfortunate part of the pendulum swinging as workplaces grapple with how best to right the wrong of harassment.

D. DECIDING WHETHER TO TAKE FURTHER ACTION

The truth is frustrating to hear: There is no one right way to respond to sexual harassment on the job. Despite the urgings of people who are leading the fight to ban harassment in the workplace and of books like this one, there still can be valid reasons not to speak up about being sexually harassed. Any complaint may make your harasser agitated, causing him to retaliate against you by making it still more difficult for you to do your job. Your co-workers may suddenly shun you, deciding that it's not worth their while to associate with a troublemaker.

Also, if you take legal action against your harasser, you will probably have to hire a lawyer, spend lots of time and money and be required to publicly air some personal matters such as your mental and physical health. Harassment investigations, whether within your company or through your state or EEOC procedure, often take a long, wearing time—and there is no assurance that they will end the unwanted behavior. So some women don't report harassment because they simply want to get on with their lives.

If the harassment you're experiencing is fairly mild and occasional, you may be able to perform your job effectively and to live with yourself comfortably without complaining about it. It may mean you will spend time and energy at work in the effort to skirt your harasser. Or you may even decide to leave your job to avoid him, although, obviously, this is a practical choice only if you have other equivalent or better job options.

Asserting your right to be treated with dignity and respect is usually your best course. One fact alone should motivate you: Men have traditionally relied on the fact that women often feel too vulnerable and violated to speak up. If you remain mum, you not only acquiesce in this strategy of male dominance, you all but guarantee that it will continue to infect your workplace.

1. Sizing up the situation

The first step in deciding whether to take informal or formal action against sexual harassment is to take a hard and honest look at the behavior that is making you uncomfortable, angry or frustrated. Be as objective as possible about the situation, weeding out the facts from any emotion you feel. It is often helpful at this stage to discuss your situation with a fair-minded friend, asking for a candid evaluation of your perceptions. Use his or her assessment to help you sort out what might be genuine harassment from what may be other workplace politics and life frustrations. This is especially helpful where the workplace behavior that's giving you cause for worry is not seriously threatening.

> *Example: The head of your department, a man about your age, acts uncomfortable around you, avoiding eye contact. He often fails to send you copies of memos or invite you to meetings that discuss projects in which you're involved. You know that he invited other co-workers to social events at his home and this, too, makes you feel cast out. You feel that you are treated differently than your co-workers, and that the difference may lead to you doing your job less well*

than you could. But you're not sure if you're being subjected to sexual harassment.

The best assessment that a knowledgeable friend could give you in this situation is to be wary. Although the lack of eye contact and lack of social invitations may make you feel excluded and shunned, they should not affect your job performance. However, consistently cutting you out of workplace information is more serious—and may amount to discrimination if it deprives you of the means you need to do your job well. It's sensible to begin to keep notes as to how your work is made more difficult and may be less effective. Spend some time thinking about how you and your supervisor can work to reduce the tension between you.

"Alas, I was never scuttled. Sometimes I would look up hopefully from my typewriter to see three or four scuttlers skulking in the doorway, mulling it over, but the decision was always the same—too young, too pale, too flat-chested. Clearly unscuttlable."

—Helen Gurley Brown, former editor in chief of Cosmopolitan magazine, recalling scuttling—a rite at a former workplace in which male higher-ups chased secretaries and tore their panties down

Example: You used to be the only person working in Accounts Receivable. Recently, two new employees have been hired. You think they may take over your job responsibilities completely, and you will be demoted back to your old position as a secretary.

To make matters worse, one of the new hires, John, has twice asked you on dates—once for a drink after work and another time to a cafe for lunch. You turned him down both times, the second time telling him you are engaged. John acted surprised. He said that at his old workplace, employees often ate lunch and socialized together; he meant nothing untoward. You suspect that he really wanted to get you alone to pick your brain about the specifics of your job so he could take it over.

In this situation, a friend might best tell you to lighten up. If you are insecure about the status of your job, talk with your supervisor, but don't blame John. His behavior isn't unreasonable so far; he may have merely been attempting to *be friendly. You've made it clear that you don't want to socialize with him, so it's probably best to assume he will take you at your word. But if he doesn't and asks again, restate your reasons for wanting to keep the relationship strictly professional.*

Example: Your co-worker, Frank, seems to spend an inordinate amount of time in your office. Each time, he closes the door behind him—and closed doors are not de rigueur at your workplace. Frank claims he needs to talk with you "because he respects your opinion" on how to package new compact discs for your employer, a music production company. You work as a film editor and have no real expertise or interest in packaging—and you resent the need to stay late to make up for the worktime you lose during Frank's frequent visits.

While Frank has made no sexual overtures, you are vaguely bothered by his too-frequent attention, recurring questions about your social life and lingering eye contact. You have not confronted him because you don't want to make an enemy or be seen as a someone who doesn't care about the company's success.

Here, a wise friend would encourage you to speak up to Frank to firmly let him know that his behavior is making it more difficult for you to do your job. If he persists, consider writing him a concise letter or telling a supervisor how you feel. (See Section F, below.)

2. What to do when you need to do more

For some women in some situations, the strategies discussed for fighting back against harassment may not suffice. They may need to take extra steps, such as:

- Making a special effort to educate themselves about how to recognize and fight back against harassment. This book, as well as a number of recently published pamphlets can help in this effort. (See the Appendix.)

- Meeting with other similarly situated women to discuss the common harassment problems and ways to deal with them. In many communities, particularly medium to large cities, there are ongoing support groups established expressly for this purpose. (See the Appendix.)

- Trying to educate management about the perils, pitfalls and seriousness of sexual harassment on the job. If your employee handbook makes no mention of the company's stance against harassment and defining how to recognize it, ask management to add one. If there is no sexual harassment policy, lobby for one. (See Chapter 4, Sections C and D.)

- Taking immediate legal action under your state laws (see Chapter 7) or with the EEOC (see Chapter 6)—especially if the harassment involves violence or the threat of it.

IT'S NOT ALL IN YOUR HEAD

According to the American Psychological Association, many women who have been harassed on the job report a cornucopia of symptoms similar to other forms of severe stress. They include:

Psychological Reactions
- *Depression, anxiety, shock, denial*
- *Anger, fear, frustration, irritability*
- *Insecurity, embarrassment, feelings of betrayal*
- *Confusion, feelings of being powerless*
- *Shame, self-consciousness, low self-esteem*
- *Guilt, self-blame, isolation*

Physiological Reactions
- *Headaches*
- *Lethargy*
- *Gastrointestinal distress*
- *Dermatological reactions*
- *Weight fluctuations*
- *Sleep disturbances, nightmares*
- *Phobias, panic reactions*
- *Sexual problems*

Career-Related Effects
- *Decreased job satisfaction*
- *Unfavorable performance evaluations*
- *Loss of job or promotion*
- *Drop in academic or work performance*
- *Absenteeism*
- *Withdrawal from work or school*
- *Change in career goals*

—Adapted from *Sexual Harassment: Myths and Realties*, by the American Psychological Association; Washington, DC.

E. CONFRONTING YOUR HARASSER

The key in assessing whether behavior is sexual harassment is whether it is unwanted. If it is, ask that it be stopped. Surprisingly often—some experts say up to 90% of the time—this works.

When confronted directly, harassment is especially likely to end if it is at a fairly low level: off-color jokes, inappropriate comments about your appearance, repeated requests for dates, tacky cartoons tacked onto the office refrigerator.

Saying no in a tangible way does more than assert your determination to stop the behavior. It is also a crucial first step if you later decide to take more formal action against the harassment, whether through your company's complaint procedure or through the legal system. And give serious thought to documenting what's going on; your case will be stronger if you can later prove that the harassment continued after you confronted the harasser.

PROCEED CAUTIOUSLY IF THERE'S VIOLENCE

Sexual harassment is sometimes associated with violent behavior. If you fear your harasser, do not confront him alone. Alternatives include getting the support of co-workers who will agree to confront him with you, filing a complaint with your company (see Chapter 4), filing a confidential harassment claim with your state agency or EEOC (see Chapter 6) or filing another court action (see Chapter 8). If his behavior is truly frightening, consider reporting it to local police.

---

1. Tell him what you don't want

If possible, deal directly with the harassment when it occurs. But if your harasser surprises you with an obnoxious gesture or comment that catches you completely off-guard—a common tactic—you may be too flabbergasted to respond at once. Or if you did respond, you may not have expressed yourself clearly. Either way, talk to him the next day.

Keep the conversation brief. Try to speak to your harasser privately—out of the hearing range of supervisors and co-workers. At the same time, avoid giving the appearance that you want a social meeting. Asking him to meet you away from work in a bar or restaurant is likely to give the wrong impression.

Do not smile, touch your harasser or give any other mixed messages when you speak.

This is not a good time to use humor to make your point. Joking may be too easily misunderstood or interpreted as a sign that you don't take the situation seriously yourself. For example, if a male co-worker flashes you a picture of a couple having sex in an unusual position and you find the picture offensive, do not say: "Unfortunately, I'm not that flexible." A better response might be: "I'm offended by these kinds of pictures. In the future, please respect my privacy."

It is usually better to make a direct request that a specific kind of behavior stop, rather than to describe to your harasser how you feel. For example, saying: "I am uncomfortable with this," may be enough to get the point across to some, but the subtlety will surely be lost on others. And of course, making you uncomfortable may be just the effect the harasser was after.

Make your point with simple, direct sentences like these:

Please do not touch me when we talk.

I will gladly discuss the BFT account with you during work hours, but I'm not interested in having dinner with you.

Please remove that picture you left on my desk—that's my private workspace.

I'm not at all interested in that kind of movie.

Keep in mind that you're not the one whose behavior is inexcusable. There is no need to offer excuses or apologies, such as: "My boyfriend wouldn't like it if we met at your apartment to discuss our new project."

If the thought of speaking up to your harasser makes you nervous, rehearse. Ask a friend to stand in for the harasser and attempt to anticipate how he might respond to you; practice your response.

If the harasser persists after you have said no, or changes tacks to performing other annoying and unwanted behavior, repeat your request that he stop, using stronger language. You may want to point out to him that his behavior is illegal— and that it is seriously affecting your ability to do your job. Let him know that if he persists, you are prepared to take action against the harassment—such as reporting the situation to company authorities or filing a legal action. Begin preparing for a formal action by documenting the situation. (See Section F.2.)

2. Put it in writing

If your harasser persists, write him a letter, spelling out what behavior you object to and why. Also specify what you want to happen next. If you feel the situation is serious or bound to escalate, let him know that you will take action against the harassment if it doesn't stop at once. If your company has a written policy against harassment, you may want to attach a copy of it to your letter.

> "It wasn't about getting money or going to court and winning. The only thing that drove me is I didn't want him to do it to anyone else. I didn't want him to make anyone feel the way I did when I left—helpless."
>
> —*Jonneigh Adrion, plaintiff in a sexual harassment lawsuit against her former boss*

SAMPLE LETTER

```
February 1, 199X

Charles Gazda
McNulty Company
Thiscity, Thisstate 00000

Mr. Gazda:

During this morning's meeting, you twice interrupted my
sales presentation to comment on the way I was dressed.

I found this demeaning and feel that it detracted greatly
from the overall professionalism of our pitch.

During your portion of our presentation, and in all our
time at work, I have treated you with respect. In the
future, please show me the same respect by confining your
comments to business matters.

Sincerely,

Marcia Malini
```

SAMPLE LETTER

February 10, 199X

Frank Stroh
Booktale Corporation
Thiscity, Thisstate 00000

Mr. Stroh:

Two weeks ago, you commented about my legs, told me I'd look better and "more accessible" in shorter skirts and asked me to meet you after work for a drink. I told you I was not interested in a social relationship and that I'd prefer that you didn't comment about my body and clothing.

Today, you brushed up against me as we passed in the hallway—and again said you "were anxious to see more of me" and asked me to meet you in the bar on the first floor of our office building "during the time after work and before my husband is expected home."

Your persistent comments on my clothing and requests to meet socially are upsetting to me and, as I have made clear, are unwelcome. I want our relationship to be purely professional, as it was during the first six months I worked at Booktale.

Should you be unwilling to comply with my request to conduct yourself more acceptably in the workplace, I will ask our Human Resources Department to investigate.

Sincerely,

Lizanne Romanowski

SAMPLE LETTER

October 1, 199X

Ernest Configliano
Consulters, Unlimited
Thiscity, Thisstate 00000

Mr. Configliano:

This morning, while reviewing the draft of the complaint in the Kyler case, you brushed against my breast and twice touched my buttocks while ostensibly reaching for other office materials.

As I told you last week, I am offended by you touching me in these suggestive ways and find it to be totally inappropriate workplace behavior.

I have attached pages of our company's policy against sexual harassment. Note that your behavior not only clearly violates the letter and intent of our policy, it is also prohibited by both state and federal law.

Should you persist in your behavior, I will take action against it at once by bringing a copy of this letter when I discuss this distressing matter with your supervisor, Cathy Henderson.

Sincerely,

Rachel Bornstein

Before you send the letter to the person you feel is harassing you, ask the opinion of someone you trust as to whether your letter is clear and to the point. Experience indicates that a surprising number of women have been too nice, too indirect—and therefore not very effective in writing down what they mean.

Make a copy of your letter before you send it. Keep your copy in a safe place away from work, preferably at home. If the situation remains or escalates, the letter will be great evidence that you were forthright and prompt in letting the harasser know that his behavior was wrong.

In most cases, the recipient of your letter will not respond or write back to you—but he may express surprise or shock about your view of his behavior. He will likely be concerned about the possibility that you will go public with the charges. But his reaction to your letter is not as important as the fact that you have sent it—making your feelings and intentions clear and beginning to document the unpleasant situation.

Best of all, in a great many situations, this will stop the harassment.

> **"I saw the Hill-Thomas developments as positive. I saw a credible, articulate woman speaking up somewhat reluctantly. I saw columnists by the droves acknowledging that sexual harassment happens to all of them (or their wives or women friends). Sexual harassment became something that not only the fringe would allege, but that everyone could acknowledge."**
>
> **—*Pat Conover Mickiewicz, Oregon State Bar Bulletin***

HOW TO SAY NO—AND BE HEARD

Elizabeth Evans, a psychotherapist in private practice in Berkeley, California, also has extensive experience teaching classes in assertiveness and communication skills, primarily aimed to help women in the workplace. She urges the following formula for a woman who wants to speak up to her workplace harasser.

Take the scenario where you are being pestered by a male co-worker or supervisor for a lunch date you don't want. I recommend starting out with a rather benign statement the first time you speak to him. You might say: "I am comfortable with our business relationship, but I'm not comfortable carrying it any further—even for lunch."

But even more important than your words is how you say them. Pay special attention to your body as you speak—posture, vocal tone, eye contact, facial expression, personal distance.

Aim for a relaxed, confident stance. Do not hunch or strut. Take time to adjust your position so that you're neither looking up at nor down at him. The tone of your voice should be even and firm. Look him in the eye. If standing, stand at a distance that feels comfortable—not too close, not so far that you have to raise your voice unnaturally. Make only appropriate gestures. Do not wring your hands, look down, stare, move in toward the person, or shake your finger under his nose.

If he persists in the unwanted behavior, make an escalated assertion, something like: "I've told you three times that I am not interested in any other relationship. I would like you to stop asking me."

If the harassment persists: "The answer is no and please don't ask again."

Another thing a woman can do is to reward the behavior that she wants repeated. For example, at the end of a meeting, you might say: "Thanks, John, for letting me express my opinions. I noticed you really listened to me."

F. WHAT TO DO IF THE HARASSMENT CONTINUES

Serious harassers will persist in their behavior—even after you have clearly made known that their advances or other wrongful conduct are unwanted. You will need to consider your next move.

You can choose to remain on the job, keep your mouth shut and hope that the harassment will stop. In some cases, the harassers simply wear themselves out or move on to another target. But most do not. In fact, sensing an easy target, many hardcore harassers escalate their obnoxious behavior.

It is impossible to offer foolproof advice on how to respond to every situation involving serious sexual harassment. But it's usually best to get official help either from your employer or a state or federal agency. Prepare to do this by collecting as much detailed evidence as possible about the specifics of your harassment.

Two areas are especially important.

Your reactions to the advances. You will want to be able to show as clearly as possible that the advances were unwanted, and practically speaking, this may be essential before anyone will act on your claim.

The timing of your complaint. The more quickly you confront your harasser—and if the harassment continues, make an official complaint—the more credibly your complaint is likely to be treated.

Here are some practical suggestions.

1. Collect evidence

Be sure to save any offensive letters, photographs, cards or notes you receive. And if you were made to feel uncomfortable because of jokes, pin-ups or cartoons posted at work, confiscate them—or at least make copies. An anonymous, obnoxious photo or joke posted on a bulletin board is not anyone else's personal property, so you are free to take it down and keep it as evidence. If that's not possible, photograph the workplace walls. Note the dates the offensive material was posted—and whether there were hostile reactions when you took it down or asked another person to do so.

2. Keep a detailed journal

Write down the specifics of everything that feels like harassment. Include the names of everyone involved, what happened, where and when it took place. If anyone else saw or heard the harassment, note that as well. Be as specific as possible about what was said and done—and how it affected you, your health or job performance.

Also include details of harassing or annoying phone calls you receive at work or home—including dates, times, lengths of time that the calls lasted and summaries of what was said. Again, keep this journal in a safe place, preferably at home.

HARASSMENT REPORTS UP, ACTION UP TOO

According to a recent study, nearly 75% of medium and large firms reported sexual harassment claims in 1996—compared to a tally of just over 50% five years earlier. Most of the more recent complaints were against co-workers rather than supervisors.

A look at the action the firms took follows.

Offender reprimanded: 35.1%

Mediation for those involved: 35%

Accuser dismissed: 16%

Allegation dismissed: 15%

Accuser transferred: 3.9%

Offender transferred: 3%

Source: American Management Association

SAMPLE JOURNAL ENTRIES

April 24, 199X

On his way in to work today, my supervisor Robert Neeson stopped by my office. As I took off my coat, he stepped behind to help, then clasped me against him with one arm. He said: "You look so sexy with your hair down—just like the star of a really hot movie I saw last night. Do you like to watch porno movies?" I felt a little scared, but I said no, took his arm off my shoulder and sat down at my desk and began to return phone calls. It was early—about 7:45—and no one else was at work yet.

April 26, 199X

When I came back from lunch today, there was an interoffice memo left on my chair that said: "Here's your look-alike. Please see me about this.—Bob" Attached was a picture of a nude woman with long brown hair and the caption Pleasure Me. The woman was on her hands and knees. A man was holding a gun to her head. This afternoon, I told Mr. Neeson that I found the picture offensive and asked him not to show me any more. He said: "It's too bad for you. Debby really went for that flick in a big way." This was the week after Deborah Utner had been promoted from my position to become Neeson's assistant.

April 27, 199X

At midnight, Mr. Neeson came to my apartment door with a bouquet of flowers in his hand. He looked drunk and slurred his words. When I refused to let him in, he became angry and shouted: "You don't know what you're missing" and "You little bitch, I'll make sure your life gets harder." He shouted and swore for about ten minutes, until Burt Griffith, my upstairs neighbor, called down to ask whether he should call the police.

3. Talk with friends

Sexual harassment usually takes place in private—with no witnesses—and a later legal action will often turn on how reliable the person complaining is considered to be. Promptly telling other people you trust about the harassment is an excellent way to create potentially valuable witnesses to verify that you were angry or upset about the harassment. And of course, telling another person about the harassment is likely to make it seem less threatening or scary, less like a terrible secret.

If you do not complain to or confide in someone when the harassment occurs, an investigator, judge or jury evaluating the situation later may conclude that you were not really offended by the incident—or that it didn't occur as you claim.

4. Talk with co-workers

Talking with co-workers can be somewhat trickier than talking with friends. You don't want to jeopardize their jobs or bring down their morale at work, but you may need to enlist their help. This is especially important if the co-workers have seen or heard your harasser at work and can back up your claim. Being familiar with your office inner workings, he or she might also be in the best position to discuss your options in dealing with the harassment.

Former co-workers may also be a grand resource for you. You may be surprised to learn that a number of them left the workplace because they were subjected to the same kind of harassing behavior that you are experiencing. Even though they chose to leave rather than suffer on, their stories will often help strengthen your claim. And because they are now safe from repercussions, they may be more likely to talk with you openly and honestly.

5. Contact a support group

If you want additional seasoned advice about how to deal with your situation and protect your safety, or want an experienced assessment of whether you are being sexually harassed from a legal standpoint, contact a sexual harassment hotline or support group. (See the Appendix for contact details.)

BEWARE OF RETALIATION

In possibly volatile cases in some workplaces, do not overlook the possibility that some company witnesses may be blackmailed with the threat—often unspoken—of losing their jobs or being demoted if they cooperate with you in documenting or investigating a sexual harassment complaint. While retaliation is illegal, it is difficult to prove. If possible, try to document the harassment by talking with witnesses both inside and outside the company.

---

6. Organize a group

If sexual harassment is pervasive and taken for granted and management appears oblivious to it, communicate your concerns to other employees. You may find that several of your co-workers have been subjected to a similar kind of harassment. Certainly if your workplace is poisoned by sexual materials, comments and jokes, you should have little difficulty rounding up allies. You can then provide a great support network for one another.

If several of your co-workers have been harassed by the same person or in the same way, several simultaneous complaints about the behavior will speak more loudly than a single one. If you are still considering whether you want to take action, you will likely find it empowering to have witnesses: If your harasser uses verbal harassment, try to make sure there are other people within hearing range when he is likely to speak to you.

But when talking with other co-workers, be discreet. Talk at first only with those who may have been harassed by the same person or who you know are likely to be sensitive to the issue. Meet in private, away from work—and preferably before or after work hours.

7. Get a copy of your work records

If your employer has conducted periodic evaluations of your work, make sure you have copies. In fact, you may want to ask for a copy of your entire personnel file—before you tip your hand that you are considering taking action against a harassing co-worker. Your records will be particularly persuasive evidence if your evaluations have been good and your employer later retaliates by trying to transfer or fire you, claiming poor job performance.

If the atmosphere becomes particularly negatively charged at your workplace, you may want to guard against your records being changed or destroyed. To do this, mail a copy of your records to yourself, but do not open it. Save the sealed, post-marked envelope for evidence.

GETTING STRENGTH FROM NUMBERS

Here are some practical ideas for organizing allies in your workplace.

Find out who else cares about the problem. Sexual harassment is an issue that affects many people. Talk with co-workers you know and ask them to talk with the people they know who may also be concerned about it.

Agree on a plan. Get together—at lunch, after work, or in the evening at someone else's home. Identify who in the company you need to deal with. List concrete suggestions to improve the situation. Figure out how to get more information if you need it. Decide whether the best tactic is a letter, a petition, a meeting with the boss or some other work action.

Take action. Involve as many people as you can, and act as a group.

Spread the word about your successes. When others see you have made a difference, they'll want to join in. Once you've gotten started, you might decide to have an ongoing group to learn more about the issues at your workplace and continue to win improve-ments.

Keep it going. A support or advocacy group can give workers a collective voice to raise issues of concern. Since such a high percentage of women workers have been sexually harassed at some time, it is likely that in any organization of women, several members will be able to share experiences, help you plan a course of action, deal with day-to-day stresses of the situation, reinforce your attitudes and otherwise advise and support you.

If you belong to a book group, church group, professional women's group or some other organization, you might also find help among the members. Local chapters of special interest groups, such as 9to5, National Association of Working Women, or Federally Employed Women have many resources for their members who want to start these type of groups. (See the Appendix for contact details.)

—Adapted from *"The New 9to5 Office Worker Survival Guide,"* published by 9to5, National Association for Working Women.

8. Build your own strength

Acknowledge that you are in the midst of a very trying situation. It is wearying to put up with harassment on the job—and going forward with a complaint about it will also require a great deal of energy.

Make a special effort to spend time with friends or family members who will support and encourage you without being judgmental. Help reduce the increased stress in your life by setting aside time for activities you enjoy that help you feel calm and strong—exercise, yoga, massage, reading, other hobbies.

Learn more about assertiveness and effective communication principles—many of them offer simple ways to help build your confidence and get you centered on solving your workplace problems. There are several good books now out on the subjects; browse through a bookstore for one that appeals to you. Many companies offer workshops or courses in assertiveness or workplace communication. If your employer does not, check with a local adult school or community college. And, as discussed above, many communities have support groups you can join.

9. Consider filing a formal action

If you have sent your harasser a letter demanding that he stop (as discussed in Section E.2), but he hasn't been deterred, you may want to take more forceful action. Consider giving a copy of your letter to his supervisor—along with a memo explaining that his behavior has become more outrageous.

If the harassment still does not abate, send the letter to the next-ranked worker or official at your workplace. Include a cover letter in which you offer your own remedy for the situation—something realistic that might help end the discomfort, such as transferring the harasser to a more distant worksite.

If it's your own supervisor who has been harassing you, consider asking to be assigned a different supervisor.

10. Use formal complaint procedures

If you have followed the steps suggested in this chapter that seem feasible to you but the harassment continues, your next option is to pursue any procedure your company has established for handling harassment. (See Chapter 4 for guidance.)

11.   Recognize the value of moving on

Fighting sexual harassment on the job or filing a claim in the hopes of ending it can be all-consuming, energy-zapping feats. And while you endure the pain, there is no assurance that the right thing will happen.

Keep in mind that you will have a working future—one that's likely to be free of harassment. Unfortunately, you can't buy a healthy dose of perspective while you're wading through the morass.

If you have filed a sexual harassment claim and are experiencing retaliation from your co-workers or management, it may be important to embrace the notion of moving on to find that utopian workplace. And if you found the harassment intolerable and quit your job because of it, you are already well aware of that reality.

Waste no time in recirculating. Take some time to research good job leads and get a copy of your current résumé in the proper hands. If no good fit seems apparent at once, use the time off work as an opportunity to take training or classes that may help prepare you for a future job. If you move quickly enough, you will have no unsightly gaps in your résumé.

But if you do have a work history gap and a prospective employer questions you about it, don't lie or use the entreaty as an opportunity to vent your spleen about your former work situation. It is usually enough to acknowledge the time off, then deflect the questioner by turning the conversation to your excitement about the prospective job.

> "The only reason I put up with it as long as I did is I really wanted to advance. You put up with a lot to try and be one of the crowd. I feel very guilty for having put up with it."
>
> —Dr. Frances Conley, a neurosurgeon who resigned from Stanford University's Medical School after 25 years, citing harassment and demeaning attitudes by male colleagues

WHY FEMINISTS LOVE TO HATE PAULA JONES

Only Paula Jones and Bill Clinton know what happened in that hotel room in Little Rock back in 1991. That hasn't stopped some people from being sure that what took place was sexual harassment. But for many others—most of them self-identified feminists—something is wrong with that picture.

Left, Right, Republican, Democrat, Conservative, Liberal. All the leanings and labels shouldn't matter a whit in eradicating illegal behavior. But something about Paula Jones' claims that Bill Clinton harassed her while he was a conventioneering governor have churned a He-Said, She-Said into a They-Said, They-Didn't-Say debate that has sharply divided the nation.

Sometimes, a Bandwagon Is Not a Bandwagon

The first mudballs were slung four years ago when conservatives targeted the mothership of feminist organizations, the National Organization for Women. Chided for not backing Jones, NOW president Patricia Ireland publicly questioned sudden support for the cause of harassment heaped on by unlikely right wing leaders including Operation Rescue's Randall Terry and the 700 Club's Pat Robertson—and concluded noncommittedly that "every Paula Jones deserves to be heard." She countered the charge of favoritism by noting that the group opposed Clarence Thomas' Supreme Court nomination and issued "I Believe Anita Hill" buttons emblazoned with the NOW logo only after hearing testimony from both of them.

True, most feminists by definition support the right to work free from discrimination—and the right to fight for that freedom in court if necessary. But thinking souls don't jump blindly behind every harassment banner that gets raised. And as a group, some thinking souls are free to be skeptical about lodged claims that don't seem to them to parse. Just as conservatives might not embrace every guy named Rush or believe every bon mot he pronounces.

Trying to Have It Both Ways

It's disconcerting whenever anyone tries to endrun that adage about having your cake and devouring it, too. And there's no shortage of that in Jones' facts. It's the little things that speak loudly.

Early on, Jones claimed that she "made small talk" with plainclothes trooper Danny Ferguson while she was posted at her spot at the hotel registration desk. She asked if she could see and touch his gun while the two had "light, friendly banter." It's easy to picture this exchange of batting lashes and manly swagger. But Jones later described Ferguson as a menacing trooper who escorted her, armed, to the Governor's room.

Then too, Jones, who worked checking in registrants at a table at the Excelsior, claims that she was excited to visit Governor Clinton in his hotel room, "thinking this might lead to a better job with the state." That strains logic, even if she made the best darn checkmarks in all of Arkansas. Jones was 23 years old when it all happened—young, by most counts. But old enough to know that most job promotions don't happen in hotel rooms. And most don't come from perfect strangers.

To some minds, these leaps in logic are hard to swallow. They create credibility problems for Jones. And as in any relationship, it's hard to embrace someone you don't think you can trust.

The Color of Money

Jones and her staunchest supporters say she's in it for justice, not money. But the line between the two seems blurry. In a recent plea for funds to the Rutherford Institute, a group backing her case, Jones addressed a four-page plea to thousands of people. In it, she wrote: "Please understand that this lawsuit is not in principle about money. [Emphasis hers.] I simply want my character and reputation cleared (and my expenses covered)." [Parenthetical qualifier hers, too.]

Truth is, outside of her own circle of family, friends and associates, no one knew Paula Jones or had formed an opinion of her character until she insinuated herself into a 1994 article in *The American Spectator* which contained the quote that Clinton might once have been briefly involved with a woman named Paula. By then, the Paula we now know had married, changed her last name from Corbin to Jones—and had moved half the world away to California. It's unlikely many *Spectator* readers would connect up the dots to her, unclear how heavy a hand she played in connecting them herself.

And in a 17-page letter only recently unsealed, Jones' former lawyers begged her not to reject a settlement in the case before it was dismissed—warning her: "you will lose all prospect of financial reward from selling your sealed affidavit." That blew the lid on what the lawyers, Gilbert Davis and Joseph Cammarata, described as Jones' plan to later market her own account of the meeting with Clinton.

Imagine that Jones were forced to sit in a Senate hearing and answer the question: What could be your motivation? She might have a readier answer than Anita Hill had when sitting in the same hot seat, given the same prompt to search her psyche. Fear of what Jones' true answer might be—not politics—is one reason why many do not support her, including those who would otherwise champion those who had suffered sexual harassment.

It's a Class Thing

What's more queasy-making for feminists ready to dismiss Jones is the charge that they won't embrace her because of her muddy roots. Jones' supporters decry quotes like this one from Clinton's former campaign manager James Carville: "You drag $100 bills through trailer parks and there is no telling what you'll find." Carville is a paid political mouthpiece—a clever one—and at times, too clever by half. Jibing that poor folks are not to be believed is mean-spirited and wrong.

And sadly, there is a ring of veracity to the charge of snobbery. Truth is, in the darkest part of our souls, we all prefer our spokespeople to be well spoken. If feminists could make an icon to order, it would be someone with smaller hair, more stylish clothes, a less brittle manner. Still, if Jones' claim had delivered more substance, it would have triumphed over the shortcomings of the form.

A Victim of Bad Timing?

Jones even tried to help by recognizing her own image problem. She hired a spokes-woman with a hyphenated moniker, had a makeover, checked out how best to offer up her story to a few publishers and media reps—and only after all that weighed in with a 700-page legal filing charging she was sexually harassed by the man who now holds the most visible position in the United States. The makeover which was later augmented by an expense-paid nose job turned out great, but the filing seemed embarrassingly padded, nearly 100 pages of it taken up by copies of newspaper cuttings and Website printouts—not the stuff of which legal claims are made.

In depositions, Jones recounted some of the recurring wrongs she was done, including these:

- On an unspecified date, she was waiting in the Governor's outer office on a delivery run when the Governor entered the office, patted her on the shoulder, and "in a friendly fashion" said, "How are you doing, Paula?"

Oh.

- She was discouraged from applying for more attractive jobs and got downgraded.

The record shows, however, that Jones did not name any positions for which she wanted to apply, did not submit an application for any and that her position with the state government was reclassified upward, increasing her salary.

- She was singled out as the only female employee not to be given flowers on Secretary's Day.

When Judge Susan Webber Wright dismissed Jones' case on April Fool's Day this year, she addressed this charge directly: "Although it is not clear why plaintiff failed to receive flowers on Secretary's Day in 1992, such an omission does not give rise to a federal cause of action."

A Woman Crying "Wolf"

There is an overriding feeling that flimsy charges denigrate the Real McCoys. Getting the courts to recognize that the law against discrimination also prohibits harassment on the job was a hard-won battle. Getting the world to recognize it as wrong was another tough one. Sexual harassment cases that have made it through courts identify a wide variety of unwanted, repeated horrors to face in the daily workplace, including:

- A model whose employer coerced her into having sex with the company's financial advisor.

- Two male employees whose supervisor threatened to fire them if they refused to participate in various sexual antics including strip poker and striptease performances at the worksite after hours.

- A bank employee whose supervisor propositioned her, fondled her in front of the other employees, followed her into the women's restroom and forced her to have intercourse with him.

- Two female workers for a construction firm in Iowa whose male colleagues repeatedly "mooned" them, flashed obscene photos, urinated in their water bottles, cornered them between trucks and reached out the windows of their trucks to rub the women's breasts and thighs.

In workplaces where workers are up against these realities, it rankles when center stage is grabbed by a woman bemoaning shoulder pats and a flowerless desk.

Why Can't We All Get Along?

In recent times, when even the world-weary members of the U.S. Supreme Court seem bound to let common sense be our guide in sexual harassment cases, we could all take a lesson from Rodney King and give a shot to getting along. Maybe we can't all agree all the time about who was a harasser, who was harassed, who's a misguided martyr and who's a victim. But we do have a starting place; we all agree that harassment on the job is a bad thing that needs to be stamped out of American workplaces as best we can. We have to concentrate on the facts. ∎

4

Workplace Policies and Programs

T his chapter sets out the policies and procedures an employer can adopt to monitor, root out and deal with sexual harassment on the job. It also guides employees who wish to lobby for a sexual harassment policy in their workplaces—or to check the strengths and weaknesses of an existing policy.

In the past, most employee manuals were little more than puff pieces—welcoming new employees, extolling the company's virtues and, occasionally, spelling out a few specifics, such as vacation and fringe benefits and the company stance on smoking in the workplace.

Now, however, employee manuals are used both to define and obtain workplace rights. And they also act as subtle legal contracts: An employer can set out the conditions of employment in a manual. And an employee can legally enforce them: insurance benefits, pay for overtime and, increasingly, a firm policy against sexual harassment and a procedure to enforce it.

Courts occasionally require a company to write up a comprehensive policy as part of the legal relief ordered in a sexual harassment case. But more often these days, the impetus to rid the workplace of sexual harassment comes from within. The link between decreased productivity and workplace harassment is now well-documented. As a result, more companies are taking an active role, adopting formal policies to prevent sexual harassment where possible and to deal with it when it occurs.

But not all employers are this enlightened. Some, especially smaller companies, still act as if ignoring the problem of sexual harassment will make it go away. Experience demonstrates that where an employer's feet drag on this issue, employees—especially if they band together—can initiate or improve policies and procedures for enforcing them.

THE EMPLOYER'S DUTY IN COMBATING HARASSMENT

In two of its most recent pronouncements on sexual harassment, the U.S. Supreme Court began to define what steps employers must take to help stamp out this unwanted behavior in their workplaces.

In one case, the Court held that an employer may be liable for sexual harassment even when an employee did not succumb to sexual advances or suffer adverse job conse-quences. But the employer could defend itself against liability and damages by showing that it used reasonable care in stopping harassment—a strong written anti-harassment policy or an investigation procedure. An employee who does not take advantage of the workplace policy by reporting the harassment has a considerably weaker case (*Burlington Industries, Inc. v. Ellerth,* No. 97-569; 6/26/98).

In another case, the Court held again that an employer could defend itself against a sexual harassment charge by showing it acted reasonably to prevent it. But it found that an employer that acted unreasonably by failing to distribute its anti-harassment policy or establishing a complaint procedure was liable for the harassment (*Faragher v. City of Boca Raton, Florida,* No. 97-282; 6/26/98).

And another recent case—this one decided by a California appellate court—commended an employer for its "textbook example of how to respond appropriately to an employee's harassment complaint." The court was impressed that, immediately after receiving a letter from an employee alleging she was sexually harassed, the employer:

- requested a meeting with her to discuss the allegations

- questioned the accused harasser

- interviewed employees and former employees the accused harasser supervised, and

- promptly gave the accusing employee a letter summarizing its investigation and the action it took.

While the company found no evidence of sexual harassment, it did find the accused had "exhibited extremely poor judgment" in a number of words and deeds. It added a written reprimand and warning to his personnel file—specifying the errors he made and warning him from "initiating any contact whatsoever" with the accuser, on pain of immediate termination (*Casenas v. Fujisawa USA, Inc.,* No. G016713; 10/7/97).

A. THE IMPORTANCE OF A SEXUAL HARASSMENT POLICY

A well-crafted sexual harassment policy, which can be incorporated as part of an employee manual or set out separately, can offer both employees and employers guidance and certainty in dealing with harassment in the workplace.

1. Benefits to employees

If an employer has a clear written policy prohibiting harassment, all who work there will have a firmer idea of what behavior will not be tolerated in the workplace. If an employee is harassed, a strong policy can provide guidance about to how to take action against it.

Despite some paranoid perceptions, very few people who bring complaints about sexual harassment on the job are seeking big bucks or vengeance. Their goal, at least initially, is to make the harassment stop—and to take all practical steps to see that it stays stopped. It is typically only where an employer offers no fair way to resolve the problem that sexual harassment complaints evolve into lawsuits.

But if an employer doesn't take heed of complaints, a worker armed with a sexual harassment policy that has been ignored will often be in a better position to pursue more formal legal options to end the harassment.

> **"To end sexual harassment is to separate work and sex and thus improve both."**
>
> *—From "Sexual Harassment in the Workplace," a pamphlet published by the Federally Employed Women Legal and Education Fund*

2. Benefits to employers

Workers who are sexually harassed on the job often become distressed, depressed, frightened or angry. It's not easy to hold a job while also working full-time to keep a harasser at bay. And the challenge often takes its toll: Sexually harassed workers often become demoralized and miss work—and even while on the job, are much less able to concentrate and to work efficiently.

All of this runs counter to every employer's prime goal: workplace productivity. A number of recent workplace studies reported in *Working Women* show the high cost of tolerating sexual harassment:

- Over 25% of women who are sexually harassed on the job use leave time to avoid the uncomfortable work situation.

- At least 15% of women who are harassed at work quit their jobs because of it.

- Nearly 50% of those harassed try to ignore it and they suffer about a 10% drop in productivity. The harassed woman's peers who know of the situation also suffer a 2% drop in productivity.

But perhaps money talks most loudly: Ignoring sexual harassment can cost the average company up to $6.7 million a year in absenteeism, employee turnover, low morale and low productivity.

In addition to these indirect costs, an employer that tolerates sexual harassment risks the high administrative costs involved in EEOC and other agency complaint investigations. Since many employers hire expensive corporate lawyers at the first scent of legal trouble, the costs of defending a sexual harassment lawsuit are extremely high.

And of course, if the harassed employee files and wins a lawsuit for sexual harassment, costs to the employer will be even higher—sometimes a lot higher. Several employers have been hard hit with jury verdicts ranging into several million dollars for emotional distress, lost wages and wrongful discharge. (See Chapter 8, Section A.)

On office romance: "Even if you were having a mad affair with the person next to you, you would avoid nasty speculation by using good manners rather than making goo-goo eyes."

—*Judith Martin, aka Miss Manners*

READING 'N WRITING 'N HARASSMENT

The U.S. Supreme Court set limits recently on a school district's liability for a public school teacher who sexually harasses a student. The case does not squarely raise the issue of sexual harassment on the job because it was decided under a different law—Title IX of the Education Amendments, rather than Title VII of the Civil Rights Act which prohibits sexual harassment in the workplace. But the case offers up a good lesson to those concerned with workplace harassment: reasonableness rules.

The schoolyard case came to light when a police officer discovered a Texas teacher having sex with a ninth grader who was a student in his college prep class. The teacher, Frank Waldrop, was fired. The student, Alida Gebser, joined with her mother in suing the school district. Neither had mentioned the sexual relationship to school officials before filing.

Echoing its most recent holdings in workplace cases, the Court used unvarnished language, decrying the fact that sexual harassment is too often part of the learning experience: "No one questions that a student suffers extraordinary harm when subjected to sexual harassment and abuse by a teacher, and that the teacher's conduct is reprehensible and undermines the basic purposes of the educational system."

But the Court also ruled that harassed students do not get to kiss and not tell. School districts are liable for sexual harassment at the hands of its teachers, the Court held, only if they know about the behavior but are "deliberately indifferent" about it—taking no action to stop it (*Gebser v. Lago Vista Independent School Dist.,* No. 96-1866; 6/22/98).

B. EVALUATING YOUR WORKPLACE

In a campaign against sexual harassment, it is not enough for employers simply to adopt the boilerplate language of some model sexual harassment policy. And it is not enough for employees to go about their daily work as if the written policy had solved the problem.

For a sexual harassment policy to be effective, it must be tailored to the needs and sensibilities of the employees. And it must be respected and enforced by the employer, not merely given lip service.

If your employer does not yet have a policy against sexual harassment, or has a poor or inadequately enforced one, use the points discussed in this section to assess whether the damaging effects of harassment may be taking their toll. The discussion should also help flag the particular trouble spots you most need to address in creating or updating a policy.

1. Evaluate the sexual hostility

Is there friction between individuals or groups that seems sex-based? Are there complaints or grievances about promotions or work performance that often pit men and women against each other? Do you often hear jokes that might be considered sexist? Check the walls. Are there pin-ups, cartoons or jokes posted that are aimed at one sex or another—and that could seem demeaning?

2. Measure the comfort level

Is there a lack of camaraderie between males and females? Do employees tend to cluster in groups of the same gender during breaks and lunchtime? Even the chosen seating arrangement at a meeting or office party may be telling. If men and women typically head for opposite sides of the room, it may signal that there is sexually-based discomfort beneath the surface.

Overly friendly office behavior can signal a problem, too. Check whether there is an inordinate amount of hugging, kissing or other touching that seems out of place or that seems to make anyone uncomfortable.

3. Take a reading of the office gossip quotient

How much backbiting and mudslinging with a sexual content goes on in a business day? For example, are there a lot of whispered conversations and averted glances when members of the opposite sex walk by? Is there an undue amount of talk about employees' personal lives? Is there frequent boasting about sexual exploits and dates?

4. Look at the professional acceptance level for women employees

Are there some tasks that are consistently labeled Woman's Work and others that are automatically assigned to men? Do men congregate in Old Boy Networks and freeze out the women?

Are men and women equally represented—and given equal credit and recognition—on important projects and on the workplace committees with real clout, such as those that target new projects that will determine the company's growth? And how about the gender division on the more drudging tasks, such as planning holiday parties or stocking the company lunchroom?

5. Compare the promotion records

Are men promoted faster than women with similar skills and seniority? Are competent women routinely placed in lower-level jobs because of sexual stereotyping?

Take a look at the numbers of men and women who hold the best-paying or most responsible positions in the company. Pay special attention to the employees promoted to those positions recently. While it is arguably possible for an employer to have a cadre of mostly senior male employees who got started with the company before a significant number of women worked there, it is plainly inexcusable for that pattern not to change.

6. Look at whether sex is traded for preferential treatment

Do women who flirt or act in other sexually suggestive ways seem to be on a fast track, while others are consistently passed over for better jobs? Are some employees routinely called in to closed door sessions that seem overlong or unnecessary?

If your workplace scores low in its sexual harassment IQ, your strongest tack may be to meet with others who share your concerns. Take the time to let everyone voice their concerns. Assuming you eventually reach common ground on what needs to be done to combat sexual harassment in your workplace, request a meeting with the personnel manager or a person in a similar position in management.

Alert him or her to the problem and urge that an excellent sexual harassment policy be adopted at once—or your current one changed. (See Section C for guidance and a sample policy.) Suggest that the most effective policies against harassment are collaborative efforts by both employers and employees. Savvy managers will grasp your point. After all, a policy handed down by management without any input from employees is likely both to fall short of meeting the needs of the workplace, and to be met with resentment as a dictate from on high. (See Section G for a Sexual Harassment Monitoring Survey—an additional method that can be used for evaluating the workplace.)

C. EFFECTIVE SEXUAL HARASSMENT POLICIES

An effective sexual harassment policy discourages harassment. And it should also encourage employees to report all serious incidents of harassment promptly—with an eye to eliminating them. Employees cannot be required to report sexual harassment; that would be coercive and illegal. But if there is a sensible and sensitively written policy against harassment, backed by good policies to deal with it as confidentially as possible and to prevent retaliation against the person making the complaint, most employees will gratefully comply.

A model policy is offered here (see Section C.2), but keep in mind that a sexual harassment policy will be effective only if it is appropriate and realistic for your workplace. A conservative, multi-tiered accounting conglomerate based in New York City, for example, may find it reasonable to have more buttoned-down strictures on permissible workplace behavior than a small computer graphics company based in San Francisco or a tractor dealership in Pocatello, Idaho.

Also, to be effective, a sexual harassment policy must be clear and comprehensible. A growing number of employers pridefully point to the fact that they have written sexual harassment policies. However, a quick look at most policies reveals that they are so replete with legalese and cross-references to other workplace documents that they are more confusing than curing. Be sure your company adopts a policy that is meaningful and written so that it can be easily understood by everyone.

Finally, a sexual harassment policy should be seen by all as a work in progress. It will surely need to be changed with the times and perhaps even altered to reflect the changing roles and numbers of employees. To make sure that this happens, the policy should be reviewed and amended regularly. One good way to do this is to pass it around to all employees each year for comments and suggestions. Forcing this periodic perusal of the policy will have the added benefit of reinforcing its provisions and will help reassure workers that management will not tolerate abusive behavior on the job.

A LESSON LEARNED THE EXPENSIVE WAY:
IGNORE HARASSMENT, PAY BIG BUCKS

In a settlement that shattered all records, Mitsubishi Motors Manufacturing recently agreed to pay $34 million to women who worked at its plant in Normal, Illinois for failing to step in and stop the widespread sexual harassment they endured for years at the company.

In a claim that came to light in 1996, hundreds of former and current female Mitsubishi workers said they were subjected to rampant bad behavior at the plant for at least the last 10 years. They said male co-workers made constant vulgar remarks and referred to them as "sluts," "bitches" and "whores." One woman alleged her manager would often stand close to her and sniff her body while smacking his lips. Another woman said a male co-worker held an airgun between her legs. Another said she was taped into a chair by two male co-workers, then shipped down the assembly line. Several women reported being sexually battered. Some former workers contend there was so much hostility toward women at the plant that they were compelled to quit; others claim they were denied promotions after refusing to fulfill supervisors' demands for sex.

In round numbers, more than 400 male workers are alleged to have harassed more than 300 of their female co-workers from 1990 to 1997.

In an interesting twist, the list of the aggrieved included women who claim to have witnessed harassment as well as those who experienced it. After 15 months of delving into Mitsubishi's business practices, one EEOC investigator said: "We believe that those women who witnessed sexual harassment have in effect been harassed themselves. Witnessing the abuse substantially affects the women's work environment."

Opting to pursue legal action separate from the EEOC investigation, 27 additional female workers filed a civil lawsuit charging similar acts of unabashed harassment at Mitsubishi. That case settled in August 1997 for $9.5 million.

Even after potentially serious problems at Mitsubishi were exposed, the company responded with what some saw as a mix of defensiveness, arrogance and sheer cluelessness.

At first, it flatly denied any wrongdoing.

Then, shortly after the charges were filed in April 1996, the automaker provided nearly 3,000 workers a paid day off and bus transportation so they could picket the EEOC's Chicago office in protest.

And at the Christmas party that year, Human Resource executives donned sumo wrestler costumes and simulated sex scenes in an apparent display of company-sanctioned Yuletide cheer.

In June, Mitsubishi agreed to pay $34 million—a sum to be divided among the workers who were harassed. Individual amounts will be based on five factors: the severity of the harassment, length of time it was endured, harm suffered, whether the worker felt forced to leave her job, and whether she complained to and cooperated with the EEOC in routing out the bad behavior. While EEOC officials predict it will take nearly a year to divvy up the money, they say individuals are likely to get as much as $300,000—or as little as a few hundred dollars "for those who file last minute claims with some validity." Each award must get the final approval of U.S. District Judge Joe Billy McDade, who approved the settlement.

As part of the deal, the Japanese automaker also issued a formal apology to the harassed women and agreed to have its new no-nonsense anti-harassment policy policed by a team of outside monitors. The settlement decree explicitly forbids Mitsubishi from retaliating against those who complained about sexual harassment at the plant.

Months after the settlement was reached, the residents of the sleepy, mostly rural town with the unassuming name of Normal are still reeling from the rancorous employment discrimination battle. "This has divided the city," said John Rowe, director of the EEOC's Chicago office, which led the investigation. "There's no question, it's been sisters hating sisters."

For many, it's not a matter of hate but of simple mathematics. Normal has long been a company town—and its company has been Mitsubishi Motors. Mark Peterson, just taking a post as city manager, has his eye on that bottom line. "Thirty-four million dollars is a lot of money by anyone's standard," he said. "Some people say how can they afford that outlay and still keep a positive balance sheet? That's the question on a lot of people's minds."

And now, even after the settlement is final, few women will talk about what happened at the plant. The settlement provides that both the EEOC and Mitsubishi must keep mum about those who are awarded money and how much they get. For Carol Knuth, one woman who has spoken out, the talk has brought mixed feelings. "I'm really thrilled they admitted they did something wrong," she told the *Washington Post* just after the settlement, but added: "It'll take me years to get to the point I'm not looking over my shoulders all the time."

There are mixed reviews on the silence the settlement has brought. Luellen Laurenti, a representative for the local branch of the National Organization for Women, lamented that because the case was settled, there will be no court hearing. And that, she said, would prevent a public airing of the parade of horribles, it would prevent people from learning what really went on at the plant.

But according to Abner Mikva, a former federal judge who helped negotiate the EEOC/Mitsubishi settlement, a public hearing would have done more harm than good. In his view, it would have decimated the community to hear women tell of the abuse they suffered at the hands of other local residents.

The record-setting settlement sends an obvious message to other companies: You can't afford to turn deaf ears and blind eyes to harassment under your noses.

"Other companies should take heed," warned EEOC Chair Paul M. Igasaki, who vowed that the government group will "actively pursue" cases of egregious harassment. At a press conference announcing the settlement, Igasaki also tipped his hand as to what others could do to help eradicate harassment from their workplaces: "The key to success in this area is having a credible policy which takes decisive, fair and timely corrective action long before a situation gets out of hand."

1. Hallmarks of a good policy

The most effective sexual harassment policies have a number of common elements.

A statement that sexual harassment will not be tolerated. A short, direct statement that sexual harassment will not be tolerated is most effective. In addition, let employees know that sexual harassment is against the law.

Define what behavior is prohibited. This used to be no small task. Fortunately, after struggling for years to come up with meaningful definitions of prohibited harassing behavior, the EEOC, legislatures and courts have made considerable progress. Today, it is possible to provide a number of clear definitions and rules. For example, it is clearly sexual harassment to suggest that future promotions will be bestowed in exchange for sexual favors.

While even the best policy cannot set out every kind of prohibited behavior, a good one should go beyond declarative language to list some specific examples. For example, a sexual harassment policy may ban:

- Verbal harassment, including making sexual comments about a person's body, telling sexual jokes or stories, spreading rumors about a co-worker's sex life, asking or telling about sexual fantasies, preferences or history

- Non-verbal harassment, such as giving unwanted personal gifts, following a person, staring at a person's body, displaying sexually suggestive material such as pornographic photos

- Physical harassment, including touching yourself in a sexual manner in front of another person, brushing up against another person suggestively.

Spell out what action will be taken for first-time offenses and repeated unacceptable conduct. Punishments should be appropriate, certain and reasonably strict. Appropriate action can range from a written warning in the employee's personnel file to counseling, suspension from work, transfer to a different position or dismissal.

Give guidelines on how to report harassment. Detail how, when and where employees can complain about harassment. For example, if the first step is to contact a particular person within the company, make clear exactly how to do that. The complaint process should be as confidential as possible. If a form is required to initiate a complaint, a copy should be included in every employee handbook—or at least be easily accessible. (See Section D.1 for a sample.)

Provide an alternative to employees who do not wish to file the complaint with their own supervisors, some of whom may either be responsible for the harassment or guilty of ignoring it. Make it possible to report the harassment to any other supervisor—or to anyone on a panel of employees designated to handle company grievances.

Provide for prompt and confidential investigations. Despite all best intentions to keep the matter hushed, news of a harassment investigation tends to circulate fast. And people often take sides quickly. Proceeding speedily and appropriately with the investigation helps take the strain from the workplace, stems the tides of worry and gossip and, above all, is the best way to get at the truth of the matter. During the investigation, as during the initial complaint filing, every effort should be made to respect the confidentiality of all involved.

If possible, appoint an outside investigator to look into the harassment complaint—or at least someone from outside the department where the problem was reported. During the investigation, both the accused and the accuser should be promptly interviewed, along with any potential witnesses to the alleged harassment and anyone who may have experienced similar behavior. (Investigations for sexual harassment are discussed in detail in Section D.2.)

BEWARE OF GAG RULES

Some harassment policies require the person making the complaint to sign a statement swearing not to discuss the matter with anyone inside the company during the investigation. Be leery of such requirements. Should your case later go to court or to the EEOC, proof that you discussed the harassment with others while it was going on may be some of the most powerful evidence in your favor. Harassment policies that prohibit confiding in others are often cynically penned by company lawyers who are trying to bottle up legitimate harassment complaints.

Make the results known. A report of the findings of a harassment investigation and a notation about whether any action is to be taken should be given to both the harassed employee and the accused harasser.

Take a strong stand against retaliation. The fear of retaliation is what keeps many employees from reporting even the most egregious workplace harassment. The retaliation may come from the harasser who, as a manager or supervisor, transfers an employee to an undesirable position, changes her work duties to be either mundane or overwhelming or fires her.

Co-workers, especially friends and supporters of the harasser, sometimes retaliate against a woman who has rocked the boat by reporting harassment. They may refuse to cooperate with the employee—so it becomes evermore difficult for her to work—or they may shun her, excluding her from workplace social functions and just plain refusing to be cordial.

A good harassment policy should also assure employees that there will not be any retaliation for filing a complaint against workplace harassment or for co-operating in the investigation of another's complaint. The policy should also spell out the kinds of discipline—reprimand, suspension, transfer, dismissal—that will be imposed against those who retaliate.

Provide training sessions and monitoring. A sexual harassment policy should also provide for regular education and training—and for periodic monitoring of the workplace. (See Sections F and G.)

SOME PEOPLE ARE MORE MOTIVATED THAN OTHERS

An Indiana woman recently filed a lawsuit against her former employer after she was fired for complaining about sexual harassment in her workplace.

Specifically, Christy R. Hubbard took issue with weekly sales meetings fondly referred to by some workers as Pie Night. Hubbard's lawsuit alleges that each Wednesday evening, the top salesperson of the week at Advertising Specialists, Inc. was urged to throw a pie in the face of the salesperson with the worst weekly record. The loser could then tell the winner to "expose his or her chest or behind for pie throwing," the complaint alleges.

Hubbard recalls that on September 1, 1993, she was told "to take off her blouse and bra and was surrounded by several yelling, laughing, swearing, intoxicated male salesmen." They then rubbed a pie over her exposed breasts.

Asked about the Pie Night antics, Damon Selle, regional manager at Advertising Specialists, said only: "That's what we do."

Selle later advised Hubbard that her complaints about the incident were "negative" and "could not be tolerated because it was having an adverse effect on sales."

The EEOC issued Hubbard a right to sue letter and she filed suit recently in Marion Superior Court.

ZERO TOLERANCE: THE COMPANY PERSPECTIVE

Individuals harass, but companies get blamed for it. Modern businesses face a host of problems, but sexual harassment is one that they should be able to solve.

Viewed from the vantage point of management, sexual harassment is an enormous waste of company time. The more serious the level of offending conduct, the more time-consuming, distracting and disruptive it is likely to be. Acts of harassment are rarely built into the work itself, but are invariably deviations from the work at hand. A company almost always suffers in productivity when someone uses office time to harass a colleague even if the target of the sexual harassment suffers in silence.

Also, companies must respect the comfort level of each employee—to protect employees from an intimidating, hostile or offensive environment. Not only does the law require it, but as a practical matter it is impossible for anyone to work productively if he or she is subconsciously squirming in anticipation of the harasser's next move. From the employer's point of view, it is important to stress the uniqueness of the workplace. Offensive conduct by any employee must be restrained so that others can get their job done. A person may have a constitutional right to be a jerk in private life, but that right does not extend to the workplace. If someone makes a sexually offensive comment in a saloon or even a salon, the person offended by it usually has the option of walking away. This isn't possible at work, where the employee is forced to stay and make the best of it.

In truth, most sexual harassment situations can—and should—be settled informally. From the company's point of view, this is the fastest and cheapest way to deal with these situations. It is clearly in the company's interest to have and to use an effective complaint procedure.

Imagine the number of potential sexual harassment cases in the American workplace as a large, fat pyramid. At the base are the cases that are settled informally. In a typical scenario, the woman (or occasionally the man) takes the man (or occasionally the woman) aside and explains that certain conduct is offensive. Sometimes the offending worker stops because he becomes genuinely enlightened about the offensiveness of his conduct. Sometimes he stops because he is afraid that he might get in trouble if he continues. Either way the company wins, because a potentially troubling and expensive situation is defused. The same is true if those involved take the dispute to the next level of the pyramid and resolve it through the company complaint procedure. It is even true if the case goes higher up the pyramid and is only resolved after an investigation by the EEOC or a state FEP agency. Although agency investigations involve expense and aggravation for the company, the company is financially ahead whenever it can resolve a sexual harassment claim out of court.

Virtually every case that has resulted in a big money judgment—the cases at the top of the pyramid—involves a company in which a manager has been in some way culpable for the harassment. The scenarios are familiar: Managers receive complaints from their employees and ignore them; managers retaliate against employees for making the complaint; managers condone the harassment; managers themselves engage in the harassment.

This pyramid analogy makes a clear point about ending sexual harassment on the job. If a company makes clear—very clear—by its conduct that it won't tolerate sexual harassment, few employees will be foolish or self-destructive enough to violate such a policy.

2. Sample sexual harassment policy

Here is a good start for a sexual harassment policy that can be modified to fit the needs of most workplaces.

SAMPLE SEXUAL HARASSMENT POLICY

[Employer name] is committed to providing a work environment where women and men can work together comfortably and productively, free from sexual harassment. Such behavior is illegal under both state and federal law—and will not be tolerated here.

This policy applies to all phases of employment—including recruiting, testing, hiring, upgrading, promotion or demotion, transfer, layoff, termination, rates of pay, benefits and selection for training, travel or company social events.

Prohibited Behavior

Prohibited sexual harassment includes unsolicited and unwelcome contact that has sexual overtones. This includes:

- written contact, such as sexually suggestive or obscene letters, notes, invitations

- verbal contact, such as sexually suggestive or obscene comments, threats, slurs, epithets, jokes about gender-specific traits, sexual propositions

- physical contact, such as intentional touching, pinching, brushing against another's body, impeding or blocking movement, assault, coercing sexual intercourse, and

- visual contact, such as leering or staring at another's body, gesturing, displaying sexually suggestive objects or pictures, cartoons, posters or magazines.

Sexual harassment also includes continuing to express sexual or social interest after being informed directly that the interest is unwelcome—and using sexual behavior to control, influence or affect the career, salary or work environment of another employee.

It is impermissible to suggest, threaten or imply that failure to accept a request for a date or sexual intimacy will affect an employee's job prospects. For example, it is forbidden either to imply or actually withhold support for an appointment, promotion, or change of assignment, or

suggest that a poor performance report will be given because an employee has declined a

---

personal proposition.

Also, offering benefits, such as promotions, favorable performance evaluations, favorable assigned duties or shifts, recommendations or reclassifications in exchange for sexual favors is forbidden.

Harassment by Non-Employees

In addition, [Employer name] will take all reasonable steps to prevent or eliminate sexual harassment by non-employees including customers, clients and suppliers, who are likely to have workplace contact with our employees.

Monitoring

[Employer name] shall take all reasonable steps to see that this policy prohibiting sexual harassment is followed by all employees, supervisors and others who have contact with our employees. This prevention plan will include training sessions, ongoing monitoring of the worksite and a confidential employee survey to be conducted and evaluated every six months.

Discipline

Any employee found to have violated this policy shall be subject to appropriate disciplinary action, including warnings, reprimand, suspension or discharge, according to the findings of the complaint investigation.

If an investigation reveals that sexual harassment has occurred, the harasser may also be held legally liable for his or her actions under state or federal anti-discrimination laws or in separate legal actions.

Retaliation

Any employee bringing a sexual harassment complaint or assisting in investigating such a complaint will not be adversely affected in terms and conditions of employment, or discriminated against or discharged because of the complaint. Complaints of such retaliation will be promptly investigated and punished.

Complaint Procedure and Investigation

[Title of person appointed] is designated as the Sexual Harassment Counselor. All complaints of sexual harassment and retaliation for reporting or participating in an investigation shall be directed to the Sexual Harassment Counselor or to a supervisor of your choice, either in writing, by filling out the attached Complaint Form, or by requesting an individual interview. All complaints shall be handled as confidentially as possible. The Sexual Harassment Counselor will promptly investigate and resolve complaints involving violations of this policy and recommend to management the appropriate sanctions to be imposed against violators.

Training

[Employer name] will establish yearly training sessions for all employees concerning their rights to be free from sexual harassment and the legal options available if they are harassed. In addition, training sessions will be held for supervisors and managers, educating them in how to keep the workplace as free from harassment as possible and in how to handle sexual harassment complaints.

A copy of the policy will be distributed to all employees and posted in areas where all employees will have the opportunity to freely review it. [Employer name] welcomes your suggestions for improvements to this policy.

D. COMPLAINT PROCEDURES AND INVESTIGATIONS

A good harassment policy is a crucial first step in ridding a workplace of offensive, unwanted behavior. But it won't count for much unless an employer also adopts a trustworthy and energetic procedure for handling and investigating complaints.

> **"No touches, no posters, no sexual remarks of any kind. Pats on the back may be fine in a baseball dugout, but are not appreciated in the workplace. A manager is in the best position to stop sexual harassment before it gets started."**
>
> **—From "What Every Manager Must Know to Prevent Sexual Harassment," a booklet published by the Alexander Hamilton Institute, Inc.**

WHAT LIES AHEAD: THE INVESTIGATION

Hallmarks of the optimal investigation of a sexual harassment complaint are discussed later in this chapter. (See Section D.2.)

The following sketch of the steps usually involved in an investigation may help you decide, at this juncture, whether to file a formal complaint with your company—and what to expect if you do. It assumes a workplace complete with a responsive human resource manager and ever-ready legal counsel—souls who may not exist on your job.

The investigation procedure generally involves the following steps:

1.   Fact gathering

- Compiling written statements from all involved in the situation, including witnesses.

- Collecting company documents that may establish facts—such as pay records, job assignments, promotions, transfers, working hours and performance appraisals.

- Interviewing the accused, victim and witnesses or others who observed or know about the incident. Signed statements are generally required by everyone interviewed.

2.   Documentation

A report is then prepared and a decision made. The human resource manager determines the validity of the complaint and any disciplinary actions to be taken. In some cases, it may be necessary to involve the company's legal counsel when investigating and determining a decision.

The complaint may be determined to be:

founded—the incident occurred as charged.

unfounded—the incident is not harassment.

inconclusive—there is insufficient evidence to make a ruling either way. This may occur when those involved give conflicting stories or there are no eyewitnesses.

3.   Resolution

If the case was determined to be founded, appropriate sanctions and corrective actions will be issued to the offender such as:

- an apology to the victim

- a written warning

- probation

- transfer

- suspension

- loss of seniority, or

- termination of the harasser's employment.

Severity of the discipline will be determined by a number of factors, including the nature and severity of the offense and whether or not it is a repeated offense.

If the case was inconclusive, there may be:

- an informal, verbal warning issued to the possible harasser

- a follow-up investigation, or

- no consequences at all.

Source: Adapted from "Preventing Sexual Harassment," a pocket guide by Business & Legal Reports, Inc.; Madison, Connecticut

1. Sample complaint form

A helpful attachment to a sexual harassment policy is a complaint form to record important dates, facts and names, and to flag important follow-up procedures.

SAMPLE SEXUAL HARASSMENT COMPLAINT FORM

Name:

Department:

Job Title:

Immediate Supervisor:

1. Who was responsible for the harassment?

2. Describe the sexual harassment.

First incident:

Approximate date, time and place:

What was your reaction?

Second incident:

Approximate date, time and place:

What was your reaction?

Subsequent incidents:

Approximate date, time and place:

What was your reaction?

3. List any witnesses to the harassment:

I UNDERSTAND THAT THESE INCIDENTS WILL BE INVESTIGATED, BUT THIS FORM WILL BE KEPT CONFIDENTIAL TO THE HIGHEST DEGREE POSSIBLE.

Employee:

Date:

FOR ADMINISTRATIVE USE

Dates of investigation of complaint:

Date of final report:

Copy sent to employee:

Action taken:

Date of follow-up conference with employee:

Results:

Date of follow-up conference with employee:

Results:

Date of follow-up conference with employee:

Results:

2. Workplace investigations

The tone and tenor of the investigation of a harassment complaint often means the difference between achieving a prompt and satisfactory resolution of the problem or having it escalate into an expensive legal battle. A shoddy, lip-service investigation not only fails to end the workplace problem, but risks becoming key evidence of the employer's failure to take harassment seriously in a later lawsuit.

A key component to resolving complaints is promptness. Not only is it extremely demoralizing to all concerned to have an unresolved harassment complaint hanging in the air, but a delayed investigation means that everyone's recollection of the events is likely to become unnecessarily hazy. A good rule is that the investigation should begin within 48 hours after a complaint is received.

BEWARE OF FILING DEADLINES

Federal and state laws impose fairly tight deadlines from the date the harassment occurred to the time in which you must file a complaint. Although deadlines vary, 180 days is a common cut-off. If you decide to use your employer's internal complaint procedure first, a logical argument can be made that these deadlines should be suspended while you await the outcome from your employer's investigation.

However, this is often not the case. If you think you may wish to file a complaint either with your state fair employment practices agency or the EEOC, file your complaint within the 180 day EEOC time limit (see Chapter 6, Section H) or the relevant state time period (see Chapter 7, Section F) even if a workplace investigation is still in progress.

It is also essential that whoever investigates the complaint be perceived by all within the workplace to be fair and objective. Depending on your workplace, it may be better to bring in an outside investigator once a complaint is filed. You may find a referral for one by contacting your state FEP agency. In other situations, especially for larger employers in which an impartial person can be brought in from another part of the company, it may work well to conduct the investigation internally.

And there are a number of subtleties inherent in conducting a good investigation. For example, some women feel uncomfortable discussing a harassment situation with a male investigator. A woman who feels this discomfort should have the option of being assigned a female investigator—or at least have a female personnel employee with her during investigation interviews.

A thorough investigation will have the following earmarks.

■ The complaining employee will be interviewed

The woman filing the complaint will be asked to recount details of the behavior she found offensive—including names, dates, places and specific behavior. This process can be painful, so referring to prepared notes can sometimes be helpful. In addition, a preprinted Complaint Form (such as the one set out in Section D.1), can help the interview be more organized and focused and less intimidating.

Confidentiality should be stressed. The investigator should assure the employee that the matter will be kept private and discussed with no more people than is necessary. And while the employee must be free to discuss the harassment incidents with confidantes and friends, once a complaint has been filed, she should not discuss specifics of the investigation too freely with co-workers.

Keeping complaints as confidential as possible should be a paramount concern. Only key management personnel, the accused, the accuser and those who must be interviewed to get more facts need to learn that a complaint is being investigated. However, it is usually not wise to allow employees to file sexual harassment complaints anonymously. Other workers who witness discipline or other strong company action set in motion by an anonymous complaint are likely to become paranoid and distrustful.

It is likely that the employee will not be able to remember all details or incidents of harassment during the initial interview. A good procedure will make it easy for her to supply more information later.

■ The alleged harasser will be interviewed

The investigator should explain the substance of the complaint filed against the harasser, interview him thoroughly—and obtain a signed, written statement detailing his recollection of the events. If he refuses to sign—or acknowledges his behavior—that should be noted on the statement, which will later be put in his personnel file.

■ Witnesses will be interviewed

Witnesses to be interviewed include employees, former employees and anyone else who may know about the workplace behavior being investigated. It is particularly helpful if a witness has seen or heard the harassment on which the complaint is based. Anyone who claims to have been subjected to similar behavior by the same person should also be interviewed as part of the investigation.

■ The evidence will be evaluated

If the versions of what happened are different—as they often are—the investigator may have to make an effort to search for relevant facts. Objective proof of the charges, such as an eyewitness to the harassment, would likely be persuasive evidence, although such evidence is often impossible to gather, since much harassment takes place in private.

The investigator may need to delve into the reputations for truthfulness of those involved and any possible motivation behind the inconsistent stories—such as a bad performance review or a broken romance. Other complaints against the same employee should also be carefully evaluated.

■ Prompt action will be taken

A decision as to whether harassment occurred should be issued as quickly as possible to avoid prolonging the angst and damaging speculation that often accompanies an investigation in even in the most gossip-free workplaces.

If no harassment is found

If the situation has been thoroughly investigated and no harassment is found, the accused employee should be notified at once. Allegations of harassment are likely to be personally stressful and damaging to his work productivity, too.

The needs of the person bringing the complaint should also be considered. A finding that harassment has not been established may leave the employee feeling angry, frustrated or scared. She should be encouraged to discuss her feelings with a willing ear—a sympathetic co-worker or supervisor, company counselor, workplace specialist, psychologist or psychiatrist. In some situations, it may be sensible to make workplace changes that separate her from the person she accused of harassment.

Also, the employee bringing the complaint should be informed that the employer's decision is not the last legal word on the matter. Whatever the decision reached during the employer's investigation, she is free to go forward with federal or state complaints or file other legal action against the workplace behavior. (See

Chapters 5, 6, 7 and 8.)

If harassment is found

If the investigator is convinced that there has been sexual harassment, management should promptly issue a written apology to the harassed woman. For many women, this is extremely welcome, as it signals the employer's understanding and acknowledgment of the problem.

The employer should also take quick disciplinary action against the harasser. (See Section E.) Note that an accused employee may sue, claiming reverse discrimination or wrongful discharge. (See Chapter 8, Section 8.)

■ A follow-up plan for monitoring will be established

Old habits may die hard. Even prompt and strict action against the harasser may not end his bad behavior. And there may also be delayed retaliation against the person filing the complaint, coming from the alleged harasser or from his friends or co-workers who harbor a grudge.

To guard against these possibilities, a sexual harassment investigation procedure should make clear that the situation will be monitored for an extended period. Follow-up meetings at regular intervals—two weeks, one month, three months, six months and yearly—should be scheduled with the employee who originally complained to be sure both that the harassment has been eliminated and that there has been no retaliation for taking action against it.

E. TAKING APPROPRIATE ACTION

If an investigation shows that harassment has occurred, the first action should be to right the wrongs suffered by the harassed employee. As mentioned, an immediate apology can often go a long way toward easing the pain. Other action should be aimed at making the harassed employee feel whole again—and may include back pay, a promotion, a new job assignment, or other job benefit.

The employer should also take quick disciplinary action against the harasser. Appropriate action against the harasser may include: a verbal or written warning accompanied by the request to attend sexual harassment training sessions, or, in more serious cases, suspension or dismissal. Where the harasser is also a supervisor, an apt response may be to switch him or her to a position that does not involve supervising duties.

What action should be meted out can be best determined by common sense; there are no hard and fast rules. What is appropriate will depend on the type and severity of harassment and on whether it is a first time or repeated offense. In cases where the harassment is not severe or repeated, a written reprimand in the employee's file may suffice. If the harassment is severe or repeated, the best option may be to fire the offending employee. All instances of harassment—from mild to severe—should be followed by a clear message from management that all harassment violates company policy.

Ideally, where emotions are running high, it may be best to try to separate the employee and the harasser, giving either or both the option of transferring to a different position within the company. If it is the harassed employee who is to be transferred, there must be total assurance that the transfer is not done in retaliation for making the complaint. This means that the transfer must be acceptable to the harassed employee, and must not be to a lower paying, geographically isolated or otherwise less desirable position.

Whatever action is taken against the harasser, the harassed employee should be informed about it at once—and urged to report any future problems.

F. TRAINING SESSIONS

Sexual harassment in the workplace can be curbed or even eliminated by training supervisors and employees to recognize its signals and head it off. Doing this will end the need for harassment-related lawsuits, increase productivity and make the workplace more comfortable for everyone. Often, such training requires guidance from experts.

Sexual harassment training can take many different forms, depending on the size and budget of a company. The best training programs involve all levels of employees so that the entire workplace gets a better understanding of sexual harassment—why it happens, who it happens to, typical reactions of both the harasser and harassed worker and effective ways to make the harassment stop.

An increasing number of employers now offer anti-harassment training on the job, according to the American Management Association—40% of the companies it surveyed provided training in 1991, 65% in 1996. Typically, a trainer will visit a workplace and diagnose what is needed there. Most trainers offer:

- help with writing a sexual harassment policy and a procedure for enforcing it—both tailored to the individual workplace

- seminars to increase staff awareness of sexual harassment, including strategies for preventing and addressing workplace harassment

- programs specifically geared to teach managers how to investigate and deal with sexual harassment complaints, so that everyone in the workplace will have some confidence in the process, and

- additional training for managers and supervisors in how to lead periodic sexual harassment prevention workshops in their own workplaces.

Large employers often require a full range of training services. Smaller employers without the resources for full-blown training and follow-up programs can still get expert, cost-effective help in designing a good sexual harassment policy. Also, for a reasonable cost, a few employees can attend one of the growing number of seminars offered by outside workplace consultants. Many trainers offer discount rates if a number of employees, such as three or more, attend their training.

CONDUCT UNBECOMING, SIMPLY DEFINED?

In response to the 1991 Tailhook Scandal, in which it was revealed that scores of women were sexually assaulted at an aviators' convention, the Navy recently issued a pamphlet defining prohibited conduct.

The Navy system encourages sailors and Navy employees to "think of behavior in terms of a traffic light with green, yellow and red zones." Green actions—performance counseling or polite compliments—are deemed not to be harassment. Yellow behavior, enumerating the oft-mentioned gray areas that may constitute sexual harassment include whistling, leering and sexually suggestive touching. The red behavior set out as punished harassment by Navy standards, includes posting sexually explicit pictures and rape.

Rear Admiral Kendell Pease, Chief of Navy Information, defended the harassment qualification system from attacks that it is overly simplistic: "We have a lot of young kids who understand automobiles and traffic signals and this gives them something they can understand and put in their own terms. You don't realize how low we have to get. You have to be simple. This is not being taught in the home."

TRAINING VIDEOS: THE SEMI-SILVER SCREEN

One widely touted training resource is videotapes defining and giving examples of sexual harassment on the job. While videotapes can efficiently reach a great number of employees, they have many drawbacks.

Most are of questionable quality. They offer little more than cursory, often condescending, glimpses of harassment on the job.

Many are outdated. Beware of training films that have not been updated within the past couple years; laws controlling sexual harassment have changed substantially.

Most are expensive. Only the largest employers are likely to find it cost-efficient to purchase a harassment training film. And even the costs of renting the films vary dramatically—from $50 to $200 for a 24-hour rental. Here, too, you do not always get what you pay for.

Many offer little further guidance. Some films are accompanied by manuals that have useful examples and devices to help employees remember the fine points of the training. However, while truly interested employees may take the time to read the information, many of those who could benefit the most from it will pitch the paperwork soon after showtime. Also, films and manuals alone will often not answer more specific questions employees may have—leaving them "trained" but frustrated.

Before investing in a training video, get information on the company producing it and whether those involved with the content have any experience in sexual harassment training. Try to get a preview copy—or at least get the names of similar employers that have used a particular training video and ask whether employees there found it useful.

---

1. Tips on choosing workplace training

A confusing array of workplace training experts have sprung up recently—some less expert than others. Training resources run the range from books such as this one, to seminars outside the office, to tailored in-house training programs. Match your specific needs with available resources.

A word to the wise is to start slowly: A solid policy against harassment may be the best first step, followed by more ambitious training as employee interest and awareness grows. If you decide to use some outside expertise, first do some research on how to spend your training dollars wisely.

Define your training needs. Focus first on the type of help that is needed most—a good sexual harassment policy, raising employee awareness about what harassment is, refreshers for employees on the changing legal options for dealing with harassment or advice for conducting investigations for the personnel manager and supervisors. Depending on the size and type of employer, an informal survey of employees may help define the workplace needs. Employees should be urged to be frank and specific about the company's current needs and shortcomings.

Put together a list of workplace consultants. You can get referrals for local training experts from the EEOC and from many women's groups. (For contact details, see the Appendix.) You can also get advice and ideas by talking with friends and business contacts in other companies.

Choose expert help that meets your needs and budget. Do not sign on at once for more than your budget can handle. Among the questions to ask potential trainers are:

What services do you offer?

Get details on the specific services. Note that in addition to training, many workplace consultants offer seminars, on-site investigation services, dispute mediation and other employment services.

What is your experience in sexual harassment training?

Avoid companies that have little experience or have just recently jumped on the sexual harassment training bandwagon, spotting it as a good money-making scheme—for example, career development firms that primarily offer help with job searches and resumes, but which have become sexual harassment experts overnight.

Also, look for companies that have worked with employees, and have not been limited to training managers. A trainer who can see both sides of the sexual harassment issue is often best. And again, it's essential that the trainer is up to date on sexual harassment laws and court cases. You might seek reassurance on this by asking the trainer what kind of training he or she received—and what steps are taken to keep the training au courant.

What types of employers have you trained in the past?

Government agencies? Large corporations? Small businesses? Training needs differ greatly. Specifically, look for trainers experienced in working with employers similar to yours in size and type of work.

Given our company's needs, what type of training do you suggest—and what will it cost?

Make sure the consultant can offer practical, down-to-earth suggestions tailored to your workplace, not just generalized information that is readily available from many other sources. And look for training services that aim at preventing harassment on the job, such as monitoring complaints in-house.

2. Effective training programs

A typical sexual harassment training seminar lasts from four hours to two days, depending on its scope. The number of employees attending ranges from a small group at the workplace to an anonymous group of hundreds from various employers who gather away from work in a conference room. Currently, the best training programs use a number of different methods—including videos and group discussions and written materials.

The first step in a training session is to get people comfortable enough to discuss sexual harassment openly and honestly. Many trainers break the ice by asking participants for examples of the kinds of behavior they consider to be sexual harassment. This usually works best in small discussion groups, where people are much more likely to bring up current workplace concerns rather than make abstract comments or refer to events that happened at a previous job.

Trainers should then take the lead in explaining the legal definition of sexual harassment. All participants should get a list of prohibited behavior, including that set out in the sexual harassment policy (discussed in Section C), supplemented by examples of behavior that is and is not considered harassment. The greatest concentration should be on the gray areas of behavior (discussed in Chapter 3, Section C) that give most employees the most difficulty. The best lessons to be learned come from actual court cases—and trainers should cover more subtle kinds of harassing behavior along with more outrageous examples.

Trainers should then bring the point home to employees by getting them involved in how harassment feels. Some trainers show videos of re-enacted harassment scenes. Roleplaying is another popular technique—with employees taking turns imagining that they are both the harassed and the harassing employees. This technique is especially effective in shifting the focus of awareness from what might happen to an accused harasser to what does happen to a harassed employee.

HARASSMENT CLAIMS UP—EVERYWHERE

The number of claims filed with the EEOC has soared since 1991, when the Thomas-Hill hearings made sexual harassment a workplace buzzword and the Civil Rights Act was amended to allow damages awards to those who make out a case.

But the bigger numbers do not mean more harassment is occurring—just more awareness of it and a greater willingness to take formal action against it.

Claims By Industry	1991	1997
Farm, Forestry, Fisheries	66	134
Construction	115	376
Mining	38	71
Manufacturing	924	2,023
Transportation, Utilities	294	906
Retail Trade	1,239	3,189
Wholesale Trade	131	266
Finance, Real Estate	362	745
Services	1,759	4,664
State & Local Government	415	1,060
Total Claims Filed	**6,883**	**15,889**

Source: Equal Employment Opportunity Commission, Office of Research, Information and Planning

G. SEXUAL HARASSMENT MONITORING SURVEY

In addition to adopting a sexual harassment policy and complaint procedure and providing employees with training, employers who are truly committed to eradicating sexual harassment should actively monitor their workplaces. The best way to do this is to regularly remind employees that sexual harassment is illegal and will not be tolerated—and to urge them to assess whether it is a problem in the workplace. A quick and confidential method is to ask each employee to complete a Sexual Harassment Survey every six months.

The survey that follows is a sample.

SAMPLE SEXUAL HARASSMENT SURVEY

To all employees:

We are committed to making every effort to have our workplace be free of sexual harassment, as defined in our sexual harassment policy. This survey is designed to assess whether sexual harassment is currently a problem here. Your answers will be used to develop policies to assure that the workplace feels safe and comfortable for everyone.

Please take a few minutes to complete this questionnaire and return it in the enclosed envelope. You need not sign your name. However, if you are now dealing with a sexual harassment problem, we urge you to report it promptly as discussed in our Sexual Harassment Policy. Thank you.

1. I am a
   - ☐ woman
   - ☐ man

2. Do you believe you have ever been subjected to sexual harassment while employed here?
   - ☐ No
   - ☐ Yes

   If your answer is no, please go to question 10.

PLEASE ANSWER QUESTIONS 3 THROUGH 9 FOR THE MOST RECENT INCIDENT OF HARASSMENT.

3. When was the most recent incident?
   - ☐ I am currently experiencing a sexual harassment problem.
   - ☐ less than six months ago
   - ☐ more than six months ago

4. Who harassed you? Check all that apply.
   - ☐ my immediate supervisor
   - ☐ higher management official
   - ☐ union official
   - ☐ co-worker

☐ clients, vendors or other non-employees

☐ other (specify)

_____

_____

5. What was the nature of the harassment? Check all that apply.

☐ unwelcome sexual relations

☐ unwelcome physical contact (touching, pinching, brushing against your body)

☐ commenting about your appearance or body

☐ obnoxious or unwanted telephone calls

☐ obnoxious or unwanted letters or other correspondence

☐ sexual propositions

☐ sexually suggestive objects or photographs displayed in the workplace

☐ offensive jokes or innuendos

☐ other (specify)

_____

_____

6. What was your response to the harassment? Check all that apply.

☐ nothing

☐ resolved the problem by talking to the harasser

☐ left the job by quitting or demanding a transfer

☐ complained to management

☐ complained to the personnel office

☐ filed a grievance through the union

☐ filed charges with the state anti-discrimination agency

☐ filed discrimination charges with the federal Equal Employment Opportunity Commission

☐ consulted an attorney and filed a lawsuit

7. Was any adverse action threatened or taken against you because you complained about the harassment or because you refused to submit to it?

☐ No

☐ Yes. Check all that apply.

    ☐ denied promotion

    ☐ denied salary increase

☐ reprimanded
☐ given a poor performance evaluation
☐ involuntarily transferred
☐ discharged
☐ other (specify)

_____

_____

8. If your answer to Question 6 was any but the first two options, did you find the assistance you sought helpful?

☐ No
☐ Yes

If no, please explain why you found the assistance lacking or ineffective. If you used several types of assistance, specify which ones you found unhelpful:

_____

_____

_____

9. What was the outcome of your effort to stop the harassment?

_____

_____

_____

10. Do you have any suggestions about how we can respond more effectively to problems of sexual harassment?

_____

_____

_____

Date survey completed: _____

(Survey adapted from "Stopping Sexual Harassment," an AFSCME Guide)

H. SPECIAL PROCEDURES FOR SOME EMPLOYEES

When it comes to being sexually harassed on the job, all women are created equal. Each one is free to attempt to end the harassment by confronting the harasser, complaining to company management, filing a complaint with a government agency or bringing a private legal action. But some workplaces, by design, also provide more comprehensive resources to deal with the problem.

1. U.S. government employees

Each federal employer has an Equal Employment Opportunity (EEO) office set up to handle complaints about sexual harassment on the job. The formal complaint procedure for federal employees differs somewhat from other harassment complaint procedures.

Most importantly, the complaint process must be started within 30 days of the most recent incident of harassment. Harassed employees should initially contact an EEO counselor, whose name and location should be posted on your agency's bulletin board. If you are unable to find such a posting, call your local EEO office and ask that a counselor be assigned to you.

If the counselor cannot resolve your problem to your satisfaction, file a formal complaint with your agency through its EEO process. In the usual progression, there will be an investigation and a hearing on your charges to determine whether harassment has occurred. The agency head will then issue a final decision in the matter. If you are not satisfied with the decision, you may appeal it—first to the EEOC (see Chapter 6) and then to the local federal district court.

(See the Appendix for listings of organizations that offer advice, attorney referrals and other services to government employees who have questions about sexual harassment on the job.)

**PLAYING BY THE NUMBERS:
LOOKS AS IF WE'RE DOING SOMETHING RIGHT**

In 1994, 44% of women surveyed in the federal workplace said that they had experienced some form of unwanted sexual attention during the preceding two years. The harassment cost the U.S. government about $327 million in productivity losses, missed workdays and staff turnovers—an apparent increase of $60 million since 1987.

But if you adjust for inflation and higher salaries in the 1990s, the costs of harassment have actually gone down. Let's hope that means women are being bothered less, too.

—From *Ms.*, March/April 1996

---

2. Union members

Harassed women workers who are also union members may have a potentially potent ally in fighting workplace harassment: the weight and authority of their union contracts.

Under the National Labor Relations Act, your union has the duty to make a good faith effort to stop employment discrimination—and to represent you on issues of sexual harassment.

While few union contracts specifically prohibit sexual harassment on the job, many contain anti-discrimination clauses. Keep in mind that harassment is simply one form of discrimination—and that a broad anti-discrimination clause also protects against harassment. In some unions, this may require you to do a certain amount of fancy lipwork, but you will be well within legal bounds.

Because of their relatively long history of providing some organized assistance to workers, a number of progressive unions and their lobby groups, such as the American Federation of State, County and Municipal Employees (AFSCME) and the United Auto Workers (UAW), have been particularly successful recently in fighting workplace sexual harassment among members by:

• establishing strong sexual harassment policies through local or council resolutions

- educating union members about harassment by conducting seminars and workshops and distributing literature

- expanding training on handling sexual harassment grievances by making it a mandatory part of all steward training, and

- negotiating anti-sexual harassment language in collective bargaining units and formulating complaint procedures.

a. Getting your union involved

If you are a union member who is being sexually harassed at work, your first course of action is usually to inform your union steward. Under most union agreements, a harassed union member will have the option of submitting her claim of harassment to the union's established grievance procedure. In a typical resolution of a harassment grievance, the union member, union representative, employer and alleged harasser will all work together to attempt a solution that ends the harassment and punishes the wrongdoer.

b. What to do if your union is hostile

Just as women are relative newcomers to many workplaces, they are new arrivals in many unions. The sad truth is that you may find yourself up against The Old Boys' Network with a vengeance if you complain about sexual harassment to your union representative.

If you feel that your grievance about sexual harassment is falling on deaf ears, take a hard look at how your union is structured. Do women hold positions of trust? Does the union take an active stand on sexual harassment? Is there a woman trained and sensitive to the problems of workplace harassment who is involved in the complaint and investigation process? If your union comes up short when measured by this yardstick of questions, keep careful note. Your union's lack of responsiveness may become part of your harassment complaint—or form the basis for a later grievance against the union.

If your union steward or other grievance-taker shrugs off your complaint or labels it as a non-grievable issue, do not become discouraged and drop your complaint. Exercise every right to appeal. Unions in some workplaces have already recognized that not all stewards are equally adept at handling sexual harassment complaints. So some have designated specific stewards—who are most often women—to handle sexual harassment grievances. If your union offers this alternative, take advantage of it.

As a union member, your message is only as strong as your messenger: your union steward. Some harassed workers who seek but are denied help from their union reps have been able to get an immediate investigation and resolution of the problem by going directly to company management themselves.

If the result of workplace investigation is not satisfactory to you, you may file a complaint directly with the state FEP agency or federal EEOC, or go directly to court to file common law action.

If your union refuses to aid you in investigating and prosecuting sexual harassment charges, you may also file an unfair labor practices lawsuit with the National Labor Relation Board (NLRB) for breach of its duty of fair representation. However, beware of this: Filing an NLRB charge against a union may later bar state and federal courts from considering the issues you raise there.

(See the Appendix for listings of organizations that offer advice, attorney referrals and other services to union members who have questions about sexual harassment on the job.)

> "After the Hill–Thomas hearings, we heard from 800 women in four days. Our phone lines couldn't handle the calls. We heard, 'I'm not this activist kind of person, but I'm really angry at what's going on here. Who can I write a check to, who can I work for?'"
>
> —*Pat Reilly, National Women's Political Caucus*

WHEN YOUR BACKERS AREN'T BEHIND YOU

In a brave and rare move, Missouri United Parcel Service worker Serita Wright sued her union recently for refusing to pursue her sexual harassment complaint against a fellow employee and union member. An excerpt from her testimony at the trial of the case, in which she charged the union with both sexual harassment and defamation for its mishandling of her claim:

Q: "When you went to Mario (the assigned union steward) and you asked him for the grievance form, what happened?". . .

A: "He said, 'You can't file a grievance.' And I said, 'Why can't I file a grievance?' And he says, 'Well, you can't, you just can't, let me talk to you.' And he pulled me over to the side between some trucks and he says, 'I told you I'll handle it. You can't file a grievance.' And I said, 'I want to file a grievance.' He said, 'You've already pissed a bunch of guys off over what's going on now.' He says, 'I've got—I've got some guys that are going to say that when a male driver grabbed his penis you asked could you grab it, too.' And I screamed at him."

Q: "And when you screamed at him, how did he respond?"

A: "He acted like he wanted to touch me but he was afraid to. He put his hands up and he said, 'Wait a minute, wait a minute, calm down.' And he was looking around to see what attention was being drawn to me screaming at him. And I told him, 'Do not touch me.' And he said, 'Calm down, calm down, let me talk to you.' And I said, 'I pay the same dues as these guys do and I have the same right to file a grievance and you can't just tell me I can't file a grievance.'"

Wright did file a grievance—on a form she obtained from three sympathetic members of management, which was submitted without a union signature. Wright's harasser was fired a few days later. (*Wright v. Over-the-Road and City Transfer Drivers*, 945 SW 2d 481 (1997).)

"There's a big difference between saying, 'You look great' and 'Wow! What a figure!'"

—*Abigail Van Buren, aka Dear Abby* ■

5

A Look at the Legal Remedies

T here are three broad legal protections that ensure a worker's right to be free from sexual harassment in the workplace:

1. The U.S. Civil Rights Act administered by the U.S. Equal Employment Opportunities Commission (EEOC)

2. State fair employment practices (FEP) statutes, and

3. Lawsuits under common law tort principles.

Although each of these is discussed individually in later chapters, this chapter compares their effectiveness in different situations. Here, we look at how a harassed employee can use the remedies to stop the harassment, recover lost wages and other job-connected losses, obtain compensation for personal injuries and make structural reforms within the company.

> **"If the first woman God ever made was strong enough to turn the world upside down all alone, these women all together ought to be able to turn it back, and get it right side up again. And now they is asking to do it, the men better let them."**
>
> **—Sojourner Truth, Address to the Ohio Women's Rights Convention, 1851**

A. LEGAL REMEDIES: AN OVERVIEW

Here is a brief description of the three legal protections generally available to employees.

1. The U.S. Civil Rights Act and the EEOC

Title VII of the U.S. Civil Rights Act—often shortened to Title VII—prohibits discrimination and sexual harassment in employment. It applies to most employers throughout the United States who employ 15 or more employees. This federal statute is administered by the U.S. Equal Employment Opportunities Commission (EEOC).

The EEOC investigates employee harassment and discrimination complaints by taking statements from the company and any witnesses, examining documents and records and using its subpoena power to compel the employer and others to turn over evidence they are reluctant to disclose. The EEOC usually tries to enforce a harassed employee's rights under the Civil Rights Act by negotiating with the employer in a process called conciliation. The agency can also file a lawsuit on behalf of the employee to enforce his or her rights if negotiation fails. However, in most cases, the EEOC simply issues a "right-to-sue" letter allowing the employee to file a lawsuit to enforce rights provided by the Civil Rights Act.

If the employee wins the case in court, the Civil Rights Act provides the following possible relief:

Reinstatement and promotion. The court can order the company to rehire and promote the employee to the job to which he or she was entitled.

Back pay and benefits. An award of any salary and benefits the employee lost as a result of being fired or forced to quit, demoted or passed over for advancement.

Money damages. An award of money for personal injuries, such as stress-related problems, caused by the harassment. The amount is limited to out-of-pocket losses, such as medical expenses and other damages up to a limit of between $50,000 and $300,000—depending on the number of people employed.

Injunctive relief. A court order directing the company to change its policies to prevent similar harassment in the future.

Attorney's fees. An amount awarded by the court to pay for the employee's attorney's fees—or at least a portion of them.

(See Chapter 6 for a full discussion of the U.S. Civil Rights Act and EEOC procedures.)

2. State Fair Employment Practices Statutes

Employees in most states also have rights under state fair employment practices (FEP) statutes. FEP statutes generally prohibit sexual harassment committed against a worker employed in that state. Not every state has an effective FEP law, but the states that do have such laws frequently cover most workers, including those employed by smaller companies that might not be covered under the 15-employee minimum of the U.S. Civil Rights Act.

Most states have adopted a definition of sexual harassment that is similar to the definition used by the EEOC. (See Chapter 2, Section C.1.) Most states have also created agencies similar to the EEOC to investigate and settle employees' claims, and a few local governments have such agencies as well. These federal and state agencies use similar techniques for investigating claims, sometimes doing the work for each other under work-sharing agreements—and allowing an employee to file a claim simultaneously under both the Civil Rights Act and state FEP law under a dual-filing arrangement.

There are important differences, however, in the procedures and remedies offered to harassed employees under the various state FEP laws. The most important differences have to do with allowing employees to recover money damages for personal injuries suffered as a result of the harassment. (See Chapter 7 for a discussion of state FEP laws generally and a state-by-state list of such laws.)

3. Common law torts

Common law tort lawsuits, such as intentional infliction of emotional distress and assault and battery, provide a legal remedy in certain types of sexual harassment cases that is totally independent of any of the statutes or governmental agencies. The common denominator in tort cases is money; these actions allow a harassed employee to be compensated for personal injuries. (See Chapter 8 for a detailed discussion of torts commonly brought in sexual harassment situations.)

The facts of a sexual harassment case can often be fitted into one or more recognized categories of torts. For example, the same facts needed to prove a sexual harassment claim might also be sufficient in some cases to prove a claim for intentional infliction of emotional distress or assault and battery. Not every sexual harassment claim fits a common law tort theory. But if a tort lawsuit is successful, an employee may recover substantial monetary damages for the sexual harassment suffered.

4. Linking the harassment with a remedy

An employee who has been sexually harassed may need one or all of the legal remedies described to accomplish one of four common objectives in taking action against sexual harassment:

1. Stopping the harassment

2. Recovering lost wages and other job-connected losses

3. Obtaining compensation for personal injuries, and

4. Making structural reforms within the company.

We have separated these objectives for analysis only. In most situations that arise in real workplaces, an employee will have a combination of goals, such as getting her job back and obtaining compensation for her injuries.

B. OBJECTIVE ONE: STOPPING THE HARASSMENT

Your main goal may be to simply end the harassment before it gets worse. Frequently, your best course of action is to use a direct approach and confront the harasser yourself. (See Chapter 3, Section E.) In other cases, a good company complaint procedure can be used for this purpose. (See Chapter 4, Section C.) And in some cases, mediation or arbitration can be used to help stop the harassment and fashion a good way to clear the air in a workplace. (See Chapter 9, Section A.)

But direct action is not appropriate in all cases and not all companies have effective complaint procedures.

1. The Civil Rights Act and the EEOC

Filing a complaint with the EEOC can be helpful if your principal aim is to stop the ongoing acts of harassment.

EEOC procedures allow you to file a complaint without disclosing your name, and the EEOC will not reveal your identity without your consent. (See Chapter 6, Section G.) The EEOC encourages employers to settle problems from within the workplace, if possible.

An EEOC investigation may uncover facts that the complaining employee and even the company management did not know about, such as additional harassment incidents against other employees. As the EEOC uncovers such information, it may induce the employer to settle the case and adopt policies to prevent further harassment.

An EEOC investigation may induce an otherwise lethargic management to correct some long-standing abuses. But it can also create more friction if the company management bristles at the idea of a government investigation. For that reason, it is sometimes better to use a good company complaint procedure, if one is available, than to look first to the EEOC for help.

> **"Sexual harassment on the job is not a problem for the virtuous woman, except in the rarest of cases. When a woman walks across the room, she speaks with a universal body language that most men intuitively understand."**
>
> **—Anti-feminist Phyllis Schlafly, testifying at 1981 Labor Commission hearings on the EEOC sexual harassment guidelines**

2. State Fair Employment Practices Statutes

Most FEP agencies have the same power as the EEOC to seek a court order to stop harassment within a company, but the normal practice within both agencies is to attempt to settle the problem through negotiations or conciliation.

3. Common law torts

A common law tort action is not an appropriate remedy if your only goal is to stop the harassment. The greatest strength of tort lawsuits is that they allow you to recover money damages for injuries. But the downside of this is that there is no administrative mechanism to preserve confidentiality, protect against retaliation, seek conciliation or encourage the company to make changes. Also, filing a lawsuit is usually considered an inflammatory act—likely to jeopardize your job status and aggravate your working relationship with your employer.

WHERE SHOULD YOU FILE?

- Since the investigative powers of state FEP agencies and the EEOC are similar, choosing the best place to file often boils down to practical considerations: which agency—state or federal—has the best staffing, smallest case loads, or largest budget in your community. In most situations, it doesn't make any difference whether you file with the state or federal agency, because the two offices will keep each other apprised of their cases and decide between themselves which will do the investigation and handle the matter. Sometimes women's groups and knowledgeable attorneys can give you a few tips on which agency is most responsive in your locale.

- There are two distinctions to keep in mind between a state FEP agency or the EEOC:

  Eligibility. The Civil Rights Act and the EEOC apply only to businesses with 15 or more employees. Many state FEP statutes protect employees who work for smaller employers. (See Chapter 6 for a discussion of how employees are counted for this purpose.)

  Confidentiality. The EEOC will maintain the confidentiality of your identity during the investigation if you request it. You should check with the state FEP agency to see if it will keep your identity confidential, if that is an important consideration in your case. (See Chapter 7 for a state-by-state list of eligibility requirements and confidentiality policies of state FEP agencies.)

C. OBJECTIVE TWO: RECOVERING WAGES AND OTHER LOSSES

You may suffer a number of losses if you are fired, demoted, reassigned or otherwise penalized. The direct losses can include loss of wages, pension contributions, medical benefits, regular overtime pay, regular bonuses, back pay, shift differential pay, vacation pay and participation in any company profit-sharing plan. You may also need legal help to recover your job, promotion or any other favorable work status lost because of the sexual harassment.

1. The Civil Rights Act and the EEOC

The EEOC can be helpful in recovering your lost wages and other job-connected benefits. If the EEOC finds merit in your claim, it will attempt to negotiate a settlement that might include reinstatement if you have been wrongfully terminated, as well as any lost promotions, wages and other job-connected benefits. If the EEOC cannot negotiate a settlement of your claim on your behalf, it can take the case to court. But more likely, it will issue you a right-to-sue letter, enabling you to file a lawsuit on your own. If you win that lawsuit, you may also be awarded attorney's fees to help defray your legal expenses.

2. State Fair Employment Practices Statutes

As with the EEOC, there are many administrative steps within a typical state FEP agency to encourage settlement. Most state FEP agencies can take a sexual harassment claim to court, but you must usually take that action on your own, with the help of an attorney.

In some states, the FEP agency has the additional power to conduct an administrative hearing and issue an order granting you money for job-connected losses. It may also order reinstatement, reassignment or other relief. (See Section D.)

3. Common law torts

A common law tort action is a good remedy for going after lost wages and other job-connected losses in some limited situations, but a poor remedy in many others.

A tort lawsuit is usually only appropriate if you want to recover money damages and are not interested in continuing to work for the company. In such a lawsuit, the court cannot order that you be reinstated or promoted to a higher paying job and it cannot protect you from being retaliated against or fired.

The common law tort remedy that may work best for recovering lost wages is wrongful discharge—which is an action against being fired unlawfully. However, this tort remedy has not been accepted in some states; in other states, it is unclear whether it protects against sexual harassment. (See Chapter 8, Section B.6.) If a court is willing to consider your claim for wrongful discharge, it may be to your advantage because you may then be entitled to substantial punitive damages—that is, money awarded to you to punish the wrongdoer.

> **"Let me listen to me and not to them "**
> —*Gertrude Stein, American writer*

D. OBJECTIVE THREE: COMPENSATION FOR PERSONAL INJURIES

The types of injuries and illnesses that can arise out of a sexual harassment situation are many and varied. Sometimes, physical injuries result directly from violent harassment. There are also mental and emotional injuries. Sometimes these grow out of work performance stress, but they can also be the result of sexual trauma, fear of sexual assault or any other medically diagnosable injury.

If you have suffered severe injuries from sexual harassment, your objective may be to recover compensatory damages and, if possible, to recover punitive damages as well.

Compensatory damages are open-ended in the sense that the money necessary to compensate you for your injuries cannot be predicted in advance. The illness or injury that you may develop—as well as the cost of treating it—may vary greatly from what another employee might experience. What you will be seeking, therefore, is compensation for the actual amount of your injuries.

You may also seek punitive damages, which is an additional amount of money that can be awarded if the harassment has been particularly outrageous. As the name suggests, punitive damages are awarded to punish the harasser and discourage future harassment. Punitive damages are only awarded if a judge or jury feels a sense of moral outrage after having heard all the evidence. That's often hard to predict.

> **"I am only speaking from what I experienced. I resent the idea that people would blame the messenger for the message rather than looking at the content of the message itself."**
>
> —*Professor Anita Hill, shortly after testifying before the Senate committee investigating her allegations that Clarence Thomas sexually harassed her*

1. The Civil Rights Act and the EEOC

The Civil Rights Act allows a sexually harassed woman to recover compensatory and punitive damages for her injuries, but the amount is limited.

You can recover the actual amount spent for out-of-pocket expenses, such as doctor and medical bills. But the total of any other compensatory and punitive damages that you can recover is limited to an amount based on the number of employees in the company:

$50,000 if there are 15 to 100 employees

$100,000 if there are 101 to 200 employees

$200,000 if there are 201 to 500 employees, and

$300,000 if there are 501 or more employees.

If the company has fewer than 15 employees, no damages can be awarded because the Civil Rights Act will not apply.

These limitations have no relationship, of course, to the severity of your injuries; your injuries are the same no matter how many people your company employs. These dollar limitations seriously limit the usefulness of the Civil Rights Act for recovering monetary damages, particularly for employees of small companies.

2. State Fair Employment Practices Statutes

Some state FEP laws provide very good remedies for recovering damages for personal injuries, while others provide no remedy at all. The effectiveness of FEP laws depends upon the particular nuances of the laws where the harassment occurred.

FEP statutes in several states allow employees to collect large amounts of money in damages for personal injuries—most often without any of the limitations contained in the Civil Rights Act. If you work in such a state and have suffered substantial personal injuries, consider pursuing your claim under the state FEP law. It is likely to be your most effective remedy.

However, if you work in a state in which the FEP statute does not allow compensation for personal injuries, you are clearly better off pursuing your sexual harassment claim for personal injuries under the U.S. Civil Rights Act; it at least allows the right to recover limited money damages.

3. Common law torts

Common law tort cases may be one of the best remedies if your objective is to recover for personal injuries, because they usually allow unlimited money damages.

However, it's often difficult to find a tort action that fits the facts of your case. Also, not all common law tort theories are recognized or interpreted the same way in every state. (See Chapter 8 for a detailed discussion of tort actions.)

But an advantage to a tort lawsuit is that it can be filed immediately in many situations. In a strong case where you and your attorney are clear on the merits and the facts, there is no need to file anything with the EEOC or a state FEP agency, or to wait around for a right-to-sue letter before filing the common law action.

Cases involving serious personal injuries are much less likely to require the buffer of an EEOC or state FEP investigation. Earlier we focused on objectives such as stopping harassment or getting your job back, and we indicated that in those situations it is important to have a government agency that can investigate your claim, protect you from retaliatory firing and try to settle the matter. But by the time you have decided to file a tort lawsuit, you have probably long since left your job and are prepared for an all-out legal battle to recover for your injuries.

E. OBJECTIVE FOUR: REFORMING THE COMPANY

Sometimes, the principal goal of you and a group of your co-workers is to force the company to make largescale reforms to end sexual harassment and change the way that it treats employees.

It usually takes a lot of money to reach this goal—and these cases are undertaken only after careful planning and with strong support from a workers' rights or similar organization. In one such frequently mentioned case, a woman shipyard worker named Robinson sued the Jacksonville Shipyards in Florida with the assistance of the NOW Legal Defense & Education Fund, claiming that the workplace was pervaded by pornography and misogynist humor. (*Robinson v. Jacksonville Shipyards, Inc.*, 760 F.Supp. 1486 (M.D.Fla. 1991).) The main thrust of the *Robinson* case was to obtain a court order forcing the company to adopt and implement an effective sexual harassment policy and complaint procedure.

1. The Civil Rights Act and the EEOC

If the EEOC wants to challenge broad patterns of illegal conduct within a particular company or industry, it can expand the scope of a case on its own to investigate sexual harassment suffered by other employees. It can also seek a court order that will force the company to correct the overall harassment problems within the workplace.

This is the larger leadership role that the EEOC is supposed to play—taking the initiative in important cases and dealing with sexual harassment issues of general importance to large groups of employees. But the agency only performs at this level when it has proper funding and strong leadership. On April 19, 1995, the EEOC adopted a National Enforcement Plan that attempted to show the types of cases to which it would give priority. This enforcement plan is quite general in its language, however, and it basically says that the EEOC will give priority to the cases that have the widest impact or involve the most serious abuses.

If you have an important case and the EEOC does not act on it, you may be able to work with public interest groups to bring the case to court. After receiving a right-to-sue letter, you can file a lawsuit under the Civil Rights Act to challenge a pattern of sexual harassment within the company and seek a strong court order that will help all the employees in the company. That is what happened in the *Robinson* case mentioned just above: Based on the harassment suffered by one employee, the court issued an order directing the company to adopt and implement a specific, detailed sexual harassment policy and complaint procedure for all employees working there.

2. State Fair Employment Practices Statutes

Most state FEP agencies have powers similar to those of the EEOC to seek an end to patterns of sexual harassment and make broad reforms within a company.

Ideally, the FEP agency would pursue such a case with its own resources after it has received a complaint from a harassed employee. But problems of caseload, budgets and institutional inertia keep state FEP agencies, just like the EEOC, from pursuing many such cases on their own.

3. Common law torts

In a tort case, the only relief that the court can award is money damages for injuries suffered. The court has no authority to order a company to stop harassment, to adopt a sexual harassment policy, to implement a complaint procedure or to do anything else.

Despite that, some lawyers will argue that a tort case is still the best way to get a company to change its practices. Their argument is that nothing catches a company's attention like the negative publicity of a big lawsuit and the prospect of a fat money judgment against it. The company will make quick changes, so the argument goes, if it is faced with the prospect of digging deep into its pocket again to pay off possible future plaintiffs.

> "The first problem for all of us, men and women, is not to learn, but to unlearn."
>
> —*Gloria Steinem* ■

6

The EEOC and the U.S. Civil Rights Act

C hapter 5 compared the different legal remedies for sexual harassment—
and discussed the most appropriate legal paths for sexually harassed employees.
This chapter takes a closer look at one of the laws prohibiting harassment, the Civil
Rights Act, which is also called Title VII. We also explain how the Equal Employment Opportunities Commission (EEOC) enforces the Act.

WHEN YOU DON'T NEED TO READ THIS CHAPTER

This chapter is intended for those who are seriously considering filing a claim with the
EEOC under the U.S. Civil Rights Act—or for those who are considering filing a claim
under their state fair employment practices law and want to know more about the
administrative procedures that are similar for both federal and state agencies.

If you do not wish to file charges, but instead want to try informally to stop the harassment, see Chapter 3.

A. WHEN TO USE THE CIVIL RIGHTS ACT

There are several reasons to file a claim with the EEOC under the U.S. Civil Rights
Act.

- It provides a system of investigating and settling sexual harassment claims
  that is comparable to, and in some cases better than, similar systems
  provided by the various state fair employment practices (FEP) agencies.

- Because of dual-filing agreements between the EEOC and most state
  agencies, filing a claim with the EEOC will ordinarily protect your rights
  under both the Civil Rights Act and the particular state FEP law. (See
  Section F.2.)

- The Civil Rights Act provides a limited amount of money damages for
  personal injuries, based on the number of employees in the company. In this
  respect, it is better than many state FEP laws but not as good as others. (See
  Chapter 7.)

B. COVERAGE AND REMEDIES

There are some limitations as to which employees are covered and what remedies are offered under the Civil Rights Act.

1. Employees who are covered

The Civil Rights Act extends protection against sexual harassment to employees of all public and private employers in the United States, including U.S. citizens working for a U.S. company in a foreign country. The Act also applies to labor unions, both to the workers they employ and to their members.

However, there is one major exception: The Civil Rights Act does not apply to any company that has fewer than 15 employees. (This 15-employee minimum is discussed in detail in Section C.1.)

2. Remedies available

Remedies that the courts or the EEOC can provide under the Civil Rights Act to a sexually harassed employee include:

Reinstatement and promotion. A court can order the employee rehired, promoted or reassigned to whatever job she lost because of sexual harassment.

Wages and job-connected losses. A court can award any salary and benefits the employee lost as a result of being fired, demoted or forced to quit because of sexual harassment. This can include loss of wages, pension contributions, medical benefits, overtime pay, bonuses, back pay, shift differential pay, vacation pay and participation in a company profit-sharing plan.

Money damages. A court can award damages to compensate for personal injuries. This can include money to cover the actual amount of out-of-pocket losses, such as medical expenses. It can also include other compensatory and punitive damages, but the amount of such damages is limited to between $50,000 and $300,000—depending on the number of people employed by the business. (See Section C.1.)

Injunctive relief. A court can direct the company to change its policies to stop sexual harassment and to prevent similar incidents in the future.

Attorney's fees. If the employee wins a case, a court can order the company to pay part of the attorney's fees incurred.

3. Filing a claim is a prerequisite

You must file a claim with the EEOC to use the U.S. Civil Rights Act. Even if you or your attorney would prefer to skip the EEOC investigation and proceed directly to court, you must first file a claim with the agency and obtain a right to sue letter. (See Section L.)

IF YOU WORK AT A LARGE COMPANY

If you work for a large company with well over 500 full-time employees, skip the next three sections and go directly to Section F.

---

4. Who may be liable

The Civil Rights Act specifies that employers may be sued for allowing sexual harassment to persist in their workplaces. Individual harassers may also be liable for their actions. And a growing number of courts hold that supervisors who know of harassment on the job but take no action to stop it may also be legally responsible. (See Chapter 2, Section E for a discussion of employers' potential liability for harassment by employees.)

C. THE IMPORTANCE OF COUNTING EMPLOYEES

If you want to use the U.S. Civil Rights Act, you must know how many people work for your employer. This number is important for two reasons:

1. The Civil Rights Act only applies to companies with 15 or more employees, and

2. The amount of money damages you can recover is based on the total number of employees in the company.

1. The 15-employee minimum requirement

The 15-employee minimum can have very harsh results: If your company has fewer than 15 employees, the Civil Rights Act does not protect you. This means that the EEOC will not accept your case, will not investigate or negotiate your claim—and you cannot sue your employer for damages under the Civil Rights Act.

The reason for this rule is not entirely clear, but Congress apparently felt that it should confine its legislative efforts to larger businesses and leave it to the states to prevent discrimination by smaller employers. If this is what Congress had in mind, it hasn't worked. Many state FEP laws also have a 15-employee minimum rule. And even among the state FEP laws with a smaller minimum requirement, several provide less effective remedies than the Civil Rights Act. (See Chapter 7 for a state-by-state listing, including required number of employees.)

Workers in small firms should carefully read the next section to be sure they are counting correctly. But, sadly, there will be some employees who will conclude that no amount of creative counting will bring them under the protection of the federal or state sexual harassment laws. Their only hope for legal redress will stem from the common law tort remedies. (See Chapter 8.)

2. The limitation on damages

The number of employees also determines what limit on money damages will be placed on your claim. Prior to November 1991, there was no need to count employees for this purpose, because there was no right to money damages at all. Then Congress amended the Civil Rights Act, giving an employee the right to sue for compensatory and punitive damages, limited to:

$50,000 if the employer has 15 to 100 employees

$100,000 if the employer has 101 to 200 employees

$200,000 if the employer has 201 to 500 employees, and

$300,000 if the employer has 501 or more.

These limits are, of course, purely arbitrary; they have nothing do with the actual damages a harassed employee may have suffered. The reason they are in the law at all is strictly political. (See Chapter 1, Section D.)

The money restrictions do not apply to back wages, nor do they apply to out-of-pocket losses, such as doctor's bills. But they do set an upper limit on the combined total of all other compensatory and punitive damages, regardless of your injuries.

> *Example: Etta works for a company that has 150 employees. She files a sexual harassment lawsuit against the company under the Civil Rights Act and convinces the jury that she has suffered severe injuries. The jury awards Etta $15,000 for her medical expenses, $150,000 for her pain and suffering and $200,000 in punitive damages.*
>
> *However, the judge reduces her award based upon the limitations in the statute: Etta gets the $15,000 in out-of-pocket expenses, but the other $350,000 in damages is reduced to $100,000. The judge reduces the damage award because the number of employees where Etta works (150) places her in a category in which the maximum allowable damages under the Civil Rights Act is $100,000.*

D. HOW TO COUNT EMPLOYEES

Any time a law sets arbitrary limits, you can expect problems. By setting a 15-employee minimum and damage limitations based on the number of employees in the company, Congress left a few ambiguities to be resolved.

The courts and the EEOC have recently clarified the rules for determining how the 15-employee limitation works (EEOC Notice, #915.002; May 2, 1997). The rules are now a little more clear with respect to satisfying the minimum requirement of 15 employees in order for a company to be covered under federal law.

However, this EEOC policy notice does not specifically refer to the methods of counting the minimum number of 101, 201 or 501 employees necessary to invoke the limitations on money damage limitations under federal law. Since the language of the statute is the same whether you are counting 15, 101, 201 or 501 employees, it's logical to assume that the rules for counting at one level will apply to all levels. However, law and logic don't always run on parallel tracks. And keep in mind that the rules described below apply with less certainty if the issue is the level of money damages that an employee can recover in a lawsuit under federal law.

Counting the number of employees in your company is more complicated than it sounds. Here are a few tips on adding up these numbers.

1. The counting period

The Civil Rights Act states that the required number of employees—whether 15, 201 or 501—must be employed "in each of 20 or more calendar weeks in the current or preceding calendar year." The language of that statute has to be looked at carefully: It requires that the company must be of the requisite size for at least 20 weeks—not necessarily consecutive—within the current or previous year.

a. Number of employment relationships

The number of employees is measured in both weeks and days. In order for a week to be included as one of the "20 or more calendar weeks," the company must have an employment relationship with the required number of employees—that is, at least 15—on each working day of that week.

The term "employment relationship" is one that the EEOC has adopted from a U.S. Supreme Court opinion (*EEOC & Walters v. Metropolitan Educational Enterprises, Inc.*, 117 S.Ct. 660 (1997)). The EEOC's position is that all workers currently on the payroll should be considered employees whether or not they are actually performing work each day of the week or whether or not they are being paid for any particular day. In other words, if a company has at least 15 employees on the payroll for an entire week, that week counts as one of the 20 required weeks.

b. Weeks need not be consecutive

There is no requirement in the statute that the "20 or more calendar weeks" be consecutive, as long as the 20 weeks fall within the "current or preceding calendar year." The courts are not entirely clear on this point, but it appears that any 20 weeks within that period will do.

Example: A fruit canning company has on staff 535 employees each week between September 1 and November 15 of one year and again between Septem-

ber 1 and November 15 of the next year. Between those two peak periods, the number of employees working each week drops to 87. On November 10 of the second year, an employee is sexually harassed. The limit for her claim should be $300,000 (more than 500 employees), because the company employed more than 500 employees for two ten-week periods during a calendar year.

c. Harassment need not be during peak employment

The language of the statute doesn't require that the sexual harassment occur during one of the "20 or more calendar" weeks in which the company has the required number of employees. The 20-week requirement only determines if the company is covered by federal law. If the company is covered, all sexual harassment is illegal, no matter when it occurs.

Example: Marika goes to work for a new real estate development firm on February 1. At the time the company only has ten employees. On February 10, her supervisor gives Marika a ride home, and while they are in the car he tries to talk her into having oral sex with him. When he won't back off, she has to force her way out of the car. Marika is under a doctor's care for several weeks, and she is fired on March 15. By June 1 of that year, the firm, which bought out another business, is up to 210 employees and stays at that level until the end of the year.

Here, the company was below the 15-employee minimum when the incident occurred. But it later exceeded that minimum for more than 20 weeks during the same calendar year, so the case is covered under the Civil Rights Act. The case also fits within the $200,000 damage limitation bracket because the company had between 201 and 500 employees for more than 20 weeks during that year.

"I don't buy into this crap that men are saying, 'You can't even say hello in the office anymore without being accused of being a harasser.'"
—Barbara Otto, 9to5 spokesperson

2. Which employees are counted

There can also be problems in determining which employees are counted for purposes of the 15-employee minimum and the damage restrictions. The harassed employee will want to count as many as possible, but the employer will want to keep the employee count down.

a.   Workers with an employment relationship

Anyone who has an "employment relationship" with the company should be counted. Anyone who is on the company payroll is assumed to be an employee for this purpose unless there is evidence to the contrary.

But even workers who are not being paid by the company in which the harassment occurs can be considered employees in some instances. For example, a secretary who is employed by and paid by a temporary employment agency will be considered an employee of the company to which she is assigned for purposes of the protection of the Civil Rights Act. The EEOC takes the position that the worker in such a situation is an "employee" of both companies. This means that she will be counted for purposes of determining the required number of employees—and also that she will be protected under federal law from sexual harassment.

b.   Employees at other worksites

All employees of the company should be counted, no matter where they work. The count is not limited to the number at the worksite, in the particular division or even at the plant or building in which the harassed employee worked. In estimating the total number of employees in a relatively small company, remember that there may be additional employees who work at home or away from the worksite who should also be counted.

c.   Employees of related companies

If the company where the sexual harassment occurs is one of a number of related companies that have some common ownership or link—for example, parent-subsidiary or franchisor-franchisee—the question frequently arises whether the employees of those related companies should be counted.

This question is answered on a case-by-case basis. According to the EEOC, its investigators will evaluate the "interrelationship of operations, common management, centralized control of labor relations, common ownership, and power of control over employees." If it finds that the companies are integrated enterprises, all of the employees will be counted.

In some cases, it may be very important for a harassed employee who works for a small company to show that it is closely connected with a large, nationwide business.

> *Example: Tamina is sexually accosted by the manager and his supervisor at the ice cream store where she works. As far as she knows, there are only 12 employees of the store who work in shifts of six at a time. The ice cream shop is part of a heavily advertised, nationwide chain. The manager claims to be president of the corporation that owns the store, but he also appears to report directly to the supervisor who works for the nationwide franchisor.*
>
> *If the individual ice cream shop is considered the "company," then there are not enough employees to meet the 15-employee minimum required by the Civil Rights Act. However, the store is part of a chain that advertises all of its stores nationwide. The store is also directly supervised by someone from the parent company—in fact, he participated in the sexual harassment. Although the manager is the president of the company, he does not act as if he or that company really owns the ice cream store.*
>
> *These and other facts may be enough to show that the parent company had substantial ownership or control of the ice cream shop and would be considered one integrated business. If so, this would mean that there would be more than enough employees to put the business over the 15-employee minimum—and that a count of all the employees in the nationwide chain would be necessary to determine which damage limitation should apply.*

"The problem is that we don't have enough men (5 men, 40 women on the editorial staff) to go around for the harassing."

—Helen Gurley Brown, former editor in chief of Cosmopolitan *magazine, when asked whether there was any sexual harassment in her office*

E. INDEPENDENT CONTRACTORS

The Civil Rights Act only prohibits discrimination and sexual harassment against employees. So if you have been classified as an independent contractor by your employer, you may have trouble using the Act.

1. True status of employee

Often a worker is required to sign a document stating that she is an independent contractor, when in fact she is treated as an employee. However, courts enforcing the Civil Rights Act may look through the label of "independent contractor" to protect an individual from sexual harassment. The question of whether someone is an independent contractor is not always easy to resolve, and it often has many tax implications beyond questions of the Civil Rights Act.

Generally, you will be considered an employee for purposes of the Civil Rights Act if you do not have true independent control over how you do your work. The control must be real, not in name only. To be a true independent contractor, you must control not just the end product of the work, but also the details and means by which that result is accomplished.

Independent contractors should not be confused with workers who are paid by temporary employment agencies or labor contractors. Unlike independent contractors, workers in this category have little or no control over the conditions of their employment. For purposes of the Civil Rights Act, temporary workers are usually considered to be both employees of the company that pays them as well as the company to which they are assigned.

2. The status of other employees

If a significant number of employees are classified as independent contractors, then they are not counted as employees for purposes of the Civil Rights Act. In a small company, you may find yourself not only trying to refute the argument that you are an independent contractor, but also arguing that your co-workers are not independent contractors, either.

"Sometimes I wonder if men and women really suit each other. Perhaps they should live next door and just visit now and then."

—*Katherine Hepburn, Actress*

HISTORY WITNESSES THE RISE OF HARASSMENT COMPLAINTS

In 1981, a total of 3,661 complaints of sexual harassment were filed with the federal Equal Employment Opportunity Commission. By 1990, the number of complaints had climbed to 5,694—an increase EEOC officials attributed to the Supreme Court's unanimous recognition in 1986 that "without question," sexual harassment is a form of sex discrimination and that hostile environment as well as sex-for-jobs harassment violates the Civil Rights Act (*Meritor Sav. Bank v. Vinson*, 477 U.S. 57 (1986)).

The number of EEOC harassment complaints again mounted dramatically in 1991 in the wake of public and publicized hearings in which U.S. Supreme Court nominee Clarence Thomas was alleged to have sexually harassed former co-worker Anita Hill while at the EEOC.

During the three months following Hill's testimony, the EEOC reported a 70% increase in the number of sexual harassment charges filed over that same period the previous year.

The fervor has not been stilled. In 1993, the EEOC resolved 9,710 claims for sexual harassment. By 1997, that number had surged to 15,889.

F. WHERE TO FILE AN EEOC CLAIM

Filing a claim with the EEOC is relatively simple. You can do it alone—or with the assistance of an attorney or other advisor.

1. File at an EEOC office

A sexual harassment or discrimination claim can be filed at any EEOC office. There is no charge for filing.

There are EEOC offices throughout the United States. (See Section M for the addresses and telephone numbers.) Normally, it is best to file the complaint in the office nearest to you or your place of employment, but you can legally file it in any office.

2. Dual filing

You also have the option in most states of filing your claim in the offices of a state FEP agency or sometimes a local FEP agency. The EEOC maintains dual filing agreements with most state FEP agencies, as well as several local FEP agencies.

Dual filing means that a claim filed in the state or local office is automatically filed at the same time with the EEOC office in the area. The reverse is true as well: Any claim filed with an EEOC office is automatically filed with an FEP office of the state where the employee works, if there is a dual-filing agreement. (See Chapter 5, Section F for an example of how dual filing works.)

Even if a claim is dual filed, there is usually only one investigation. Ordinarily the agency in which the claim is first filed does the actual work of investigation, but sometimes the two agencies also have a work-sharing agreement that allows them to shift the work of investigation back and forth.

Dual filing can be important, because it allows you to get the benefit of both the Civil Rights Act and the state FEP law. This is particularly important if you have not hired an attorney. If you are unsure whether state or federal law offers the best protection, you can dual file with both agencies and decide later which avenue to pursue after receiving legal advice.

If you file a claim with the state FEP agency or with the EEOC, ask if it will be dual filed with the other agency. The EEOC does not have these agreements with every state FEP agency, and the agreements change without notice. If your claim has been dual filed, you should receive a letter within a week or so confirming that fact. If you don't receive a letter, check with the other agency to confirm that it has been filed.

If the two agencies do not dual file the claim, do it yourself. Tell the second agency that you are only filing this second claim to protect your rights under both federal and state law.

EXPECT THE UNEXPECTED WITH EEOC PROCEDURES

For the most part, the EEOC does what it is supposed to do, but you shouldn't expect every case to proceed exactly as described in this chapter. EEOC offices differ in caseloads, local procedures and the quality of their personnel. Investigations are usually slow, sometimes taking as long as three years or more. The EEOC takes only a small portion of its cases to court—as few as 1% of those that are filed with it. These and other factors can have an impact on how a case is actually handled.

Some things to keep in mind:

Stay alert. Don't assume that the EEOC will do everything right and on time. Check periodically to find out what is happening with your case.

Be assertive. If some EEOC action—or, more likely, inaction—is causing you serious problems, call that to the attention of the people handling your case. If you are not happy with the work of the investigator assigned to your claim, ask that your claim be reassigned to another investigator.

Keep your options open. Filing a claim with the EEOC does not prevent you from taking other action to deal with your case. You still have a right to use a company complaint procedure or try to solve the problem on your own—or to hire an attorney to file a lawsuit, if that is appropriate for your situation.

G. HOW TO FILE A CLAIM

An EEOC claim can either be filed in your own name or by someone else acting for you to keep your identity confidential.

1. Filing in person or by mail

A sexual harassment claim can be filed in person or by mail at any office of the EEOC. It must be in writing to be valid. Certified mail is not necessary, but if you're filing a claim close to the deadline (see Section H), you should use certified mail with a return receipt or some other method that proves the date of delivery.

If you have the time and are able to do so, file the claim in person. Not only can you be sure that it has been received, but you can also become acquainted with some of the staff and pick up information on local office procedures. The claim does not have to be filed on any particular form to be valid, but if you file it in person, you can file it on the EEOC's specially designed charge form.

If the particular EEOC or state FEP office requires you to make an appointment before coming in to file a complaint, be careful about the timing. You must file your claim within a certain time period (see Section H), and you have to be sure that the date set for your appointment is within the required time. Merely calling for an appointment within the required time is not enough to comply with the filing deadline.

2. Keeping your identity confidential

EEOC procedures permit another person or organization to file the claim on your behalf to keep your identity secret. This can be done by an attorney, a union, an employment rights group or any other person acting on your behalf.

This confidentiality rule has two purposes:

- to protect you from retaliation while the investigation is proceeding, and

- to encourage employees to file charges promptly after the sexual harassment has occurred.

Anyone filing on your behalf must do it in the same form and within the same time limits as you would if you were doing it yourself. The person or agency actually filing the claim must provide the EEOC with your name, address and phone number in a separate document so that EEOC personnel can contact you and verify that you authorized filing the charge. If at that point you continue to request that your identity remain confidential, the EEOC must honor your request.

Most state FEP laws do not have this type of confidentiality procedure. If you want to file confidentially at a state office, check first to be sure that the agency will protect your identity to the same extent as the EEOC. It is also a good idea to make sure that the confidentiality of your identity will be preserved when the EEOC dual files your claim with the state FEP agency.

BEWARE OF RETALIATION

Although the EEOC may keep your identity confidential, there is nothing to prevent company management from figuring out your identity from the specific charges in the sexual harassment claim. If you are the only mailroom supervisor in the company and your complaint relates to harassment in the mailroom, it won't take long for the company to determine who is bringing the complaint. In this situation, all you can do is watch for acts of retaliation and ask the EEOC to take protective action on your behalf if necessary.

Many EEOC investigations proceed to the point where conciliation or some other specific remedy for the employee is discussed, and it is usually impossible to resolve the case without telling the employer your name. Usually when settlement is in the offing, confidentiality of your identity will not be so critical. But if you are still concerned about possible retaliation by your employer, ask the EEOC staff if it will go to court, if necessary, to prevent the employer from retaliating against you.

H. TIME LIMITS FOR FILING A CLAIM

Despite the fact that the EEOC is a nationwide agency, there is no uniform rule about the time limit in which a claim must be filed.

1. Within 180 or 300 days

The EEOC has two different time limits, called "statutes of limitation" in legal jargon, for filing sexual harassment claims. In some states, it's 180 days from the date of the sexual harassment incident; in others, it's 300 days from the incident.

The EEOC tends to allow a longer filing limit in states that have longer time limits under their own FEP law, and to use shorter time limits in other states.

There is no penalty for filing early, but there are serious problems if you file late. Therefore, you should assume that the time limit for filing a claim is 180 days from the date of the harassment unless you are clearly told, preferably in writing, by the EEOC or state FEP agency that you have a longer time.

2. Claim must be actually filed

The written sexual harassment claim must be actually filed within the 180-day period—or 300 days, if that applies. Talking on the phone with the EEOC personnel or setting up an appointment within the time period is not sufficient. The written claim must be on file.

3. Company procedure does not extend time

The time for filing with the EEOC is not extended if you attempt to resolve your claim through a company complaint procedure. However, under some state FEP laws, the time you spend using a company complaint procedure extends the time you have to file.

If you are engaged in a lengthy negotiation procedure with your employer over your claim but don't want to give up any of your other rights, file your claim within the 180 days and ask the EEOC to defer action until negotiations are finished.

4. Determining the date of the harassment

The 180-day period for filing the complaint begins on the day the act of sexual harassment actually occurs. But even though the events of the harassment may be etched in your mind, it is sometimes difficult to determine as a legal matter what incident triggers the 180-day period. The safest course is to file your claim within 180 days of the earliest harassment incident.

Example: Sondra has been bothered by a co-worker who has pestered her for dates and made sexual innuendoes to her. On November 1st, a friend tells her that one month earlier, the same man sent a photo of a woman to another male worker. The woman in the photo was naked with an arrow pointing toward her crotch. Attached was a note that read: "Looks just like Sondra Felipo to me." Sondra complains of this incident to her supervisor. It turns out that the co-worker is a friend of her supervisor, and on December 1st, Sondra is fired.

The date of the incident that would begin the 180-day filing period may be December 1st when the most significant injury occurred to Sondra—the loss of her job. However, it could also be argued that the time period began on November 1st when she discovered the most serious act of harassment—the pornographic photo. Or it could be October 1st, when the actual incident occurred. The safest course for Sondra is to file her claim promptly. As long as she is within 180 days of the October 1st incident, there is no need for her to pinpoint the exact date of the harassment.

5. Exceptions for late claims

If you miss the deadline for filing a claim, the EEOC or the courts will allow you to file late in a few circumstances. Here are some of them:

a. Being misled about the facts

If you can show that you were misled about the real reason behind certain important events, you may be able to convince the EEOC to accept a late claim if you file promptly after discovering the facts.

Example: Roberta is sexually accosted in the lunchroom by a co-worker—and she calls company security to get him away from her. Two weeks later, Roberta's supervisor tells her that she is being laid off because the company has to cut back on her department. One year later, she learns that there was no cutback in her department and that the supervisor who fired her is the brother-in-law of the co-worker who accosted her. In this case, the EEOC would likely allow Roberta to file a claim for sexual harassment if she did so promptly after learning the truth.

b. Being misled about the law

If you complain about a sexual harassment incident to your employer and the employer misleads you about your rights, then the EEOC filing date may be extended. A common example of this would be if your employer tells you that you can protect your rights by participating in a lengthy complaint procedure—and then fails to tell you when the time is running out for you to file your claim with the EEOC.

c. Hardship

If you have a legitimate reason why you were unable to file the charge with the EEOC within the proper time period, the agency may extend the filing deadline. If, for example, you had a lengthy illness, file the charge with the EEOC and give a plausible and detailed explanation as to why you should be granted an exception.

6. Restructuring the claim to stress later events

Even if an incident is barred by the 180-day or 300-day filing rule, there may be a later incident that is within the filing period. In this situation, you may not be able to recover damages for the earlier incident, but the later incident may be strong enough to sustain a damages award, particularly if there is strong evidence that the sexual harassment was part of a long pattern of behavior.

In this situation, you should file a claim based on the incidents that occurred within the filing period. But be prepared to point out to EEOC investigators how the earlier events had an impact on your injuries.

Example: Patrice received a series of six bizarre letters over a period of three years from one of her co-workers, expressing in strong terms his desire to go out with her. Patrice considers his behavior at work for the few weeks or so after each letter to be threatening and weird. During that period, he also phoned her at home and parked in front of her house. Patrice reported each of the incidents to her supervisors, but they did nothing about it. Finally, after the last incident, Patrice sought psychiatric care. Within 180 days after the last incident, she filed a claim with the EEOC.

Patrice's EEOC claim was within 180 days of the last incident, but the earlier incidents would technically not be covered because they are beyond the 180-day period. However, the courts and the EEOC would probably allow evidence of the earlier incidents to be considered to show a pattern of conduct. Also, she could probably show that her need for psychiatric care, although triggered by the latest incident, was built up over a period of time. In other words, her injuries are current, but they are aggravated by what had happened before.

"Sexual harassment is a subtle rape, and rape is more about fear than sex."
—John Gottman, psychologist at the University of Washington

I. CONTENTS OF THE SEXUAL HARASSMENT CLAIM

A sexual harassment claim does not have to be filed on a government form. Any written document containing the necessary information will do. According to the EEOC regulations, a claim need only identify the people involved and generally describe the harassment.

However, if you file a claim containing only the bare minimum of information, the EEOC will later ask for further information. So to save time, include all the important information from the start. EEOC regulations also ask that you state in your claim whether or not you have already filed a claim about the same sexual harassment incident with any other governmental agency.

According to EEOC regulations, the claim should include:

1. The full name, address and telephone number of the person making the charge, or that of the person or organization filing a confidential complaint

2. The full name and address of the person charged with harassment, if known

3. A clear and concise statement of the facts, including dates when the alleged unlawful employment practices occurred, and

4. If known, the approximate number of employees of the employer or the approximate number of members of the labor organization, as the case may be.

This information seems relatively straightforward, but you should be careful in writing up your charge. In fact, this may be a good time to get legal advice from an employee's organization or women's group. Many of them will be willing to review your claim with you before you file it. (See the Appendix for contact details.)

Here are some points to remember while completing your claim paperwork.

1. Name and address of the employee

In most cases, you will simply write down your own name, address and telephone number.

SAMPLE LETTER

April 1, 199X

Equal Employment Opportunity Commission
330 South Second Avenue
Suite 430
Minneapolis, MN 55401

Dear Madame or Sir:

I am writing to you to file a charge of sexual harassment against my employer under Title VII of the U.S. Civil Rights Act.

I have not filed a previous complaint with any government agency.

My name, address and telephone number are:

Ms. Rose Riveter
4321 South Spring Street
Minneapolis, MN 55401
612/123-4567

If someone else is filing the claim on your behalf so that your identity will remain confidential, a little more paperwork is required. Do not include your name on the claim letter. Instead, write in the name, address and telephone number of the person or organization filing the claim for you. This person or organization should also include a separate letter or document that states your name, address and telephone number with an indication that the claim is being filed on your behalf.

The claim or charging letter will at some point be shown to your employer and the individuals charged with the harassment. However, the cover letter, which includes your name, should remain in the EEOC files and not be shown to anyone.

SAMPLE COVER LETTER REQUESTING CONFIDENTIALITY

April 1, 199X

Equal Employment Opportunity Commission
330 South Second Avenue
Suite 430
Minneapolis, MN 55401

Dear Madame or Sir:

Enclosed is a charge of sexual harassment against Minnesota Builders that this organization is filing on behalf of Ms. Rose Riveter, an employee of that company.

We are filing this charge on behalf of Ms. Riveter because she wishes her identity to remain confidential pursuant to 29 C.F.R. 1601.7.

We request that this letter remain confidential and that the information in it not be provided to any representative of the people or organizations named in the charge.

Ms. Riveter's address and telephone number are:

4321 South Spring Street
Minneapolis, MN 55401
612/123-4567

Sincerely yours,

Thelma Barrett
Minneapolis Women's Advocates
3214 Well Street
Minneapolis, MN 55401
612/765-4321

SAMPLE LETTER WITH CONFIDENTIAL CLAIM

```
April 1, 199X

Equal Employment Opportunity Commission
330 South Second Avenue
Suite 430
Minneapolis, MN 55401

Dear Madame or Sir:

We are writing to you to file a charge of sexual harassment
against an employer under Title VII of the U.S. Civil
Rights Act.

We are filing this complaint on behalf of the employee to
maintain the confidentiality of her identity pursuant to 29
C.F.R. 1601.7. We have sent you a separate letter giving
her name, address and telephone number.

We have not previously filed a complaint in this matter
with any other government agency.

Our name, address and telephone number are:

Minneapolis Women's Advocates
3214 Well Street
Minneapolis, MN 55401
612/765-4321
```

2. Name and address of the person charged

When naming those charged in your claim, you should ordinarily include at least two names:

- the name of the person or people who sexually harassed you, and
- the name of your employer. If your employer is a franchisee, subsidiary or affiliate of some other company, or if you're not sure of the proper name of the company, list all the names you know.

Both the harasser and the employer should be named, because you will ordinarily want to establish that both are responsible for the sexual harassment and should be held liable for it.

Name any parent or affiliated companies as well. There are several reasons for doing this. You may want to establish that a parent company is liable for the harassment, because the subsidiary or affiliated company you work for may be unable to pay off any judgment for damages. There may also be some uncertainty about whether you and the harasser are technically employed by the same company, and you will want to show that all of the affiliated companies should be held liable. Also, you should be sure that all the employees in the affiliated and parent companies are counted together to bring your case into a higher damage limitation bracket. (See Section C.1.)

SAMPLE

```
The name and address of the businesses and person against
whom the charge is made are:

Minnesota Builders
8976 Industrial Parkway
Minneapolis, MN 55401

Minnesota Construction Associates
(an affiliated company at the same address)

Roy Harlow
(address unknown, but he works at Minnesota Builders)
```

3. The approximate number of employees

The EEOC requests that you give the approximate number of employees for two reasons:

- to determine whether the company meets the 15-employee minimum under the Civil Rights Act, and

- to determine the appropriate damages limitation for your claim based upon the number of employees in the company.

It is unlikely that the EEOC will make a determination about the size of the company based on your estimate alone. But avoid making a low estimate of the number of employees whenever possible. If you estimate the number of employees at 500 or less, that could limit your potential damages to something less than the $300,000 maximum allowed against larger companies. It is never advisable to state a number of employees that is less than 15.

Since you're unlikely to be in a position to know the precise number of employees, state an approximate amount with an open upper limit, such as: at least 500 to the best of my knowledge. If you have no idea of the number of employees, simply state that you don't know.

SAMPLE

> I don't know the total number of employees at all of the offices of Minnesota Builders, but I believe that there are more than 500 employees.

4. A statement of the facts

You must include a brief statement of what happened to you in your claim to the EEOC. It should be written in plain English, rather than legalese, and the precise form is not important. You technically only have to include enough information to allow the EEOC to begin its own investigation, but it's best to include enough information to impress the agency with the seriousness of your sexual harassment claim.

If someone else is filing a claim on your behalf to protect your confidentiality, be sure the facts are stated so that they do not inadvertently reveal your identity. Sometimes the only way to do this is to make a statement of facts that is somewhat incomplete. If you are faced with this problem, explain the situation to someone at the EEOC and ask what information it will allow you to leave out of your claim letter.

SAMPLE STATEMENT OF THE FACTS

A statement of the facts is as follows:

On March 2, 199X, I started work as an assistant truck dispatcher for Minnesota Builders in Minneapolis. I was the only woman employee in my office.

During the first week I was there, one of the truck drivers, Roy Harlow, came into my office several times and made rude, sexual comments about my breasts, my lips and my buttocks. I told him to stop, but he continued.

On Friday, March 6th, I complained to my supervisor, but right after that, Mr. Harlow made a very hostile statement to me, which indicated that he had heard about my complaint but was still going to keep harassing me.

The next week, some of the other truck drivers began calling me by a derogatory nickname first used by Mr. Harlow. I don't know all of their names, but one of them is named John Harris. Also I received several anonymous phone calls and a note left on my desk with a pornographic picture. There was a very disparaging comment about me next to it. This happened on March 12th.

On March 13th, I filed a complaint with the company grievance committee, but they told me later they couldn't do anything about it. The following week on March 19th, someone left a photo on my desk of a naked woman on a dartboard.

The tension from all of this has left me ill, and I've found it hard to concentrate on my job. I've had nausea and a shaking problem I can't control. I had to take some time off from work, and while I was home I received an anonymous call from someone mocking me for taking time off.

When I got back to work on March 20th, my supervisor told me that I was being demoted and assigned to another office because he said my work wasn't adequate and I took too much time off. However, my work was fine when I wasn't being harassed by Mr. Harlow and whoever else is involved. I think his real reason for demoting me was that I had reported that I was being harassed.

Sincerely,

Rose Riveter

5. Tips for writing an effective EEOC claim

While charges to be filed with the EEOC can be informal, there are a few tips you can follow to be sure your claim is as effective as possible.

Give the important facts, including attitudes. Include everything that might be important. This includes facts about the events: "After I wouldn't go out with him, he gave the promotion to a less experienced person." It may also include facts about the attitudes of the harasser or management: "He always made a lot of disparaging comments about women," or "He got hostile towards me when I rejected his advances."

Don't worry about legal theories. You don't have to know what legal theory applies to your case or to use technical legal language. Take, for example, a 48-year-old black woman who rejected her supervisor's advances and was then passed over for a promotion. She may not know what his exact motivation was, but she should state the facts clearly so that the EEOC can investigate: "I am a 48-year-old black woman and I was passed over for promotion under the following circumstances… "

The EEOC may ultimately decide that she was discriminated against because of her sex, her race, her age, her refusal of his sexual advances or some combination of the four.

Don't exaggerate or understate your case. Avoid exaggerations and sweeping generalities in the charge you file with the EEOC, but don't be falsely modest or apologetic. Simply state the facts favorable to your position and avoid mentioning any doubts you may have.

If you state in your charge: "I felt that he was making a sexual advance to me," stop the sentence at that point. If you add an apology, such as: "maybe I was overreacting" or "maybe someone else wouldn't have taken it that way," you're only weakening your case. State your side of things, and leave it to the employer to argue against you.

Watch the dates. You must include the dates on which you were harassed, so be sure that the dates fit within the limits for the filing deadlines discussed earlier. (See Section H.) Always include the most recent or ongoing acts of sexual harassment that fall within the proper time limits. If you describe only an act of sexual harassment that occurred a year or so ago, the EEOC may decide that you filed your claim too late.

Be brief. You need to cover all of the pertinent facts, but you don't have to go into elaborate detail with any one of them. The EEOC will interview you and investigate the claim thoroughly later.

J. EEOC INVESTIGATION OF THE CLAIM

Once the claim is filed, the EEOC follows its own routine in investigating the complaint and trying to resolve it. There is little you can do to speed up the process except to be prompt and thorough in responding to EEOC requests for information. Investigations take anywhere from several months to several years.

1. Investigative procedures

The EEOC has a number of different investigation techniques.

The first thing the EEOC does is notify the employer and other people charged within 10 days after the sexual harassment claim is filed. This is normally done by sending it a copy of the claim or charge filed by the employee. The employer and the others charged with harassment then have the right to file their own versions of what happened.

The EEOC will accept any additional evidence or statements from friendly witnesses that either side wishes to present.

If the EEOC needs more information, it may ask you to make a more detailed statement. It may also request a fact-finding conference, at which you and your employer will sit down with EEOC investigators to figure out what facts you agree on—and those facts in dispute.

The EEOC can go to court while the investigation is going on to seek a court order, if necessary, to prevent your situation from getting worse. This is not something that the EEOC does very often. If you are faced with retaliation or some other threat from your employer during the course of the EEOC investigation, tell the agency and ask it to seek a court order, if necessary, to stop your employer from retaliating against you.

2. Subpoena power

The EEOC can also issue subpoenas to gather information. A subpoena is a court order that forces a witness to answer questions, to produce documents or give other information.

The EEOC can use this power to force an employer or any other witness to answer questions, disclose records or bring forth other evidence that might have a bearing on the case. Frequently, the crucial evidence that will make or break your case will be in the company files and the employer probably wouldn't give it to you without a subpoena. This could include performance reports, investigative reports of harassment incidents, personnel or hiring policies, or other documents.

Example: Lisa files a claim with the EEOC, stating that she was fired from her job in a consulting firm because she complained about the sexual advances of a co-worker. The company files a response saying that Lisa was really fired because of poor job performance. At this point, Lisa remembers that a few months earlier, her supervisor had sent a letter to a prospective client, describing the consulting services they would perform, and praising her talents on the subject. She also remembers being told several months before that she had received a favorable job evaluation. She doesn't have a copy of either letter.

Although Lisa didn't have these crucial documents, by telling the EEOC investigators that they exist, she enabled the agency to subpoena documents from both her employer and the client company.

K. EEOC ACTION AFTER COMPLETING THE INVESTIGATION

After the investigation is complete, the EEOC decides either to conciliate or dismiss the case.

1. Conciliation by the EEOC

If the EEOC decides there is reasonable cause to believe you were sexually harassed, it attempts to a negotiate a settlement informally.

Before trying to settle the case, the EEOC staff will normally meet with you to find out your bottom line. You may, for example, no longer want your job back but only be interested in recovering lost earnings and money damages resulting from the harassment. Once the EEOC knows how you want the case to be resolved, it attempts to get the employer to give you whatever you would get if you took the case to court and won. In other words, the agency has no authority to force you to accept anything other than your full legal rights by way of settlement.

If you agree, the EEOC ordinarily presents a proposal to the employer, requiring it to end its illegal practices and give you the agreed recovery in exchange for your agreement to waive your right to sue. If the employer agrees to this settlement, the EEOC must continue to monitor the case until it gets proof that your employer has fulfilled its obligations to you under the settlement. That ends the case.

If the employer rejects the settlement, then the EEOC will either file a lawsuit on your behalf or issue a right to sue letter that allows you to file your own lawsuit. (See Section L.2.) All efforts at settlement are confidential, so none of the discussions or records from the conciliation process can be used later in court.

2. A finding of no cause by the EEOC

The EEOC will issue a "no cause" determination if it feels that your sexual harassment claim cannot be proven. If you receive a no cause letter from the EEOC, you have the right to appeal that decision. You can also treat the EEOC's no cause determination as the equivalent of a right to sue letter and take the case to court yourself.

If the EEOC dismisses your case or issues a no cause determination, consider carefully the reasons why it did so before taking the time and expense of pursuing the case further. Look at all the evidence, including any evidence the EEOC has uncovered. The EEOC can and does make mistakes, but ask yourself this question: Why would I be any more likely to succeed in front of a judge or a jury than in front of the EEOC? Review your case with a women's support group or a knowledgeable friend and get their opinions.

Although the EEOC dismissal or no cause determination does not stop you from bringing your own lawsuit, your employer can use that evidence in a later trial to try to convince a judge or jury that you were not harassed.

L. LAWSUIT BY THE EEOC OR BY THE EMPLOYEE

Either the EEOC itself or you and your attorney can bring a lawsuit if you have a right to sue letter.

1. Lawsuit by the EEOC

Once the EEOC has finished investigating and trying to settle the case, it can file a lawsuit itself based on the issues raised in your claim. However, this happens only in a tiny percentage of the cases that are filed with the EEOC.

If the EEOC files a lawsuit in your case, you can simply let it handle the entire matter and wait to see what happens. If you want your own attorney to be involved in the case, you can petition the court to make you an official party to the case. You and your attorney would then be formally involved in the entire decision-making process.

2. When the right to sue letter is issued

If the EEOC decides not to file a lawsuit itself, you can file a suit on your own. But you can't do so until the EEOC issues a right to sue letter.

Theoretically, the EEOC is required to complete its investigation within 180 days after the claim is filed, and is supposed to issue the right to sue letter at that point. But as a practical matter, the investigation usually takes a lot longer—sometimes three years or more. If left alone, the EEOC will not issue a right to sue letter until it feels that its investigation and conciliation efforts are complete. That may be several years down the line.

However, if the EEOC has not finished its investigation by 180 days after the claim is filed, you can demand a right to sue letter. Also, upon request, the EEOC can issue a right to sue letter even before the 180 days are up if it determines that it probably will be unable to complete its investigation by the end of the 180-day period.

You ordinarily have only 90 days from the date you receive a right to sue letter to file a lawsuit, so it is very important that you receive it promptly. The right to sue letter is usually sent to you, so keep the EEOC informed of your current address to be sure you actually receive it.

There is a great deal of confusion about how the 90-day period should be measured. It is supposed to begin when you receive the letter. But while some courts have held that you must personally receive the letter to start the 90-day period, others have ruled that the period begins when it is received by a responsible person living at that address. If it is sent to your attorney, the 90 days runs from that date if it can be proven that you authorized the attorney to receive it for you.

To complicate matters further, some courts will assume that the 90 days begins five days after the letter was sent. Also, if you did not tell the EEOC of your current address, the 90 days will probably begin when the letter arrived at the last address you filed with the agency unless you have some very good reason for the miscommunication.

Failure to file the lawsuit within 90 days does not absolutely prevent you from bringing a lawsuit, because the court can allow you to proceed late if the delay was not your fault. However, you should not rely on the court's discretion. File your case well within the 90-day period to be sure you can bring a lawsuit.

WHEN TO DEMAND A RIGHT TO SUE LETTER

As mentioned, you can insist that the EEOC send you a right to sue letter 180 days after you file your claim. This will allow you to proceed with your case quickly and avoid any further delay. But before doing so, there are two things you should consider.

• If the EEOC sends you a right to sue letter, it will ordinarily stop its investigation. From that point on, you are on your own, and whatever benefit you might have gotten from a further investigation is lost.

• Once you get the right to sue letter, you have a relatively short period of time to file your lawsuit. Ninety days may seem like a long time, but its not very long by a court's timetable. You will have to move quickly to get your case filed on time, so you should never ask the EEOC to issue a right to sue letter unless you have already retained an attorney who is ready to move on the case quickly.

3. Filing a lawsuit under the Civil Rights Act

Once the EEOC has issued a right to sue letter, you can then file a lawsuit in federal court—or, in some cases, in state court—to enforce your rights under the U.S. Civil Right Act.

"They just don't get it. Those men just don't understand how injurious, how demeaning and how frightening sexual harassment really is. So it took a massive eruption of outrage from women across America—and across party lines—to shock those senators into delaying the vote on Thomas so the charges could be investigated."

—Molly Yard, President of the National Organization for Women, in an October 10, 1991 plea to members to help finance campaigns of women for Congress

M. EEOC DISTRICT OFFICES

As mentioned, there are EEOC offices throughout the United States. Normally, it is best to file a sexual harassment complaint at the office nearest to you or your place of employment. But if there is not one nearby or not one in your state, you can legally file it in any office.

To be automatically connected with the nearest field office, call: (800) 669-4000; TDD: (800) 669-6820.

ALABAMA

Birmingham District Office
1900 Third Avenue, North, Suite 101
Birmingham, AL 35203
(205) 731-1359
TDD: (205) 731-0095

ARIZONA

Phoenix District Office
3300 North Central Avenue, Suite 300
Phoenix, AZ 85012
(602) 640-5000
TDD: (602) 640-5072

ARKANSAS

Little Rock Area Office
425 West Capitol Avenue, Suite 625
Little Rock, AR 72201
(501) 324-5060
TDD: (501) 324-5481

CALIFORNIA

Fresno Local Office
1265 West Shaw Avenue, Suite 103
Fresno, CA 93711
(209) 487-5793
TDD: (209) 487-5837

Los Angeles District Office
255 East Temple, 4th Floor
Los Angeles, CA 90012
(213) 894-1000
TDD: (213) 894-1121

Oakland Local Office
1301 Clay Street, Suite 1170-N
Oakland, CA 94612
(510) 637-3230
TDD: (510) 637-3234

San Diego Area Office
401 B Street, Suite 1550
San Diego, CA 92101
(619) 557-7235
TDD: (619) 557-7232

San Francisco District Office
901 Market Street, Suite 500
San Francisco, CA 94103
(415) 356-5100
TDD: (415) 356-5098

San Jose Local Office
96 North Third Street, Suite 200
San Jose, CA 95112
(408) 291-7352
TDD: (408) 291-7354

COLORADO

Denver District Office
303 East 17th Avenue, Suite 510
Denver, CO 80203
(303) 866-1300
TDD: (303) 866-1950

DISTRICT OF COLUMBIA

Washington Field Office
1400 L Street, NW, Suite 200
Washington, DC 20005
(202) 275-7377
TDD: (202) 275-7518

FLORIDA

Miami District Office
One Biscayne Tower
2 South Biscayne Boulevard, Suite 2700
Miami, FL 33131
(305) 536-4491
TDD: (305) 536-5721

Tampa Area Office
501 East Polk Street, 10th Floor
Tampa, FL 33602
(813) 228-2310
TDD: (813) 228-2003

GEORGIA

Atlanta District Office
100 Alabama Street, Suite 4R30
Atlanta, GA 30303
(404) 562-6800
TDD: (404) 562-6801

Savannah Local Office
410 Mall Boulevard, Suite G
Savannah, GA 31406
(912) 652-4234
TDD: (912) 652-4439

HAWAII

Honolulu Local Office
300 Ala Moana Boulevard, Room 7123-A
P.O. Box 50082
Honolulu, HI 96850
(808) 541-3120
TDD: (808) 541-3131

ILLINOIS

Chicago District Office
500 West Madison Street, Suite 2800
Chicago, IL 60661
(312) 353-2713
TDD: (312) 353-2421

INDIANA

Indianapolis District Office
101 West Ohio Street, Suite 1900
Indianapolis, IN 46204
(317) 226-7212
TDD: (317) 226-5162

KANSAS

Kansas City Area Office
400 State Avenue, Suite 905
Kansas City, KS 66101
(913) 551-5655
TDD: (913) 551-5657

KENTUCKY

Louisville Area Office
600 Dr. Martin Luther King Jr. Place, Suite 268
Louisville, KY 40202
(502) 582-6082
TDD: (502) 582-6285

LOUISIANA

New Orleans District Office
701 Loyola Avenue, Suite 600
New Orleans, LA 70113
(504) 589-2329
TDD: (504) 589-2958

MARYLAND

Baltimore District Office
10 South Howard Street, 3rd Floor
Baltimore, MD 21201
(410) 962-3932
TDD: (410) 962-6065

MASSACHUSETTS

Boston Area Office
1 Congress Street, 10th Floor, Room 1001
Boston, MA 02114
(617) 565-3200
TDD: (617) 565-3204

MICHIGAN

Detroit District Office
477 Michigan Avenue, Room 865
Detroit, MI 48226
(313) 226-7636
TDD: (313) 226-7599

MINNESOTA

Minneapolis Area Office
330 South Second Avenue, Suite 430
Minneapolis, MN 55401
(612) 335-4040
TDD: (612) 335-4045

MISSISSIPPI

Jackson Area Office
207 West Amite Street
Jackson, MS 39201
(601) 965-4537
TDD: (601) 965-4915

MISSOURI

St. Louis District Office
122 Spruce Street, Room 8.100
St Louis, MO 63103
(314) 539-7800
TDD: (314) 539-7803

NEW JERSEY

Newark Area Office
1 Newark Center, 21st Floor
Newark, NJ 07102
(201) 645-6383
TDD: (201) 645-3004

NEW MEXICO

Albuquerque Area Office
505 Marquette Street, NW; Suite 900
Albuquerque, NM 87102
(505) 248-5201
TDD: (505) 248-5240

NEW YORK

Buffalo Local Office
6 Fountain Plaza, Suite 350
Buffalo, NY 14202
(716) 846-4441
TDD: (716) 846-5923

New York District Office
7 World Trade Center, 18th Floor
New York, NY 10048
(212) 748-8500
TDD: (212) 748-8399

NORTH CAROLINA

Charlotte District Office
129 West Trade Street, Suite 400
Charlotte, NC 28202
(704) 344-6682
TDD: (704) 344-6684

Greensboro Local Office
801 Summit Avenue
Greensboro, NC 27405
(910) 333-5174
TDD: (910) 333-5542

Raleigh Area Office
1309 Annapolis Drive
Raleigh, NC 27608
(919) 856 4064
TDD: (919) 856-1296

OHIO

Cincinnati Area Office
525 Vine Street, Suite 810
Cincinnati, OH 45202
(513) 684-2851
TDD: (513) 684-2074

Cleveland District Office
1660 West Second Street, Suite 850
Cleveland, OH 44113
(216) 522-2001
TDD: (216) 522-8441

OKLAHOMA

Oklahoma Area Office
210 Park Avenue
Oklahoma City, OK 73102
(405) 231-4911
TDD: (405) 231-5745

PENNSYLVANIA

Philadelphia District Office
21 South Fifth Street, 4th Floor
Philadelphia, PA 19106
(215) 451-5800
TDD: (215) 451-5814

Pittsburgh Area Office
1001 Liberty Avenue, Suite 300
Pittsburgh, PA 15222
(412) 644-3444
TDD: (412) 644-2720

SOUTH CAROLINA

Greenville Local Office
15 South Main Street, Suite 530
Greenville, SC 29601
(803) 241-4400
TDD: (803) 241-4403

TENNESSEE

Memphis District Office
1407 Union Avenue, Suite 521
Memphis, TN 38104
(901) 544-0115
TDD: (901) 544-0112

Nashville Area Office
50 Vantage Way, Suite 202
Nashville, TN 37228
(615) 736-5820
TDD: (615) 736-5870

TEXAS

Dallas District Office
207 South Houston Street, 3rd Floor
Dallas, TX 75202
(214) 655-3355
TDD: (214) 655-3363

El Paso Area Office
The Commons Building C, Suite 100
4171 North Mesa Street
El Paso, TX 79902
(915) 534-6550
TDD: (915) 534-6545

Houston District Office
1919 Smith Street, 7th Floor
Houston, TX 77002
(713) 209-3320
TDD: (713) 209-3367

San Antonio District Office
5410 Fredericksburg Road, Suite 200
San Antonio, TX 78229
(210) 229-4810
TDD: (210) 229-4858

VIRGINIA

Norfolk Area Office
101 West Main Street, Suite 4300
Norfolk, VA 23510
(804) 441-3470
TDD: (804) 441-3578

Richmond Area Office
3600 West Broad Street, Room 229
Richmond, VA 23230
(804) 278-4651
TDD: (804) 278-4654

WASHINGTON

Seattle District Office
909 First Avenue, Suite 400
Seattle, WA 98104
(206) 220-6883
TDD: (206) 220-6882

WISCONSIN

Milwaukee District Office
310 West Wisconsin Avenue, Suite 800
Milwaukee, WI 53203
(414) 297-1111
TDD: (414) 297-1115 ■

7

State Fair Employment Practices Laws

State fair employment practices (FEP) statutes provide a harassed employee with a legal remedy that is often similar to the U.S. Civil Rights Act. The effectiveness of these statutes varies considerably from state to state. Many states have a weak FEP statute that provides little help, while in other states the FEP statute can be the single most effective legal weapon against sexual harassment.

SIMILARITIES TO EEOC PROCEDURES

Be sure to read Chapter 6. Although that chapter deals with the Civil Rights Act and the Equal Employment Opportunities Commission (EEOC), much of the discussion also applies to state FEP agencies—and is not repeated in this chapter.

Techniques for presenting your claim and for determining your eligibility are basically the same in dealing with a state FEP agency as with the EEOC. State FEP agencies use many of the same administrative processes as the EEOC, including subpoenas to gather evidence and negotiation and conciliation to settle cases. Unfortunately, most state agencies suffer from the EEOC problems of excessive caseload and delay.

A. EEOC RELATIONSHIP WITH STATE FEP AGENCIES

The EEOC and most state FEP agencies work together to avoid unnecessary duplication of work and to simplify their investigative procedures.

1. State agencies designated by the EEOC

The EEOC places most state FEP agencies in a category referred to as "designated." If an FEP agency is designated, it means that it meets certain standards set by the EEOC regarding staffing, funding and enforcement.

The EEOC and designated FEP agencies often defer to each other—that is, they accept each other's investigation of a case or refer cases back and forth in what is called a "work-sharing" agreement. Because the investigative work done by the designated state FEP agency must meet EEOC standards for this system to work, procedures will not vary that much from agency to agency or from state to state.

All of the agencies described in this chapter have been designated by the EEOC unless otherwise noted.

2. Dual filing agreements

The EEOC maintains dual filing agreements with most—but not all—designated FEP agencies. This means that when you file a claim with one agency, it is automatically filed with the other agency as well. You then get the benefits of whatever rights are available under both the state and federal law.

Although dual filing agreements are in force between the EEOC and most FEP agencies, they may change without notice. If you file a claim with one agency, ask whether it will be dual filed. (See Chapter 6, Section F.2.)

LOCAL AGENCIES MAY HAVE DIFFERENT LAWS

Many counties and cities also have their own laws prohibiting sexual harassment. Many of them have administrative agencies—similar to the EEOC or state FEP agencies—and some of these local agencies have also been designated by the EEOC.

If you are trying to decide where to file a harassment claim, find out whether there are any local agencies in your city or county that handle sexual harassment. Ask representatives at your local EEOC or state FEP office if they know of any—or look in the City and County Government listings in the telephone book under Employment Discrimination or Sexual Harassment.

Taking the time to do this bit of research could make a big difference in the outcome of your claim. Because local laws may be different from the laws of the state in which you live, you may find that a city or county ordinance:

*   *Covers more categories of employees. For example, some states require a minimum number of employees, and a local law may not have this restriction.*

*   *Covers more kinds of discrimination. A local law may define sexual harassment differently than the state law, or may prohibit other discrimination, such as discrimination based on sexual orientation.*

*   *Gives better remedies. Even in a state which allows no compensatory or punitive damages, a local law may authorize such an award.*

---

3. No guarantees of effectiveness

Each designated FEP agency has the power to stop ongoing acts of harassment and provide some help to the employee in recovering lost wages and other job-connected losses, but many FEP laws stop at that point. In about half of the states, the FEP agencies have only those minimum powers. In other states, the legislatures have gone further with their FEP laws and have established remedies in money damages for sexually harassed employees.

The mere fact that the EEOC has designated a state agency does not mean that agency administers an FEP law that offers an effective remedy.

> "Even if men admit that *some* women have to work, they acknowledge only *financial* necessity as forcing women to work outside the home, as if women had no need to use talents and capacities not drawn on in the household, or to spend their days in the company of fellow workers, rather than in isolation."
>
> —*Marilyn French, The War Against Women*

B. EXCLUDING CERTAIN EMPLOYEES

Most state FEP laws exclude various categories of employees from protection under the law. These exclusions vary greatly from state to state, but they fall into two general categories:

- exclusions based on the number of employees, and
- exclusions based upon the type of employment.

1. Minimum number of employees

Many states exclude employees from protection of the law unless their employer has a certain minimum number of employees, but no state imposes a minimum that is higher than the 15-employee minimum under the U.S. Civil Rights Act. A few states set their own minimum number at 15, but most states that have a minimum set it at a lower number. For example, the Connecticut FEP statute covers companies with three employees or more, while Iowa covers companies with four or more.

If you fear you may be excluded from the protection of the state FEP law because your employer falls short of the minimum number of employees, ask the FEP agency for a copy of the statute or regulation and find out exactly what is required. In many instances, you can use some of the arguments suggested in Chapter 6, Section D, for making sure that the maximum number of employees are counted.

2. Exclusion by type of employment

Many state FEP laws exclude certain categories of employees. These categories also vary greatly from state to state, but there are certain similarities. Many states, for example, exclude domestic employees. Others exclude employees of religious groups or other nonprofit groups. People employed by a parent, spouse or child is another common exclusion.

Be wary of any question on an FEP claim form that asks if you work in domestic employment or some similar type of work. If you answer yes, the FEP agency may decide that you are not protected by the law. If you have any doubt as to how to answer the question, ask to see the exact language of the statute or regulation. Sometimes the precise wording will clearly indicate that the exclusion does not apply to the particular type of work you do. Other times, you may be able to characterize the work you do in a way that the exclusion will not pertain to you.

Example: Ken Arnold hires Jackie Baker. From the job interview, Jackie expected to do secretarial and editorial work for Ken's writing projects in his home office. But in reality, Jackie ends up spending most of her hours cleaning Ken's house, taking care of his kids and running errands for him. She does some secretarial work, but on those days, Ken sexually harasses her.

When Jackie files her claim with the state FEP office, she describes her work as secretarial rather than domestic service for two reasons: That is the type of work she thought she was getting and also, she considers that the most important part of her job.

Because sexual harassment is abusive and sometimes violent, you may be able to convince a judge or the FEP agency not to apply these exclusions too strictly.

These exclusions were written into the FEP laws mainly so that the anti-discrimination provisions of these laws would not apply in certain types of hiring situations. The state legislatures wanted to give employers the right to hire a close relative, despite equal opportunity restrictions—and to allow employers to hire whomever they wish for extremely personal work, such as domestic service or work that requires the employee to live in the employer's home, such as personal care.

But there is a big difference between allowing a man to hire whomever he wants as an assistant or a housekeeper and allowing him to sexually harass the woman that he does decide to hire. You may be given the benefit of the doubt in some cases because of the possibility of serious injury and abuse in sexual harassment situations.

STATES ACT AGAINST EMPLOYER INACTION

A few states have taken the initiative against sexual harassment in the workplace by passing laws that require employers to take action to prevent it from occurring. Typical new laws require that employers post their sexual harassment policies. And several more states set out tougher standards.

- California makes it unlawful for employers, labor organizations or employment training programs to fail to take all reasonable steps necessary to prevent discrimination and harassment (Cal. Gov't. Code §12940(i)). A Vermont statute states that the employer has an obligation to ensure that the workplace is free of sexual harassment (Vt. Stat. Ann. tit. 21, §495h).

- California (Cal. Gov't. Code §12950), Massachusetts (Mass. Ann. Laws ch. 151, §3a), Rhode Island (R.I. Gen. Laws §§28-51-2 & 3) and Vermont (Vt. Stat. Ann. tit. §495h) require employers to display a poster defining sexual harassment, giving examples of harassing behavior and describing the state's complaint process. In addition, these states require that the employer provide a written statement informing each employee that both sexual harassment and retaliating against those who complain about it are illegal.

- Maine also requires a workplace poster and written statement about harassment—and also requires employers with 15 or more employees to train all new employees about how to recognize and take steps against against harassment at work (Maine Rev. Stat. tit. 26, §807).

C. CHOOSING A REMEDY: THE IMPORTANCE OF DAMAGES

The most significant difference among the various state FEP laws is between those that allow money damages to be awarded for personal injuries and those that do not. About one-half of the states award these damages. This is a key issue, because the availability of money damages will often be the determining factor in deciding whether to pursue a claim under the state FEP law or deciding to pursue another remedy.

1. If no money damages are allowed

If you feel you have a claim for personal injuries, there is no good reason for you to use a state FEP law that makes no provision for money damages. You should probably pursue your claim under the U.S. Civil Rights Act instead, since that Act allows at least a limited award of money damages—between $50,000 and $300,000 based on the number of employees in the company. (See Chapter 6, Section B.)

The EEOC and the state FEP agencies are roughly equal in their investigative powers and their abilities to provide other types of help to harassed employees, so the existence of a potential remedy in money damages under the federal law will often be the decisive consideration. Of course, not every sexual harassment case involves personal injuries. But if you have suffered them, you will want to be compensated adequately.

You may not be eligible under the Civil Rights Act because you work for a company with fewer than 15 people. (See Chapter 6, Section C.) This rules out the Civil Rights Act as a remedy in your case, but it doesn't make a poor FEP statute any more attractive. If you are in this situation, you will probably have to look for a common law tort lawsuit as your best option to recover damages for your injuries. (See Chapter 8.)

2. If money damages are allowed

If you work in a state with an FEP law that allows money damages for personal injuries, that statute may provide your best remedy for sexual harassment.

The FEP laws in these states often allow a remedy that is more generous than the remedy under the U.S. Civil Rights Act. State FEP laws that provide for money damages almost always allow them to be awarded in their actual amount, without any of the limitations contained in the Civil Rights Act.

For example, an employee in New York who can prove damages of $700,000 for pain and suffering is entitled to recover the full amount under the state FEP law. By contrast, she would be limited to between $50,000 and $300,000 under the U.S. Civil Rights Act, depending upon the number of employees in the business. (See Chapter 6, Section B.)

Even if your state FEP law provides for damages for personal injuries, the U.S. Civil Rights Act may still be the best choice. Some state FEP laws, for example, permit damages to compensate the worker for injuries, including pain and suffering, but do not allow punitive damages to punish the harasser when his actions were particularly outrageous. And sometimes, state court decisions put crippling restrictions on a state FEP law that looks good on its face. The best legal remedy in these situations may be a combination of claims under the U.S. Civil Rights Act, the state FEP law and various common law torts. (See Chapter 5, Section F for an example of this.)

D. MONEY DAMAGES: STATE DIFFERENCES

The FEP laws in roughly half of the states allow some form of money damages for personal injuries in sexual harassment cases. However, there are significant differences in these laws and how they are administered.

1. Administrative hearings

Several state FEP laws offer an alternative to going to court that allows a sexually harassed woman to be awarded money damages in an administrative hearing. This is usually an alternative procedure; you retain the right to go to court if you choose not to use this hearing process.

If you work in a state that allows money damages to be awarded through an administrative hearing, give serious thought to using it. This is simpler—and typically faster—than filing a lawsuit. It can be much cheaper as well, because some state agencies will either provide you with an attorney or have a staff member act as your advocate at the hearing. You have the option, however, of filing a lawsuit instead of using the administrative hearing process if you feel that you are likely to get a larger damages award from a judge or jury in court.

2. Punitive damages

In some states, the money damages award can include an amount for punitive damages—exacted to punish the harasser for particularly outrageous acts. About half the states that allow money damages to be awarded also allow an award of punitive damages.

There are also differences in how punitive damages can be awarded. Some FEP laws allow punitive damages to be awarded along with compensatory damages through an administrative hearing. Other state FEP laws allow punitive damages only if you take your case to court.

These restrictions on punitive damages may be important if you are trying to decide whether to use the state FEP law or bring a common law tort suit.

3. Filing an administrative claim first

In some states, you must first file your claim with the FEP agency before you can file a private lawsuit. In California, for example, you must file your complaint with the Department of Fair Employment and Housing, the California FEP agency—and obtain a right to sue letter before filing the lawsuit.

However, in other states, such as Illinois, you don't have to file with the FEP agency before filing a lawsuit.

THE IMPORTANCE OF PHONING FIRST

Your state FEP agency should be able to answer any questions you might have, tell you if the law has changed and send you documents, such as copies of the state laws and regulations, that may help you make your decision. A few things you should keep in mind when dealing with a state agency:

Call before you do anything else. Some state agencies require you to file your complaint over the phone, others require you to come in for an interview, and still others require you to file your complaint by mail. Before you make any decisions about whether to use your state FEP law, or waste time doing the wrong thing, call and ask.

Be sure you are talking to the right person. The person who answers the phone will rarely know the answers to all of your questions. If you want to know when, where or how to file a complaint, ask to speak with an intake person or investigator. They can also answer questions about the investigation and conciliation process. If you have legal questions about the state FEP law, or want to know if the law has changed, ask to speak with someone on the legal staff—either a lawyer or someone who can give legal assistance.

Ask them to send you written materials. Most state agencies are willing to send you any pamphlets or other materials they have describing how their administrative procedures work, as well as copies of the state law and regulations. Also ask for a copy of the complaint form or any other forms you will be asked to fill out.

Ask whether the law has changed. Many state legislatures are in the process of changing their FEP laws to conform to the changes in the U.S. Civil Rights Act. Always make sure the information you have is current.

Be persistent. State agencies tend to be understaffed and overworked. If you cannot get through to the person you need to reach, keep trying. Don't expect your call to be returned immediately. And if you find yourself on the line with someone who cannot or will not answer all of your questions, call back later and speak with someone else.

> "Men hardly ever ask sexual favors of women from whom the certain answer is no."
>
> *—Anti-feminist Phyllis Schlafly, testifying at Labor Commission hearings on the EEOC sexual harassment guidelines*

E. FEP LAWS AND PROCEDURES: STATE SUMMARIES

This section gives some basic information about each state's FEP law and administrative procedures. We have compiled the most up-to-date facts available, but be careful. The law of sexual harassment is changing rapidly—and many states are amending their laws. Before you take action based on the information given here, call your state agency and make sure it remains accurate.

How to Use These Listings

The information here is divided into a number of categories.

Statute. The legal citation to your state FEP law, if there is one. (See Chapter 9, Section C on how to read statute citations.)

State agency. The name, address and phone number of the state organization responsible for administering and enforcing the FEP law. Only the main office is listed here. There may also be local offices that are more convenient. Call the state agency for information on how and where to file a claim.

Exclusions. Individuals who are not entitled to the protections of the state FEP law. If you think you may fall under one of these categories, see Section B and Chapter 6, Section B.

Time limits. The time within which you must file a claim. Unless otherwise indicated, the time limit starts with the incident of harassment. So, for example, in Arizona, an employee would have 180 days from the date she was harassed to bring a claim with the Commission. If she tried to bring a claim after 180 days, she would not be allowed to do so. It is very important to keep on top of these limits. Call your state agency if you have questions about when to file. When in doubt, file early.

Exhaustion. Whether you must file a claim with your state agency before bringing a private lawsuit based on the state FEP law. The term is shorthand for "exhaustion of administrative remedies." Some states require you to follow all available administrative procedures before you can resort to a lawsuit.

If there is a "yes" listed for your state, you must file a claim with the state agency as a prerequisite to a lawsuit. If there is a "no" listed, you are not required to file a claim before bringing a lawsuit. Some states follow a procedure similar to the EEOC. They require you to file a claim with the state agency, but they will give you permission to bring a private lawsuit—either through a right to sue letter or by some other method—after a certain number of days.

Monetary damages. The kinds of damages that can be awarded under the state FEP law. We specify here whether these damages are available from an administrative hearing, a private lawsuit, or both. Unless otherwise indicated, all states will award job-connected losses, such as back pay and lost benefits. In addition, some states award:

- compensatory damages, or money to compensate for personal injuries, pain and suffering, mental distress and humiliation, and

- punitive damages, or money to punish the harasser for particularly heinous behavior.

Administrative procedure. Some details about how your state agency works. Unless otherwise indicated, every agency will investigate your claim and make an attempt to reach a settlement between you and your employer. Some agencies will also hold an administrative hearing, like a court case. Many agencies provide an attorney to argue for your complaint at this hearing; others require that you hire your own attorney. Some states will also award attorney's fees.

Private lawsuit. The requirements for bringing a private lawsuit based on state law. Some states don't allow you to bring a lawsuit at all. Others require you to obtain a right to sue letter before bringing a lawsuit or imposing other limitations.

ALABAMA

No state FEP law.

ALASKA

Statute: Alaska Stat. §§18.80.010 to 300 and §22.10.020
State agency: Alaska State Commission for Human Rights
          800 A Street, Suite 202
          Anchorage, AK 99501-3669
          (907) 276-7474

Exclusions: Those who work for nonprofit social, religious, fraternal, charitable or educational organizations; domestic employees

Time limits: 180 days after incident of harassment, but 300 days if incident occurred before 8/22/97

Exhaustion: No

Monetary damages: Compensatory and punitive damages can be awarded in a private lawsuit, but not by the administrative agency.

Administrative procedure: If you choose to bring your complaint to the Commission, an administrative hearing is available. The complaint will be represented by the Commission, but you can also hire your own attorney. Attorney's fees are available.

Private lawsuit: You can bring a lawsuit directly in state court. You must file it within two years.

ARIZONA

Statute: Arizona Rev. Stat. §§41-1461 to 1465, §§1481 to 1484
State agency: Arizona Civil Rights Division
          1275 West Washington Street
          Phoenix, AZ 85007
          (602) 542-5263

Exclusions: Those who work for employers of fewer than 15 employees, for the United States, for Native American tribes or for bona fide tax-exempt private membership clubs; appointed staff of elected officials

Time limits: 180 days after incident of harassment

Exhaustion: Yes. After 90 days, if the Division has not completed its administrative process, you can request a right to sue letter.

Monetary damages: No compensatory or punitive damages are available under state law.

Administrative procedure: The Division does not hold an administrative hearing. If, after investigation, the Division decides that there is reasonable cause to believe that harassment took place, it can bring an action on your behalf in state court against your employer, but it is not required to do so.

Private lawsuit: You can bring a private action only with a right to sue letter. If the Division decides not to bring a lawsuit itself, you can bring your own lawsuit starting 90 days after the complaint was originally filed. You can apply for a court-appointed attorney to represent you in this lawsuit, or you can petition the court for permission to begin the action without paying fees or court costs. Attorney's fees are available.

ARKANSAS

Statute: Arkansas Stat. Ann. §§16-123-101 to 108

State agency: None; contact the EEOC

Exclusions: Those who work for employers of fewer than nine employees; those employed by their parent, spouse or child; those working as vocational rehabilitation trainees

Time limits: One year after incident of harassment—or within 90 days of receiving a right to sue letter or notice of determination from federal EEOC, whichever is later.

Exhaustion: No

Monetary damages: Compensatory and punitive damages may be awarded in a private lawsuit according to these limits: from an employer with fewer than 15 employees, up to $15,000; with more than 14 and less than 101 employees, up to $50,000; with more than 100 but fewer than 201 employees, up to $100,000; with more than 200 but fewer than 501 employees, up to $200,000; with more than 500 employees, up to $300,000.

Administrative procedure: No administrative procedure; you must file in state court.

Private lawsuit: You must bring a private action. Attorney's fees are available.

CALIFORNIA

Statute: Ca. Gov't. Code §§12900 to 12996

State agency: California Dept. of Fair Employment and Housing

           2014 T Street, Suite 210

           Sacramento, CA 95814

           (916) 227-0551

           (800) 884-1684

Exclusions: Those who work for employers with fewer than four employees or for nonprofit religious organizations

Time limits: One year after incident of harassment

Exhaustion: Yes. If the Department has not completed its administrative process after 150 days, you can request a right to sue letter.

Monetary damages: Compensatory up to $50,000 and punitive damages can be awarded.

Administrative procedure: The Department will hold an administrative hearing. At this hearing, an attorney for the Department will represent the complaint.

Private lawsuit: You can bring a lawsuit for up to one year after receiving a right to sue letter.

COLORADO

Statute: Colorado Rev. Stat. §§24-34-301 to 406
State agency: Colorado Civil Right Commission
         1560 Broadway, Suite 1050
         Denver, CO 80202
         (303) 894-2997
Exclusions: Those who work for religious organizations not supported by public taxes; domestic employees
Time limits: 180 days after incident of harassment
Exhaustion: Yes. If the complaint is dismissed after a finding of no probable cause, you can have the right to sue (within 90 days of dismissal). You can also request a right to sue letter at any time before the hearing notice is sent.
Monetary damages: No compensatory or punitive damages can be awarded under state law.
Administrative procedure: The Commission will hold an administrative hearing. The complaint will be represented by an attorney for the Commission. You may also hire your own attorney.
Private lawsuit: You can bring a private lawsuit only after receiving a right to sue letter.

CONNECTICUT

Statute: Conn. Gen. Stat. §§46a-51 to 99
State agency: Connecticut Commission on Human Rights and Opportunities
         1229 Albany Avenue
         Hartford, CT 06112
         (860) 566-7710
Exclusions: Those who work for employers with fewer than three employees; domestic employees, those employed by their parent, spouse or child
Time limits: 180 days after incident of harassment
Exhaustion: Yes
Monetary damages: Compensatory damages can be awarded both by the Commission and in a private lawsuit. Punitive damages cannot be awarded under state law.
Administrative procedures: If the Commission finds probable cause that you were sexually harassed and has sent a notice of hearing, you may choose to have your complaint heard in an administrative hearing or in state court. In a hearing, the complaint will be represented by the Commission. You can hire your own attorney if you wish. Attorney's fees are not available from the Commission.
Private lawsuit: You can elect to move your claim to state court if you get to the hearing stage of the administrative procedure.

DELAWARE

Statute: Del. Code Ann. tit. 19, §§710 to 718
State agency: Delaware Department of Labor, Anti-Discrimination Section
                 4425 North Market Street
                 Wilmington, DE 19802
                 (302) 761-8200
Exclusions: Those who work for employers with fewer than four employees or for religious, fraternal, charitable or sectarian organizations not supported by government appropriations; agricultural workers, domestic employees, those employed by their parent, spouse or child, those who live with their employers as part of their job
Time limits: 90 days after incident of harassment or 120 days after its discovery, whichever is later
Exhaustion: Yes
Monetary damages: No compensatory or punitive damages can be awarded under state law.
Administrative procedure: If the Department finds that there is cause to believe harassment took place, there will be a hearing before the Equal Opportunity Review Board. You may request an attorney from the Commission or hire your own attorney. Attorney's fees are available. The Board will have to petition the Court of Chancery to enforce its decision.
Private lawsuit: You cannot bring a private lawsuit.

DISTRICT OF COLUMBIA

Statute: D.C. Code §§1-2501 to 2557
State agency: D.C. Department of Human Rights
                 441 4th Street NW, Suite 970N
                 Washington, DC 20001
                 (202) 724-1385
Exclusions: Those employed by their parent, spouse or child; domestic employees who work in the employer's home
Time limits: One year after incident of harassment or its discovery
Exhaustion: No
Monetary damages: Compensatory and punitive damages can be awarded both by the Department and in a private lawsuit.
Administrative procedure: The Department will hold an administrative hearing, called a fact-finding conference. You can hire an attorney for this conference, but you are not required to have one. If you do get an attorney, attorney's fees are available.
Private lawsuit: You can bring a lawsuit directly in district court.

FLORIDA

Statute: Fla. Stat. Ann. §§760.01 to .11
State agency: Florida Commission on Human Relations
325 John Knox Road
Suite 240, Building F
Tallahassee, FL 32303-4149
(904) 488-7082
Exclusions: Those who work for employers with fewer than 15 employees
Time limits: One year after incident of harassment
Exhaustion: Yes. If the Commission has not made a decision on probable cause within 180 days, you may withdraw your complaint and bring a private lawsuit.
Monetary damages: No compensatory or punitive damages can be awarded by the Commission. Compensatory and punitive damages may be awarded by state court; punitive damages are limited to $100,000.
Administrative procedure: The Commission will hold an informal hearing, at which attorneys are ordinarily not present. If the Commission finds there is probable cause, you may either elect to bring a civil action or request a formal hearing before the Department of Administrative Hearings. The Commission suggests that you hire an attorney for this hearing. Attorney's fees are available.
Private lawsuit: You can bring a lawsuit either after 180 days or after the Commission makes a finding of probable cause on your behalf.

GEORGIA

Note: Only applies to employees of the state of Georgia
Statute: Ga. Code Ann. §§45-19-20 to 45
State agency: Georgia Commission on Equal Employment Opportunities
710 International Tower
229 Peachtree Street, NE
Atlanta, GA 30303-1605
(404) 656-1736
Exclusions: Those who work for state departments or agencies with fewer than 15 employees; employees of private employers, appointed staff of elected officials
Time limits: 180 days after incident of harassment
Exhaustion: Yes
Monetary damages: No compensatory or punitive damages can be awarded under state law.
Administrative procedure: Only state employees are protected, and they are limited to this state remedy. All actions are confidential. The Commission holds an administrative hearing, at which you will be represented by an appointed attorney. If the Commission finds probable cause, your claim will go on to a hearing with a special master. The state will provide counsel, but if you hire your own, no attorney's fees are available.
Private lawsuit: You can bring a private lawsuit if the Commission dismisses your claim. You must request a right to sue letter.

HAWAII

Statute: Hawaii Rev. Stat. §§368-1 to 17, §§378-1 to 9
State agency: Hawaii Civil Rights Commission
                   830 Punch Bowl Street, Suite 411
                   Honolulu, HI 96813
                   (808) 586-8636
Exclusions: Those who work for the United States; domestic employees
Time limits: 180 days after incident of harassment—or after the most recent incident if there was a pattern
Exhaustion: Yes.
Monetary damages: Both compensatory and punitive damages can be awarded by the Commission and in a private lawsuit.
Administrative procedure: The Commission will hold an administrative hearing. If you choose to hire an attorney for this hearing, attorney's fees are available.
Private lawsuit: You may bring a private lawsuit after you request and receive a right to sue letter. You must bring the lawsuit within 90 days of receiving the right to sue letter.

IDAHO

Statute: Idaho Code Ann. §§67-5901 to 5912
State agency: Idaho Human Rights Commission
                   1109 Main Street
                   Boise, ID 83720
                   (208) 334-2873
Exclusions: Those who work for employers with fewer than five employees or for bona fide private clubs not open to the public; domestic employees
Time limits: One year after incident of harassment
Exhaustion: No
Monetary damages: No compensatory damages can be awarded under state law. Punitive damages of up to $1,000 can be awarded if you or the Commission bring a lawsuit in state court.
Administrative procedure: The Commission has no administrative hearing. If there is cause to believe that sexual harassment has occurred, the Commission will bring a lawsuit on your behalf in state court. You may hire your own attorney if you are bringing claims that do not fall within the state statute, such as a common law tort action. Attorney's fees are available.
Private lawsuit: You can bring a lawsuit directly in state court. You must file the lawsuit within two years of the incident of discrimination or within one year of filing the complaint.

ILLINOIS

Statute: Ill. Ann. Stat. ch. 68, §§1-101 to 2-105, §§7A-101 to 104, §§8-101 to 105, §§8A-101 to 104; or
Ill. Comp. Stat. Ann. Chapter 775 §§5/1-101 to 5/2-105, §§5/7A-101 to 104, §§5/8A-101 to 104

State agency: Illinois Department of Human Rights
            100 West Randolph Street
            Chicago, IL 60601
            (312) 814-6245

Exclusions: Those who work for private employers with fewer than 15 employees or for nonprofit religious organizations, domestic employees, appointed staff of elected officials, administrative officers of state and municipal governments, trainees in vocational rehabilitation facilities

Time limits: 180 days after incident of harassment

Exhaustion: No

Monetary damages: Compensatory damages can be awarded both by the Department and in a private lawsuit, but punitive damages cannot be awarded under state law.

Administrative procedure: The Department will hold an administrative hearing. You can hire an attorney for this hearing, and attorney's fees are available.

Private lawsuit: You can bring a lawsuit directly in state court.

INDIANA

Statute: Indiana Stat. Ann. §§22 9 1 1 to 18

State agency: Indiana Civil Rights Commission
            100 North Senate Avenue, Room E 103
            Indianapolis, IN 46204
            (317) 232-2600

Exclusions: Those who work for employers with fewer than six employees or for nonprofit fraternal, religious or social clubs or organizations; domestic employees, those employed by their parent, spouse or child

Time limits: 180 days after the incident of harassment

Exhaustion: Yes

Monetary damages: No compensatory or punitive damages can be awarded under state law.

Administrative procedure: The Commission will hold an administrative hearing. An attorney will be provided for you. No attorney's fees are available.

Private lawsuit: You can only bring a private lawsuit if the defendant agrees and if a hearing on probable cause is not underway.

IOWA

Statute: Iowa Code Ann. §§601A.1 to .19 or Iowa Code §§216.1 to .20
State agency: Iowa Civil Rights Commission
                    Grimes State Office Building
                    211 East Maple Street, 2d Floor
                    Des Moines, IA 50319
                    (515) 281-4121

Exclusions: Those who work for employers with fewer than four employees (family members do not count as employees), domestic employees, personal services employees, live-in employees
Time limits: 180 days after incident of harassment
Exhaustion: Yes. After 60 days, you can request a right to sue letter. However, you can't get a right to sue letter if there has already been a finding of no probable cause, if a conciliation agreement has already been reached or if notice of the administrative hearing has already been issued.
Monetary damages: Compensatory damages can be awarded, both by the Commission and in a private lawsuit, but not punitive damages.
Administrative procedure: The Commission will hold an administrative hearing. The complaint will be presented by a Commission attorney. You can also hire your own attorney. Attorney's fees are available.
Private lawsuit: You can bring a lawsuit only with a right to sue letter. You must file the action within 90 days of receiving the right to sue letter.

KANSAS

Statute: Kan. Stat. Ann. §§44-1001 to 1013 and §44-1044
State agency: Kansas Commission on Human Rights
                    Landon State Office Building
                    300 SW 10th Street
                    Topeka, KS 66612
                    (913) 296-3206

Exclusions: Those who work for employers with fewer than four employees, domestic employees, those employed by their parent, spouse or child, nonprofit fraternal or social associations
Time limits: Six months from incident of harassment, or from the most recent occurrence if there was a pattern
Exhaustion: Yes; but you can request a right to sue letter immediately
Monetary damages: The Commission can award compensatory damages, but only up to $2,000. It is unclear whether compensatory or punitive damages can be awarded in a private lawsuit.
Administrative procedure: The Commission holds a public hearing if there is probable cause to believe discrimination has taken place. You will be provided with an attorney at this hearing.
Private lawsuit: You can bring a private suit only after receiving a right to sue letter. You will be granted a right to sue letter if the Commission has not, within 300 days of the filing of the complaint, issued a finding of probable cause or no probable cause or dismissed the complaint.

KENTUCKY

Statute: Ky. Rev. Stat. §§344.010 to .450
State agency: Kentucky Commission on Human Rights
          332 West Broadway, Suite 700
          P.O. Box 69
          Louisville, KY 40202
          (502) 595-4024
Exclusions: Those who work for employers with fewer than eight employees, domestic employees, those employed by their parent, spouse or child
Time limits: 180 days after incident of harassment
Exhaustion: No
Monetary damages: Compensatory damages can be awarded both by the Commission and in a private lawsuit, but punitive damages cannot be awarded under state law.
Administrative procedure: If there is probable cause to believe that discrimination has occurred, there will be an administrative hearing. You can hire an attorney for this hearing, but the Commission will provide an attorney for you, if you wish. Attorney's fees are available.
Private lawsuit: You can file your own lawsuit directly.

LOUISIANA

Statute: La. Rev. Stat. Ann. §23:1006
State agency: None
Exclusions: Those who work for employers of fewer than 16 employees, for private educational or religious institutions or for nonprofit corporations
Time limits: None indicated. If you are planning to bring a lawsuit, consult with an attorney about the appropriate statute of limitations.
Exhaustion: No, because there is no administrative procedure at the state level.
Monetary damages: Compensatory damages can be awarded in a private lawsuit.
Administrative procedure: None
Private lawsuit: You must bring a private lawsuit.

MAINE

Statute: Maine Rev. Stat. Ann., tit. 5, §§4551 to 4633
State agency: Maine Human Rights Commission
Statehouse Station 51
Augusta, ME 04333
(207) 624-6050

Exclusions: Those who work for nonprofit religious or fraternal organizations; those employed by their parent, spouse or child
Time limits: Six months after the incident of harassment
Exhaustion: No. You may have fewer remedies, however, if you do not file a complaint first. See the summary of monetary damages, below.
Monetary damages: Compensatory damages are available. Attorney's fees and punitive damages may be awarded only if the Commission files the lawsuit on your behalf or if you file your own lawsuit, but had filed a complaint first with the Commission and: 1) the complaint was dismissed after a finding that there were no reasonable grounds to believe that discrimination took place; 2) the harassment could not be conciliated within 90 days of a reasonable grounds finding; or 3) if you received a right to sue letter and you file the private lawsuit within two years of the original complaint. Punitive damages may then be awarded, if you cannot recover under federal law, from an employer with more than 14 and less than 101 employees, up to $50,000; with more than 100 but fewer than 201 employees, up to $100,000; with more than 200 but fewer than 501 employees, up to $200,000; with more than 500 employees, up to $300,000.
Administrative procedure: After investigating and attempting to conciliate, the Commission, if it finds probable cause, will either bring a lawsuit on your behalf in state court within 180 days or give you a right to sue letter. The Commission will not hold its own hearing. If it does not find probable cause, you may request a right to sue letter.
Private lawsuit: You may bring a private lawsuit anytime, but see the discussion of monetary damages, above.

MARYLAND

Statute: Md. Ann. Code, art. 49B, §§9 to 39
State agency: Maryland Commission on Human Relations
6 St. Paul Street, Suite 900
Baltimore, MD 21202
(410) 767-8600

Exclusions: Those who work for employers with fewer than 15 employees, bona fide private membership clubs, appointed staff of elected officials
Time limits: Six months after the incident of harassment
Exhaustion: Yes
Monetary damages: No compensatory or punitive damages can be awarded under state law.
Administrative procedure: The Commission will hold an administrative hearing. You can hire an attorney if you wish, but no attorney's fees are available.
Private lawsuit: You cannot bring a private lawsuit.

MASSACHUSETTS

Statute: Mass. Ann. Laws ch. 151B, §§1 to 10
State agency: Massachusetts Commission Against Discrimination
            One Ashburton Place, Room 601
            Boston, MA 02108
            (617) 727-3990
Exclusions: Those who work for employers with fewer than six employees or for nonprofit social or fraternal organizations; domestic employees, those employed by their parent, spouse or child
Time limits: Six months after the incident of harassment
Exhaustion: Yes; but you may request a right to sue letter immediately
Monetary damages: Compensatory damages can be awarded by the Commission, and both compensatory and punitive damages can be awarded in a private lawsuit.
Administrative procedure: You can file your complaint anonymously if you wish. The Commission will hold an administrative hearing. An attorney will be provided by the Commission. You may hire your own attorney; attorney's fees are available.
Private lawsuit: You can bring a lawsuit only after initially filing with the Commission if it issues a right to sue letter, or after 90 days from the filing of the complaint without a right to sue letter.

MICHIGAN

Statute: Mich. Comp. Laws Ann. §§37.2101 to .2804; Mich. Stat. Ann. §§3.548(101) to (804)
State agency: Michigan Department of Civil Rights
            303 West Kalamazoo
            Lansing, MI 48913
            (517) 335-3164
Exclusions: Those employed by their parent, spouse or child
Time limits: 180 days after incident of harassment
Exhaustion: No
Monetary damages: Compensatory damages can be awarded, both by the Department and in a private lawsuit. No punitive damages can be awarded under state law.
Administrative procedure: The Department will hold a hearing. An attorney from the Department will represent you, but you can also hire your own attorney if you wish. Attorney's fees are available.
Private lawsuit: You can bring a lawsuit directly in state court.

MINNESOTA

Statute: Minn. Stat. Ann. §§363.01 to .15
State agency: Minnesota Department of Human Rights
              Bremer Tower
              Seventh Place and Minnesota Street
              St. Paul, MN 55101
              (612) 296-5665
Exclusions: Those employed by their parent, spouse or child; domestic employees
Time limits: One year after incident of harassment
Exhaustion: No. However, if you do file with the Department, you must wait to bring a private lawsuit until after dismissal of the claim and then you must file a private action within 45 days of notice of dismissal. You can also file a lawsuit after 45 days from the filing of the complaint, if the Department has not held a hearing or entered into a conciliatory agreement—and then you must give notice to the Department and file a private action within 90 days.
Monetary damages: You can recover compensatory damages up to three times the amount of your actual damages. In addition, you can recover unlimited damages for mental suffering and up to $8,500 in punitive damages. These damages can be awarded both by the Department and in a private lawsuit.
Administrative procedure: After 180 days have passed since the complaint was filed, you can request that the case be heard by the Department of Administrative Hearings. The Department will pay your costs, but will not provide an attorney. Attorney's fees are available.
Private lawsuit: You can bring a lawsuit directly in state court.

MISSISSIPPI

Statute: Miss. Code Ann. § 25-9-149
Although there is a state law prohibiting discrimination against state employees, no damages, exclusions or other specifics are mentioned in the statute.

MISSOURI

Statute: Mo. Ann. Stat. §§213.010 to .137

State agency: Missouri Commission on Human Rights
            3315 West Truman Boulevard
            P.O. Box 1129
            Jefferson City, MO 65102
            (314) 751-3325

Exclusions: Those who work for employers with fewer than six employees or for religious or sectarian groups

Time limits: 180 days after incident of harassment

Exhaustion: Yes. You can request a right to sue letter 180 days after the harassment occurred if the Commission has not completed its administrative process.

Monetary damages: Compensatory damages can be awarded, both by the Commission and in a private lawsuit. Punitive damages are available in a private lawsuit only.

Administrative procedure: The Commission will conduct an administrative hearing. At this hearing, the complaint will be presented by the attorney general. You can join in the hearing and have your own attorney, if you wish. No attorney's fees are available. Or, within 30 days of receipt of a notice of hearing letter, you may elect to have your claim heard in court. The Commission will bear the costs.

Private lawsuit: You can bring a lawsuit only after filing a complaint and receiving a right to sue letter.

MONTANA

Statute: Mont. Code Ann. §§49-2-101 to 49-2-601

State agency: Montana Human Rights Division
            Department of Labor and Industry
            Post Office Box 1728
            1236 6th Avenue
            Helena, MT 59624
            (406) 444-2884

Exclusions: Nonprofit fraternal, charitable or religious organizations

Time limits: 180 days after incident of harassment. However, if you first go through a valid company or union grievance procedure, this time can be extended by the amount of time spent using the grievance procedure, up to an additional 120 days.

Exhaustion: Yes. You can request a right to sue letter if the Division has made a finding of no reasonable cause, it has completed its investigation or 12 months have passed since the filing of the complaint without an administrative hearing.

Monetary damages: Compensatory damages can be awarded both by the Division and in a private lawsuit. No punitive damages can be awarded under state law.

Administrative procedure: If there is a finding of reasonable cause, your claim will be certified for an administrative hearing. At this hearing, you can have an attorney. No attorney's fees are available from the Division, but you can petition the state court for a rehearing solely on the issue of attorney's fees. Attorney's fees are routinely granted in this manner.

Private lawsuit: You can bring a lawsuit only with a right to sue letter.

NEBRASKA

Statute: Neb. Rev. Stat. §§48-1101 to 1126
State agency: Nebraska Equal Employment Opportunity Commission
                301 Centennial Mall South, 5th Floor
                P.O. Box 94934
                Lincoln, NE 68509
                (402) 471-2024
Exclusions: Those who work for employers with fewer than 15 employees, or any employer financed in part by the Nebraska Investment Finance Authority Act regardless of the number of employees, for the United States, for Indian tribes, for religious organizations and private membership clubs; domestic employees, those employed by their parent, grandparent, spouse, child or grandchild
Time limits: 300 days after incident of harassment
Exhaustion: You should file your complaint with the Commission first, but if you have suffered physical, emotional or financial harm, you may file a private lawsuit with the district court at any stage of the proceeding before dismissal.
Monetary damages: No compensatory or punitive damages can be awarded under state law.
Administrative procedure: You will be included in a hearing conducted by the Commission. Attorney's fees are available in district court and on appeal.
Private lawsuit: If you have suffered physical, emotional or financial harm, you may file a private lawsuit with the district court at any stage of the proceeding before dismissal.

NEVADA

Statute: Nev. Rev. Stat. Ann. §§613.310 to .430, §§233.160 to .210
State agency: Nevada Equal Rights Commission
                1515 East Tropicana, Suite 590
                Las Vegas, NV 89158
                (702) 486-7161
Exclusions: Those who work for employers with fewer than 15 employees, for nonprofit private membership clubs, for the United States or for Indian tribes
Time limits: 180 days after incident of harassment
Exhaustion: Yes. If the Commission finds that there is no probable cause to believe that you have been harassed, you can bring a private lawsuit.
Monetary damages: No compensatory or punitive damages are available under state law.
Administrative procedure: After investigation and conciliation efforts, if the Commission finds that there is probable cause to believe that discrimination has occurred, it will hold a formal hearing.
Private lawsuit: You may bring a lawsuit if the Commission makes a finding of no probable cause.

NEW HAMPSHIRE

Statute: N.H. Rev. Stat. Ann. §§354-A:1 to A:14
State agency: New Hampshire Commission for Human Rights
163 Loudon Road
Concord, NH 03301
(603) 271-2767
Exclusions: Those who work for employers of fewer than six employees or for nonprofit social, fraternal, educational, charitable or religious organizations; domestic employees, those employed by their parent, spouse or child
Time limits: 180 days after incident of harassment
Exhaustion: No
Monetary damages: No compensatory or punitive damages can be awarded under state law.
Administrative procedure: The Commission will hold a hearing. It must either hold the hearing or close the case within 24 months of the filing of the complaint. The complaint will be presented by an attorney for the Commission, but you can have your own attorney if you wish. Attorney's fees are available.
Private lawsuit: You may bring a lawsuit directly in state court.

NEW JERSEY

Statute: N.J. Stat. Ann. §§10:5-1 to 28
State agency: New Jersey Division on Civil Rights
P.O. Box 46001
Newark, NJ 07101
(609) 984-3100
Exclusions: Domestic employees
Time limits: None indicated. Call the state agency for more information.
Exhaustion: No.
Monetary damages: Compensatory and punitive damages can be awarded, both by the Division and in a private lawsuit, according to a recently enacted law. Check with the Division about how this law is being interpreted.
Administrative procedure: The Division will hold an administrative hearing. The complaint will be presented by an appointed attorney.
Private lawsuit: You may bring a lawsuit directly in state court. Attorney's fees are available.

NEW MEXICO

Statute: N.M. Stat. Ann. §§28-1-1 to 15
State agency: New Mexico Human Rights Division
            Aspen Plaza
            1596 Pacheco Street
            Santa Fe, NM 87505
            (505) 827-6838
Exclusions: Those who work for employers with fewer than four employees
Time limits: 180 days after incident of harassment
Exhaustion: Yes. If the Division has not settled the complaint or held a hearing within 180 days, you can request a letter of no determination, which will allow you to bring a private lawsuit.
Monetary damages: The Division cannot award compensatory or punitive damages. State law is unclear as to whether compensatory damages can be awarded in a private lawsuit.
Administrative procedure: The Division will hold an administrative hearing. You must get your own attorney for this hearing. The Division may then file a formal complaint of its own and take it to district court. Attorney's fees are available.
Private lawsuit: You can bring a lawsuit directly in state court only after the Division has issued a letter of non-determination or held its hearing.

NEW YORK

Statute: N.Y. Exec. Law §§290 to 301
State agency: New York State Division of Human Rights
            55 West 125 Street, 13th Floor
            New York, NY 10027
            (212) 961-8400
Exclusions: Those who work for employers with fewer than four employees; domestic employees, those who work for their parent, spouse or child
Time limits: One year after incident of harassment
Exhaustion: No
Monetary damages: Compensatory damages can be awarded both by the Division and in a private lawsuit, but punitive damages can be awarded only in a private lawsuit.
Administrative procedure: The Division will decide if there is probable cause within 180 days of the filing of the complaint. It must either dismiss the case or send notice of a hearing within 270 days. The state will provide you with an attorney at the administrative hearing.
Private lawsuit: You can bring a lawsuit directly in state court, but not if you have already filed a complaint with the Division.

NORTH CAROLINA (HAS TWO STATE AGENCIES)

Statute: N.C. Gen. Stat. §§143-422.1 to .3

For state and county employees and employees of the University of North Carolina:
State agency: North Carolina Office of Administrative Hearings
     1203 Front Street, Room 240
     Post Office Drawer 27447
     Raleigh, NC 27611-7447
     (919) 733-0431
Exclusions: Private employers
Time limits: 180 days after incident of harassment
Exhaustion: Yes
Monetary damages: No compensatory or punitive damages can be awarded under state law.
Administrative procedure: There will be an administrative hearing, at which you must provide your own attorney. Attorney's fees are available.
Private lawsuit: You cannot bring a private lawsuit.

For private employees:
State agency: North Carolina Human Relations Commission
     217 West Jones Street
     Raleigh, NC 27603
     (919) 733-7996
Exclusions: Those who work for employers with fewer than 15 employees
Time limits: 180 days after incident of harassment
Exhaustion: Yes
Monetary damages: No compensatory or punitive damages can be awarded under state law.
Administrative procedure: The Commission has no enforcement power. The Commission will defer the claim to the EEOC.
Private lawsuit: You cannot bring a private lawsuit; you must file with the EEOC.

NORTH DAKOTA

Statute: N.D. Cent. Code Ann. §§14-02.4-01 to .4-21
State agency: North Dakota Department of Labor
          State Capitol Building
          600 East Boulevard
          13th Floor, State Capitol
          Bismarck, ND 58505
          (701) 328-2660
Exclusions: Appointed staff of elected officials, domestic employees, those employed by their parent, grandparent, spouse, child or grandchild
Time limits: 300 days after incident of harassment
Exhaustion: No
Monetary damages: No compensatory or punitive damages can be awarded under state law.
Administrative procedure: There is no administrative hearing. After investigation and conciliation, if the Department finds that there is cause to believe harassment has occurred, it will send you to the EEOC.
Private lawsuit: You can bring a lawsuit directly in state court. Attorney's fees are available.

OHIO

Statute: Page's Ohio Rev. Code Ann. §§4112.01 to 99
State agency: Ohio Civil Rights Commission
          220 Parsons Avenue
          Columbus, OH 43215
          (614) 466-2785
Exclusions: Those who work for employers with fewer than four employees, domestic employees
Time limits: Six months after incident of harassment
Exhaustion: No
Monetary damages: Compensatory and punitive damages can be awarded in a private lawsuit. No compensatory or punitive damages can be awarded by the Commission.
Administrative procedure: If conciliation fails, the Commission will file a formal complaint and hold a hearing, at which the Attorney General will present the complaint. You may also have your own attorney, if you wish.
Private lawsuit: You may bring a lawsuit directly in state court within one year of incident of harassment. The state will provide an attorney.

OKLAHOMA

Statute: Oklahoma Stat. tit. 25 §§1101 to 1706
State agency: Oklahoma Human Rights Commission
         2101 North Lincoln Boulevard, Room 481
         Oklahoma City, OK 73105
         (405) 521-3441
Exclusions: Those who work for employers with fewer than 15 employees, for bona fide nonprofit private membership clubs or for Indian tribes; domestic employees, those employed by their parent, spouse or child
Time limits: 180 days after incident of harassment
Exhaustion: Yes. If the Commission has not completed its administrative process in 180 days, you can request a right to sue letter.
Monetary damages: No compensatory or punitive damages can be awarded under state law.
Administrative procedure: The Commission will hold a hearing, at which the complaint will be presented by Commission staff. You may also have your own attorney if you wish. Attorney's fees are available. The Commission's order has no legal effect without a corresponding order from the state court. The Commission must bring an action for review by the state court to get such an enforcement order.
Private lawsuit: You can bring a private lawsuit with a right to sue letter.

OREGON

Statute: Or. Rev. Stat. §§659.010 to .990
State agency: Oregon Bureau of Labor and Industry
         Civil Rights Division
         800 NE Oregon, Suite 1070
         Portland, OR 97232
         (503) 731-4075
Exclusions: Domestic employees, those employed by their parent, spouse or child
Time limits: One year after incident of harassment
Exhaustion: No
Monetary damages: Compensatory damages can be awarded by the Bureau. State law is unclear as to whether compensatory damages can be awarded in a private lawsuit. No punitive damages are available under state law.
Administrative procedure: The Bureau will hold a hearing, and a Bureau attorney will present the complaint. You may also have your own attorney if you wish. Attorney's fees are available. If the Bureau has not sent a hearing notice or come to a conciliation agreement within one year, you may move your case to state court.
Private lawsuit: You may file a lawsuit directly in state court. You must bring this action within one year of the harassment, if you don't file a complaint with the Bureau.

PENNSYLVANIA

Statute: 43 Pa. Stat. Ann. §§951 to 962.2

State agency: Pennsylvania Human Relations Commission
                101 South 2nd Street, Suite 300
                Harrisburg, PA 17101
                (717) 787-4412

Exclusions: Those who work for employers with fewer than four employees; agricultural workers, domestic employees, those employed by their parent, spouse or child or those who live in their employer's residence as part of their employment

Time limits: 180 days after the incident of harassment

Exhaustion: No

Monetary damages: Compensatory damages can be awarded in a private lawsuit, but not by the Commission. No punitive damages can be awarded under state law.

Administrative procedure: If the Commission has sent a notice of hearing, you may choose to have your complaint heard in state court, costs paid by the state. Attorney's fees are available for a hearing or an action in state court. If you choose a hearing, the Commission must petition the courts to enforce its order.

Private lawsuit: You can bring a lawsuit directly in state court.

RHODE ISLAND

Statute: R.I. Gen. Laws §§28-5-1 to 40

State agency: Rhode Island Commission for Human Rights
                10 Abbott Park Place
                Providence, RI 02903
                (401) 277-2661

Exclusions: Those who work for employers with fewer than four employees; domestic employees, those employed by their parent, spouse or child

Time limits: One year after incident of harassment

Exhaustion: Yes. After 120 days, but not after two years, you can request a right to sue letter.

Monetary damages: Compensatory damages can be awarded both by the Commission and in a private lawsuit. Punitive damages can be awarded only in a private lawsuit.

Administrative procedure: The Commission will file a formal complaint and hold a hearing, at which you must be represented by your own attorney. Attorney's fees are available. The Commission must petition the courts to enforce its order.

Private lawsuit: You can bring a private lawsuit only with a right to sue letter.

SOUTH CAROLINA

Statute: S.C. Code tit. 1, §§1-13-10 to 110
State agency: South Carolina Human Affairs Commission
            P.O. Box 4490
            Columbia, SC 29240
            (803) 253-6336
Exclusions: Those who work for employers with fewer than 15 employees, for bona fide private membership clubs or for Indian tribes; appointed staff of elected officials
Time limits: 180 days after incident of harassment
Exhaustion: Yes. If the Commission doesn't bring a lawsuit within 180 days of your complaint, or if it dismisses your claim, you can get a right to sue letter.
Monetary damages: No compensatory or punitive damages can be awarded under state law.
Administrative procedure: There is no administrative hearing. If the Commission makes a finding of probable cause, it can bring a lawsuit against your employer. If the Commission doesn't bring a lawsuit within 180 days, you can bring a private lawsuit.
Private lawsuit: You may bring a private lawsuit only with a right to sue letter.

SOUTH DAKOTA

Statute: S.D. Codified Laws, §§20-13-1 to 56
State agency: South Dakota Division of Human Rights
            118 West Capitol Street
            Pierre, SD 57501
            (605) 773-4493
Exclusions: None
Time limits: 180 days after incident of harassment
Exhaustion: Yes. A right to sue letter is available after 60 days.
Monetary damages: Compensatory and punitive damages can be awarded in a private lawsuit, but not by the Division.
Administrative procedure: If the Division finds probable cause to believe that discrimination has occurred, there will be an administrative hearing. You may choose to have your case heard in state court instead. You must get an attorney for this hearing, but no attorney's fees are available.
Private lawsuit: You may bring a private lawsuit only with a right to sue letter. Attorney's fees are available.

TENNESSEE

Statute: Tenn. Code Ann. §§4-21-101 to 408

State agency: Tennessee Human Rights Commission
         530 Church Street, Suite 400
         Nashville, TN 37243
         (615) 741-5825

Exclusions: Those who work for employers with fewer than eight employees; domestic employees, those who work for their parent, child or spouse

Time limits: 180 days after incident of harassment

Exhaustion: No

Monetary damages: Compensatory and punitive damages can be awarded, both by the Commission and in a private lawsuit.

Administrative procedure: You are entitled to an attorney at the administrative hearing. You can choose your own attorney, or have one appointed for you. Attorney's fees are available.

Private lawsuit: You can file a lawsuit directly in state court within one year. If you file a complaint with the Commission, you can withdraw it at any time to file your own lawsuit.

TEXAS

Statute: Tex. Lab. Code 21.001 to .259

State agency: Texas Commission on Human Rights
         8100 Cameron Road, #525
         P.O. Box 13493
         Austin, TX 78753
         (512) 837-8534

Exclusions: Those who work for employers with fewer than 15 employees; appointed staff of elected officials, participants in U.S. Department of Labor's statewide hometown plan, those who work for their parent, spouse or child

Time limits: 180 days after incident of harassment

Exhaustion: Yes. After 180 days, you can bring a private lawsuit.

Monetary damages: Compensatory and punitive damages are available under state law, according to the following limits: from an employer with more than 14 and less than 101 employees, up to $50,000; with more than 100 but fewer than 201 employees, up to $100,000; with more than 200 but fewer than 501 employees, up to $200,000; with more than 500 employees, up to $300,000.

Administrative procedure: If the evidence supports the complaint, the Commission will recommend a finding of harassment to an administrative panel. If two of the three members of this panel agree that harassment has taken place, the Commission can decide to file suit in the state court to enforce its finding. You can join this lawsuit, with or without an attorney. The case for the complaint will be presented by Commission staff. Attorney's fees are available.

Private lawsuit: You must first file a complaint with the Commission. You can request a right to sue letter if the Commission dismisses your claim or does not bring a suit in state court within 180 days of the filing of your complaint. You must then file in state court within 60 days.

UTAH

Statute: Utah Code Ann. §§34A-5-101 to 108
State agency: Utah Labor Commission, Anti-Discrimination Division
          160 East 300 South, 3rd Floor
          Salt Lake City, UT 84114
          (801) 530-6801
Exclusions: Those who work for employers with fewer than 15 employees or for religious organizations
Time limits: 180 days after incident of harassment
Exhaustion: Yes
Monetary damages: No compensatory or punitive damages are available under state law.
Administrative procedure: You may have an attorney at the administrative hearing. Attorney's fees are available.
Private lawsuit: You cannot bring a private action.

VERMONT

Statute: 21 Vt. Stat. Ann. §495
State agency: Vermont Attorney General's Office
          Civil Rights Division
          109 State Street
          Montpelier, VT 05609
          (802) 828-3171
Exclusions: None
Time limits: Three years after the incident of harassment
Exhaustion: No
Monetary damages: Compensatory and punitive damages can be awarded in a private lawsuit only.
Administrative procedure: There is no administrative hearing. If, after investigation and conciliation efforts, no solution has been reached, you must litigate in state court.
Private lawsuit: You may bring a lawsuit directly in state court.

VIRGINIA

Statute: Va. Code Ann. §§2.1-714 to 725
State agency: Virginia Council on Human Rights
       1100 Bank Street
       Washington Building, 12th Floor
       Richmond, VA 23219
       (804) 225-2292
Exclusions: None
Time limits: 180 days after incident of harassment
Exhaustion: Yes
Monetary damages: Compensatory and punitive damages can be awarded.
Administrative procedure: The Council has no enforcement powers. The Council will handle your complaint and investigate the charges. If attempts to conciliate fail, the Council will give the claim to the appropriate state or federal agency.
Private lawsuit: You must bring a complaint with the Council first.

WASHINGTON

Statute: Wash. Rev. Code Ann. §§49.60.010 to .330
State agency: Washington State Human Rights Commission
       Evergreen Plaza Building
       711 South Capitol Way, Suite 402
       Olympia, WA 98504-2490
       (360) 753-6770
Exclusions: Those who work for employers with fewer than eight employees or for nonprofit religious or sectarian organizations; domestic employees, those employed by their parent, spouse or child
Time limits: Six months after incident of harassment
Exhaustion: No
Monetary damages: The Commission can award up to $10,000 in compensatory damages for humiliation and mental suffering, but no punitive damages. Unlimited compensatory and punitive damages can be awarded in a private lawsuit.
Administrative procedure: There will be an administrative hearing, at which the Commission will represent the complaint. If you wish to have your own attorney, you may do so. Attorney's fees are available.
Private lawsuit: You may bring a lawsuit directly in state court.

WEST VIRGINIA

Statute: W. Va. Code §§5-11-1 to 19
State agency: West Virginia Human Rights Commission
1321 Plaza East, Room 106
Charleston, WV 25301
(304) 558-2616
Exclusions: Those who work for employers with fewer than 12 employees; those employed by their parent, spouse or child
Time limits: 365 days after incident of harassment
Exhaustion: No
Monetary damages: Compensatory damages may be awarded by the Commission and in state court. No punitive damages can be awarded under state law.
Administrative procedure: At the administrative hearing, the attorney general will present the complaint. You can have your own attorney, if you wish. If you do retain an attorney, attorney's fees are available from the Commission.
Private lawsuit. You can bring a lawsuit directly in state court.

WISCONSIN

Statute: Wis. Stat. Ann. §§11.31 to 39
State agency: Wisconsin Equal Rights Division
Department of Industry, Labor and Human Relations
P.O. Box 8928
201 East Washington Avenue
Madison, WI 53708
(608) 266-6860
Exclusions: Those employed by their parent, spouse or child
Time limits: 300 days after incident of harassment
Exhaustion: Yes
Monetary damages: No compensatory or punitive damages can be awarded under state law.
Administrative procedure. You may have an attorney at the administrative hearing. Attorney's fees are available.
Private lawsuit: You cannot bring a private lawsuit.

WYOMING

Statute: Wyo. Stat. Ann. §§27-9-101 to 108
State agency: Wyoming Fair Employment Commission
            Herschler Building
            6101 Yellowstone Ave., Suite 259C
            Cheyenne, WY 82002
            (307) 777-7261
Exclusions: Those who work for employers with fewer than two employees, religious organizations
Time limits: 90 days after incident of harassment
Exhaustion: Yes. You can get a right to sue letter if the matter is not resolved within 180 days.
Monetary damages: Compensatory damages can be awarded in a private lawsuit, but not by the Commission. Punitive damages cannot be awarded under state law.
Administrative procedure: You may have an attorney at the administrative hearing if you wish; however, no attorney's fees are available. The Commission will have to petition the state court for enforcement of its findings.
Private lawsuit: You may not bring a private lawsuit. If the Commission does not resolve your claim, you may go to the EEOC. ■

8

Common Law
Tort Actions

T itle VII of the U.S. Civil Rights Act and state fair employment practices (FEP) laws that prohibit discrimination and other unfair employment practices (discussed in Chapters 6 and 7) provide some measure of relief for those who are subjected to sexual harassment on the job. This chapter discusses several additional legal actions, referred to broadly as common law torts, often filed in sexual harassment cases.

Common law torts, or civil wrongs, include assault and battery, intentional infliction of emotional distress, interference with contract and defamation. They are filed in state courts like any other lawsuit based on a personal injury. And they may provide a wider range of remedies than those available under the Civil Rights Act and most states FEP laws, including both compensatory damages for the emotional and physical distress suffered because of the workplace harassment and the possibility of large punitive damages aimed at punishing the wrongdoer.

CLAIMS WILL USUALLY OVERLAP

Although several of the principal common law tort actions are discussed here separately, in practice, a number of them are often filed in the same sexual harassment lawsuit, along with claims for violations of federal and state laws banning harassment.

Lawyers often recommend that you file as many claims as possible, even though they may be repetitious. The reasoning is that you'll have a number of different legal alternatives to fall back on if some prove unsuccessful.

A. WHEN TO FILE A TORT ACTION

However welcome and needed the state and federal anti-discrimination laws are, they offer limited relief. In many states, fair employment practices laws compensate only for easily-documented losses, such as back pay for time lost from work. Even the U.S. Civil Rights Act—which does allow damages to compensate women for physical and mental injuries—limits covered employers to those with 15 or more employees and caps the damages at $300,000 even for the largest employers.

There are a number of situations in which filing a common law tort may be the best action you can take against sexual harassment.

1. If you work for a small employer

While a tort action may be the best option for some harassed workers, it's the only possible remedy for others. As mentioned, if your employer has 14 or fewer employees, you are not covered by the U.S. Civil Rights Act and cannot file an EEOC complaint or a federal lawsuit for damages.

And unfortunately, while the local laws in some bigger cities may provide relief for employees of any size company, many state laws either do not cover employees who work for small companies at all, or limit damages to compensation for lost pay—and sometimes medical expenses—due to physical injuries. Not many state laws allow compensation for stress-related claims or punitive damages—that is, damages charged to the wrongdoer to specifically punish him for his actions.

2. If your injuries are severe

Common law tort actions allow, at least in theory, unlimited dollar verdicts for some of the most severe injuries wrought by the harassment: emotional and physical harm. These tort actions are particularly appropriate where a woman has suffered extreme trauma from the psychological remnants of harassment—embarrassment, fright, humiliation—which can cause a permanent loss of self-esteem. Also, the daily prospect of facing a workplace fraught with unpleasantness commonly takes a heavy toll on a worker's emotional and physical health. Tort actions can often compensate for these harms.

3. If your claim is unclear

Claims brought under state FEP laws or the Civil Rights Act look much the same legally. Employees must prove to administrative authorities or a court that, according to previous interpretations and the guidelines set out, they were sexually harassed at work.

But if a situation does not quite fit within the bounds of a sexual discrimination claim under federal or state law—for example, you are an independent contractor and not an employee—picking and choosing among the suitable tort actions may allow you to tailor your case more specifically to the actual workplace wrong. A woman who has been sexually harassed at work in various ways will often combine several tort actions when seeking legal relief for the wrong.

4. If your claim is filed late

Both state and federal laws prohibiting sexual harassment have strict time limits, called statutes of limitation, within which claims must be filed—commonly either 180 or 300 days from the harassment incident. There are statutes of limitations on tort actions, too, but they are less stringent. Depending on which tort you are suing for and in which state you live, you usually have one year to three years to file.

B. COMMON TORT ACTIONS AGAINST SEXUAL HARASSMENT

While creative legal minds have been able to shoehorn harassment actions into a number of different legal theories, the actions discussed here have been the most successful most often.

1. Assault and battery

Assault and battery are actually two separate legal wrongs. But because they frequently occur together, they are very often paired in legal complaints. These offenses may also be crimes and, if they are particularly serious, should be reported to local law enforcement authorities. The two actions forbid physical contact in the workplace, or the threat of contact, that you consider to be harmful or offensive.

STRIKING BACK AT HARASSMENT: THE OLD-FASHIONED WAY

Filing assault and battery charges was one of the first ways to legally combat workplace harassment. As early as 1875, a Wisconsin woman was awarded $1,000 in damages in an assault and battery action for both mental suffering and "being wronged" when a male train conductor put his soiled hand in the muff she was wearing to keep her hands warm—and then kissed her five or six times. (*Croaker v. Chicago and Northwestern Ry. Co.*, 36 Wis. 657 (1875).)

Still, even the most sympathetic early courts that considered workplace harassment were skeptical—and hesitant. When evaluating evidence of outrageous and sometimes brutal attacks by a male co-worker, court opinions would quaintly ponder for pages whether a man had "put his hands upon a woman with a view to violate her person."

---

a.   Assault

To prove an assault, you must show that:

- the person who assaulted you intended to cause physical contact, and

- you feared or apprehended the contact.

   Generally, more than verbal abuse is required for a legal claim of assault, although repeated verbal threats accompanied by menacing gestures may qualify.

b.   Battery

Battery is actual contact that is harmful, offensive or insulting. You must show that the person who battered you:

- intended to touch you—although he need not have intended to harm you, and

- contacted you physically.

   Clearly, when a battery—which may include touching, kissing, embracing or rubbing up against your body—occurs in the workplace, you may often anticipate or fear the action, so it also qualifies as an assault. That may not always be the case, however, if the abuse took you by surprise. Nevertheless, if your harasser has physically contacted you, or if you have had reason to expect that he will, it is usually best to file both assault and battery charges unless an attorney advises you to limit your pleadings to one action or another.

If, during an assault, your harasser had or attempted to have intercourse with you, it is advisable to file rape charges against him, also. (See Section B.7.)

If your harasser's offensive conduct has been limited to verbal attacks—slurs, insults or threats to fire you—you will not likely succeed with an assault or battery claim. Most courts will require that there be some actual harmful or offensive touching or threat of touching. Some courts will even require that the touching cause an observable physical injury.

> *Example: While they were attending an out-of-town convention, a male supervisor asked his female employee to come to his hotel room to discuss an upcoming business meeting. When she did, she walked in on a decidedly unbusinesslike setting: brimming glasses of wine and the television tuned to pornographic films on a pay channel. When the woman protested and attempted to leave the room, her boss grabbed her by both shoulders and blocked her way. The court held that while the touching was intentional and "it may have been mildly offensive to her," there was no assault and battery since the woman was not physically or mentally harmed. (Boyd v. James S. Hayes Living Health Care Agency, 671 F. Supp. 1155 (W.D. Tenn. 1987).)*

Fortunately, a growing number of courts that require that an injury as a result of an assault and battery produce are enlightened enough to realize that mental suffering is also a serious injury. Even one offensive instance may be enough for a battery charge. But again, the reality is that if you are able to prove the abuse took place more than once, you will have a better chance of winning your lawsuit.

> *Example: A female executive secretary filed a lawsuit for assault and battery against the plant manager after he repeatedly touched her breasts and buttocks, ignoring her pleas to stop. The court held that while the offensive touching caused no cuts or bruises, the emotional and psychological harm she suffered from the frequent abuse was sufficient to support a common law legal action for assault and battery. (Newsome v. Cooper-Wiss, Inc., 347 S.E.2d 619 (1986).)*

If you have been subjected to assault and battery in the workplace, it is especially important to notify your employer of the abuse. If your supervisor has assaulted you, the company may automatically be liable; but if it was a co-worker who did wrong, the company may not be liable unless it knew or had reason to know of the offense.

> "Companies are starting to get the message. Everyday, it becomes more unacceptable to sexually harass, because there are more punishments and sanctions, damages to pay, jobs lost—and it will all affect the bottom line."
> —*Judith Lichtman, president of the Women's Legal Defense Fund*, Washington Post, *February 16, 1994*

ADDED PROTECTION: RESTRAINING ORDERS

If you have been assaulted or battered at work, causing you to fear for your own safety, consider filing a formal complaint with local law enforcement authorities. You should also consider getting a civil or criminal restraining order against your harasser.

A restraining order is a judgment issued by a court that is tailored to stop the harassment. Restraining orders may state, for example, that your harasser must stay a certain distance away from you, must stop contacting you at home or work, or must not contact you by mail. Those who violate a restraining order can, at a minimum, be held in contempt of court and in more severe cases, may be fined or even jailed.

One advantage of a restraining order is that police are more likely to respond to future pleas for help if you can produce a judge's order requiring that the harassment stop. In most communities, specialists at women's rights groups or victim witness counselors working within local police departments to counsel those subjected to violent wrongs can advise you on how to get a restraining order—and may refer you to other local resources to help you with the necessary paperwork.

2. Intentional infliction of emotional distress

Intentional infliction of emotional distress, sometimes simply called outrage, is one of the broadest common law tort actions—and one of the most difficult to define precisely. Aimed at preserving a person's peace of mind, it is the most common of the tort actions filed in sexual harassment situations—and historically, the one most likely to secure money for harassed workers who have suffered mental anguish.

You can file an action for intentional infliction of emotional distress against a co-worker, supervisor or your employer. To win such a case, you must prove that:

- your harasser acted outrageously

- your harasser either intentionally caused you emotional distress, or at least should have known that his actions would distress you

- you suffered severe emotional distress, and

- your distress was caused by the harasser's conduct.

The biggest problem with the legal action of intentional infliction of emotional distress is defining it. To win this type of lawsuit, the harasser's conduct must be pretty outrageous, but it is unclear just how appalling the conduct must be before courts will allow you to base a legal action on it.

Courts grappling for a description of a case that might meet the legal requirements for outrageousness often fall back on a pseudo-definition set out long ago by legal scholar William Prosser:

> Liability has been found only where the conduct has been so outrageous in character, and so extreme in degree, as to go beyond all possible bounds of decency, and to be regarded as atrocious, and utterly intolerable in a civilized community. Generally, the case is one in which the recitation of facts to an average member of the community would arouse his resentment against the actor, and lead him to exclaim, "Outrageous!"

Obviously, those looking for real guidance from this definition find scant help. Probably the best that can be said is that the conduct required to prove intentional infliction of emotional distress must evoke a strong gut reaction approaching revulsion, an I-know-it-when-I-see-it response. The requisite emotional distress may include fright, horror, grief, shame, humiliation, embarrassment, anger, chagrin, disappointment and worry.

This points up another problem with the tort of intentional infliction of emotional distress: It is extremely subjective. In this tort, more than most other legal actions, cases with nearly the same facts, brought in different states, or in different years or before different judges, commonly produce different results. Even in the same state in the same year, each court will analyze the evidence according to its own standards.

Theoretically, all sexual harassment in the workplace should qualify as outrageous. Just as racial slurs against workers of color should not be tolerated, lewd comments about a female worker's body and other harassing conduct are abhorrent and inappropriate.

But the reality is that the type of harassment that will be considered an intentional infliction of emotional distress must meet a tougher standard. A few lewd remarks—even a few very obnoxious ones—probably will not qualify. Physical injury is not required to prove the intentional infliction of emotional distress, but it is much easier to prove a case if there have been some physical repercussion—illness, shock, nausea, insomnia. Generally speaking, the more outrageous a harasser's conduct, the less severe the harassed woman's injuries need to be to prove her case.

> *Example: A union officer, representing employees in California restaurants and bars, sexually harassed several women who came to him to discuss grievances. He solicited them to have sex with him and with others—and forewarned that his position with the unions and connections to underworld figures made it risky for them not to comply.*
>
> *The harassed women claimed they were fearful and intimidated by the harassment and they were able to show by evidence from their physician or psychiatrist that this affected them physically. Based on this evidence, the court upheld their claims for intentional infliction of emotional distress. (Seritis v. Lane, 30 Fair Empl. Prac. Cas. (BNA) 423 (Cal. Super. Ct. 1980).)*

Several courts have attempted to eliminate some of the nebulousness in intentional infliction of emotional distress cases by listing requirements for bringing a case. For example, a Pennsylvania court recently ruled that a claim for intentional infliction of emotional distress based on workplace harassment must include evidence of:

- direct sexual advances
- threats of retribution
- unconsented physical contact, or
- sexual references about the employee to other workers.

Courts in other states have adopted similar standards, but most are less concrete. In general, courts seem to prefer the guesswork of deciding whether particular behavior is sufficiently outrageous or shocking on a case-by-case basis. Sadly, from the view of the harassed woman, the guesses of the predominantly male judges evaluating the cases too often seem to miss the mark.

Example: A Georgia woman resigned from her transportation job and later brought an action for intentional infliction of emotional distress. The woman alleged her co-worker subjected her to a number of offensive acts and comments, including: showing her a drawing he made of fecal matter moving through a colon, showing her a hole in the crotch of his pants and asking her, in the presence of co-workers, if she would like to staple the hole closed and making lewd gestures to indicate sex acts she engaged in on her vacation. The court held that the acts the woman found to be sexually offensive were "simply instances of tasteless and crude conduct which is not actionable." (Hendrix v. Phillips, 207 Ga. App. 394 (1993).)

Example: A woman hired as a manager trainee in a shoe store claimed that, over a period of three years, her supervisor grabbed her breasts, pinched her buttocks and crotch and frequently questioned her about her sex life and the kind of underwear she was wearing. The supervisor contested the woman's claim for intentional infliction of emotional distress, arguing that she attended only two psychotherapy sessions the year following her resignation. But the court on appeal found substantial evidence of emotional distress, focusing on the woman's testimony that she suffered panic attacks, depression and recurring flashbacks of the harassing events. (Kelly-Zurian v. Wohl Shoe Co., Inc., 22 Cal. App. 4th 397 (1994).)

Example: Three women who worked as waitresses at a country club alleged that they had been harassed by the manager and a co-worker, causing them mental and emotional distress. The first woman claimed the club manager assigned her work that she was physically unable to do because she was pregnant. The second woman claimed the manager screamed and shouted at her, called her names, interfered with her supervision of the other waitresses and once threw a menu at her in anger.

The third woman complained about the chef at the club, alleging that he shouted profanities at her, threatened her and made sexually derogatory remarks and sexual advances toward her, causing her to fear he would harm her. She also claimed she was fired in retaliation for reporting the harassment to the club manager.

The court held that only the third woman had a valid claim for emotional distress. It noted that while the manager's conduct toward the first two women was "intemperate," it did not "exceed all bounds usually tolerated by a decent society" and so was not sufficiently outrageous to support a legal claim. (Hogan v. Forsyth Country Club Co., 340 S.E.2d 116 (1986).)

Retaliation may boost your intentional infliction of emotional distress claim. It seems evident that retaliation accelerates the level of a harassed woman's workplace angst. So courts generally consider evidence that a worker was shunned, ostracized or threatened after complaining about harassment to augment a claim for intentional infliction of emotional distress.

Example: An Illinois woman complained that her supervisor caused her to suffer severe emotional distress. For two months, he told her sex-related jokes daily, bragged of his sexual exploits with multiple partners, invited her and other co-workers out for weekend sex orgies, interrogated them about their preferences for anal and oral sex and described his penis to them in grand terms.

When the woman complained about his behavior to the vice president of the company, her supervisor retaliated—threatening that he would get even, undermining her authority and making it more difficult for her to do her job well. The court ruled that, taken on its own, the harassing sexual comments did not amount to intentional infliction of emotional distress, but the retaliation did. (Class v. New Jersey Life Ins. Co., 746 F. Supp. 776 (N.D. Ill. 1990).)

One additional point: Evidence of retaliation may also help establish an employer's liability if company management participates in the retaliation or pays no heed to it.

> **"Lawsuits are clumsy tools for shaping human behavior: They are expensive, eat up a lot of time, and usually exacerbate whatever tensions already exist; they often have unforeseen consequences; they tend to enrich the lawyers far more often than they satisfy the parties."**
>
> **—*Alex Kozinski, Ninth Circuit Court of Appeal judge,* Sexual Harassment in Employment Law**

A CHECKLIST TO HELP YOU EVALUATE YOUR CASE

Here are some factors to look at when evaluating workplace behavior to see whether it is likely to be considered sufficiently outrageous to support a claim of intentional infliction of emotional distress.

Coercion. Where the harasser has some power over you in the workplace, such as supervising your work or controlling your raises or promotions, your chances of success increase. Some courts have actually required that some work benefit—a raise, promotion, new job—be denied or threatened before they will find any intentional infliction of emotional distress.

Frequency. A claim is more likely to succeed where the harassing behavior happens regularly, or recurs several times, as opposed to an isolated instance.

Duration. Again, a single instance of harassment may be enough, but if the bad behavior has continued over a long span of time, it may be more likely to be considered outrageous.

Physical contact. While there is no legal requirement that your harasser actually touch you, some courts seem more inclined to find intentional infliction of emotional distress if there has been unwanted touching as opposed to solely verbal heckling or threats.

Physical symptoms. If the sexual harassment you endured also caused physical suffering, a court is more likely to find that the harassment was outrageous—and illegal. Symptoms range from nervousness, depression and sleeping disorders to headaches, rashes and severe stress-related circulatory problems. Proof that you have been treated by a physician, psychiatrist or psychologist is not essential for a legal claim, but is very persuasive evidence with a court.

Retaliation. Evidence of retaliation bolsters your claim. Evidence of co-workers shunning you, or your harasser interfering with your ability to get your work done, can often mean the difference between success and failure for a claim of intentional infliction of emotional distress.

Union members beware: Your claim of infliction of emotional distress may be barred by a court if you are a union employee and your collective bargaining agreement states that the Railway Labor Act or the National Labor Relations Act controls workplace disputes. Other union employees, however, are not banned from filing this legal action.

3. Defamation

Defamation is a legal action with the chivalrous-sounding intent of protecting a person's reputation and good standing in the community.

To sue for defamation, you must show that the person who defamed you:

- made a false or damaging statement about you

- told or wrote that statement to at least one other person

- was negligent or intentional in communicating the statement, and

- the communication harmed you in some way, such as by causing others to shun you, or resulted in you losing a job or a promotion.

Defamation cases are often difficult to prove. To win a case of defamation, you must prove that the hurtful words were more than malicious watercooler gossip: "She wore that same suit to work yesterday. Kind of makes you wonder where she spent the night," probably would not qualify.

The words must also be more than a personal opinion. It is ordinarily legal for anyone to voice an opinion, no matter how unflattering: "She looks awful in that puce dress."

Statements that have been ruled to sufficiently harm a worker and qualify as defamation are false claims that she:

- committed a crime

- performed job duties incompetently

- improperly used drugs or alcohol, or

- acted in some other way that clearly implies she was unfit for a particular job.

Because a few unflattering comments or even a small dose of mean-spiritedness don't usually qualify as defamation, it is extremely important to scrupulously document cases where false or damaging statements are made. You can do this by recording not only the exact offensive words that were said and who said them, but when and where they were said and whether there were any witnesses. (See Chapter 3, Section F, for details on documentation.) Again, courts will generally be most persuaded by words that clearly damaged your work reputation. For example, your defamation case may be stronger if you can show that a formerly friendly co-worker began to shun you after hearing the false, damaging statements about you.

In workplace harassment situations, the strongest cases are where the defamatory statements have a lasting sting—resulting in additional job-related harm, such as where a woman is passed over for a job or promotion because of the damaging words. In fact, most successful defamation cases have been against employers who have made false statements about an employee to co-workers or to other prospective employers.

> *Example: After firing a female employee, the media conglomerate ABC packed and removed all documents and other work paraphenalia from her former office. When curious co-workers asked what was going on, members of management told them "they didn't want to know" and should "mind their own business." They also made derisive comments about the woman's mental and emotional health to co-workers. Although the trial court threw out her case, an appellate court ruled that the woman may have a valid claim for defamation and that she should be given the chance to prove that the statements were made with malice.* (Coleman v. American Broadcasting Corp., *38 Fair Empl. Prac. Cas. (BNA) 65 (D.D.C. 1985).)*

Some cases against co-workers have succeeded where it is shown that the defamatory words or actions were likely to harm a woman's reputation among co-workers. To be defamatory, the statements must usually call into question her ability to do her job well or her suitability to hold the position.

> *Example: An appellate court held that a female police officer may have been defamed when several male officers photographed a nude, lifesize inflatable doll and posted the pictures in the squadroom under a teletyped message that the doll was "Wanted" for impersonating her. It sent the case back to the original court that heard it to determine whether the officer was defamed by the squadroom antics.* (Carpenter v. County of Chenango, *522 N.Y.S.2d 339 (1987).)*

DAMNED IF THEY ARE, DAMNED IF THEY AREN'T

As a practical matter for litigation, it might be noted, "attractiveness" will likely arise as an implicit credibility issue that cuts two ways—both of them against the women. A conventionally attractive woman will be more likely to be believed when she charges sexual harassment. But it will also be believed that she asked for it, since attractiveness in women so largely consists in the projection of sexual availability, although in veiled and denied ways. Conventionally unattractive women, who would be more credible in asserting that they did not ask for it, by the same token, would be less credible in asserting, over a man's derogatory denial, that it happened at all.

—From *Sexual Harassment of Working Women,* by Catherine MacKinnon

---

4. Interfering with an employment contract

Another tort action sometimes filed in workplace sexual harassment cases is quaintly called tortious interference with contractual relations or, in some states, intentional interference with an economic relationship. More simply put, this mouthful means that it is illegal for a person to make it impossible for you to get or keep employment. This legal action may be appropriate whenever there are negative employment consequences from a woman's refusal to meet sexual demands placed on her.

Under this legal theory, you may recover damages directly from the person who harassed you if you can prove that:

- you were validly working when the harassment took place

- the person who harassed you knew of the employment relationship

- your harasser intentionally and improperly interfered with your employment relationship, and

- you suffered damages such as loss of your job, a demotion or a failure to get a promotion because of the interference.

In addition, if you are able to prove that a harassing co-worker or supervisor acted maliciously in interfering with your employment relationship, you may be able to get punitive damages—an award of money aimed at punishing the wrong-doer.

This legal action is most appropriate and most common where the harasser is a supervisor or a co-worker who persuades your employer to retaliate against a woman worker by firing or demoting her.

Unfortunately, there are potentially severe limits to this legal action. The most significant is that some courts allow it only for employees who work under a written employment contract that spells out the length of employment.

While workers in upper-echelon executive positions sometimes have written employment contracts, the vast majority of workers do not have such arrangements and are considered to be employees at will. This means they can be fired or quit their jobs for any legal reason. Thus, if a court requires a written employment contract as a prerequisite to a lawsuit for interference with a contractual relationship, very few women employees who are sexually harassed can use this legal remedy. (See the discussion of wrongful discharge in Section B.6.)

But the legal trend is for courts to deal harsher blows to employers who cling to and hide behind the employment at will doctrine. Workers have persuaded courts that they were not employees at will by presenting evidence that their employer:

- made repeated assurances that the job was secure

- awarded consistent promotions, salary increases and bonuses

- did not follow a required discipline procedure before terminating the employee, and

- required that the employee sign an extended agreement not to compete with the employer after being terminated

And, fortunately, a growing number of courts recognize that even at-will employees should be able to bring actions for interference with employment in some situations. A few courts reason that where a company has an employee manual setting out specific workplace rights such as paid time off, health plan policies and pension rights, that manual may legally be considered an employment contract for purposes of this legal action. Other courts have gone much further, and allowed the action based on the simple and persuasive reasoning that at-will employees have as much interest in the integrity and security of their employment relationship as those working under a written contract.

Example: An Oregon woman took a position as a beauty supply warehouser and was soon promoted to head the company's telemarketing operations. When she spurned the sexual advances of a co-worker who was the business owner's son, he became belligerent, swearing and throwing things at her. He told co-workers that she would not be working at the company much longer and then refused to provide her with the information she needed to do her job. After management ignored her complaints, she resigned. The court found that the woman suffered harassment that was intentionally aimed at forcing her to leave her job. (Lewis v. Oregon Beauty Supply Co., 733 P.2d 430 (1987).

Example: One of the few female industrial engineers in the computer department of a large plant claimed that her supervisors and co-workers forced her to quit by making her work environment intolerable. She testified that her co-workers ridiculed and harassed her, calling her irrational and advising her that she "should become a school teacher, the best profession a woman can have."

She also presented copious statistical evidence showing that her employer tacitly approved of discrimination against its women workers, by clustering them in the lowest grades of jobs and systematically banning them from training programs that could lead to advancement. The court ruled that several supervisors and co-workers had "acted to intentionally deprive her of an economic benefit" and so had maliciously interfered with her employment contract. (Kyriazi v. Western Elec. Co., 647 F. 2d 388 (1981).

There are limitations on the types of damages that can be recovered in these actions. Employees are usually limited to damages for job-connected losses, such as loss of pay and other employment benefits. Normally, they cannot recover for mental distress or other mental injuries they may have experienced when their harasser interfered with their employment contract. For most employees, this also bars compensation for medical problems that result from being harassed.

Also, such a claim may only be brought against a third person who interfered with employment, not against your employer. The essence of this legal action is that the person who has harassed you has somehow come between you and your employer and harmed that employment relationship. For that reason, the actions are not attributed to the employer in a legal sense.

If you sue your harasser under this legal theory, you will not be able to reach the likely larger financial resources of his employer. This may make no difference if the person causing the problem is financially solvent, but suing the harasser and getting a money judgment only against him will do you little good if he is a co-worker who owes more than he earns.

COVERING THE HIGH COSTS OF HARASSMENT

While suffering through sexual harassment is not a preferred method for getting rich quick, there have been a number of cases recently in which large amounts of money were awarded.

Because most sexual harassment cases that are filed are settled, and the terms of settlements are often kept secret, there is no way of keeping tabs on final tallies. But some jury verdicts—the results of which are generally trumpeted publicly—have reached as high as tens of million dollars for emotional distress, lost wages and wrongful discharge.

While such high stakes are a rarity, a few verdicts and settlements in recent sexual harassment cases speak loudly. This is true despite the penchants of a number of judges to later reduce large jury awards to amounts they find less shocking. Then, too, daily reports in the sensation-fueled news bring the issue of sexual harassment to the public fore.

The big money and heightened awareness have caused many employers to turn to an unlikely source for refuge: insurance.

Employment Practices Liability, or EPL, is a type of insurance spawned in the early '90s to cover the costs of sexual harassment and other claims related to employment.

At first, the fledgling product was available only through a handful of providers. Premiums were expensive—from $50,000 to $100,000 for mid-sized companies. And many employers viewed the product suspiciously, as if investing in the insurance might somehow assure their chances of ending up with a boardroom of boors.

But headlines blaring big verdicts combined with insurance agent portents that every employer is at risk from every employee have changed the sales picture. Premiums have plunged to a more affordable $5,000 or so. And trusted insurers, including the vaunted Lloyd's of London, have jumped on the EPL bandwagon to offer the coverage.

Before signing on any dotted lines, most insurers claim they check employers' anti-harassment policies and past records of claims filed. Once a policy is in place, some insurers offer preventative advice such as places to contact for good training. And salespeople claim business is booming—especially in weeks after a big verdict or harassment-related business or government scandal is announced.

This boom has occurred despite the fact that EPL is labeled dangerous by some and illegal by others.

Some workplace experts posit that EPL insurance may make employers smug and complacent about sexual harassment in their midsts, less proactive about stamping it out.

And some legal experts warn that it is questionable to use insurance to cover an intentional act of discrimination such as harassment on the job. Courts in a number of states—including California and New York—refuse to allow employers to use insurance to cover punitive damages imposed to prohibit workplace wrongs.

For now, it's too soon to tell whether EPL insurance is a solid investment for employers—or a roadblock to ending sexual harassment on the job.

"Do not suffer your hand to be held or squeezed without showing that it displeases you by instantly withdrawing it."

—**Guide to Good Manners for Young Women,** *published in 1853*

---

5. Intrusion

A number of tort offenses are grouped under the general heading of invasion of privacy. Of them, intrusion is the one most likely to arise in a sexual harassment situation. Unlike the broader claim of intentional infliction of emotional distress that protects your mental well-being, the tort of intrusion is meant to protect your solitude. Simply put, it prohibits offensive nosiness.

To prove a case of intrusion, you must show:

- that your harasser intentionally intruded upon your private matters or concerns

- the intrusion would be highly offensive to a reasonable person, and

- you were damaged by the intrusion.

While it is not a legal requirement, some courts will strictly require that there be some actual physical violation for this action.

Example: A woman employed at a paper processing plant was found to have a legal case of intrusion against several male co-workers who heckled her and put an air hose between her legs, simulating a penis. (Waltman v. International Paper Co., 47 Fair Empl. Prac. Cas. (BNA) 671 (W.D. La. 1988).)

To prove intrusion, most courts do not require a physical touching, but some require that the harasser physically enter a place where he is clearly unwanted and that the harassed woman would reasonably think was private, such as a restroom or locked office. Fortunately, the strong trend is also to find intrusion where a workplace harasser follows, telephones or questions a co-worker about her sex life. Here, intruding into a person's privacy is often key. In addition, the more that the workplace harasser's comments seem to venture from the strictly work-related and the more they fixate on a woman's personal and sexual life, the more likely an illegal intrusion will be found.

Example: An assistant manager at a hotel and restaurant claimed that her supervisor not only frequently pestered her at work with telephone calls in which he regularly steered the conversation to her personal and sex life, but telephoned her at home asking the same prying types of questions. The court, strongly swayed by the fact that the phone calls were made to the woman's home, found there was an intrusion—that the supervisor had clearly transgressed "the sphere from which the woman could reasonably expect her supervisor should be excluded." (Rogers v. Loews L'Enfant Plaza Hotel, 526 F. Supp. 523 (D.D.C. 1981).)

An increasing number of courts are becoming more lenient, and find that intrusion claims may be pressed against those who violate not only physical space, but psychological bounds of privacy. This is particularly true if the harasser's offensive conduct seems especially outrageous, persistent and inappropriate.

Example: A woman whose employer constantly pestered her with questions about her sex life and frequently demanded that she have sex with him was held to have a valid complaint for intrusion. The court seemed particularly taken by the fact that the harasser was relentless and pestering in his demands for sex, causing the woman to suffer extreme and obvious health problems requiring medication and counseling. It noted that a person's "emotional sanctum is certainly due the same expectations of privacy as one's physical environment." (Phillips v. Smalley Maintenance Servs. Corp., 435 So. 2d 705 (Ala. 1983).)

"Unfortunately, sometimes people don't hear you until you scream."
—*Stephanie Powers, Actress*

CAN YOU COLLECT IF YOU WIN?

Even a multi-million dollar court award will be worth only the paper it's written on unless the person or company found liable is able to pay. In most sexual harassment cases, collecting what's due and owing to you is not a problem because your employer as well as the harasser is liable—and either or both are likely to be solvent. Some larger employers also purchase a form of specialized insurance that covers attorneys' costs in defending against a harassment lawsuit.

As a general rule, employers are responsible for sexual harassment by supervisors and managers who work there. And they may even be held financially responsible for harassment you suffer at the hands of a co-worker if a supervisor either knew or should have known about the wrongful behavior.

Where a co-worker commits one act of harassment with no prior history or workplace pattern of such treatment, the employer may not be liable. When the employee alone is liable, it will probably be difficult to collect. And if the employer is small and has limited cash supply and no insurance to cover attorney's fees for defending a sexual harassment lawsuit, it may be impossible to collect a large judgment.

---

6. Wrongful discharge

Workers who have been fired illegally may be able to sue their former employers for wrongful discharge—and if they succeed, may be able to claim compensation for all injuries suffered in the process, including lost wages and mental distress.

Historically, there was a nearly insurmountable impediment to bringing this legal action: the doctrine of employment at will. (See Section B.4.) Most workers are legally deemed to be employees at will, meaning that they can be fired for any legal reason, without violating the law. While the legal doctrine of employment-at-will is still technically the law in many states, there is also a well-recognized exception that provides many sexually harassed employees a way around it. Courts in nearly every state have held that an employee cannot legally be fired for refusing to tolerate conduct that violates a public policy—such as sexual harassment on the job.

One of the strongest arguments that a woman who has been fired after being subjected to harassment can make is this: Sexual harassment violates public policy—and that she has the right to a workplace free from it. This argument sets the stage for a lawsuit for wrongful discharge.

Example: A California woman was hired as telephone dispatcher and management trainee at a drapery cleaning company. Once she was on the job, the company president quickly lived up to his self-proclaimed status as the resident dirty old man. He tried to get her into a hot tub, into a game of strip poker, grilled her about what kind of underwear she wore and accosted her sexually—one time knocking her to the floor. After two months on the job, she was fired for rejecting his advances. The court found that the company not only tolerated but aided the harasser's efforts to get sexual favors from employees. It held that the woman's termination was wrongful because it clearly violated a strong public policy against harassment in employment. (Coit Drapery Cleaners, Inc. v. Sequoia Ins. Co., *14 Cal. App. 4th 1595 (1993).)*

Many courts also reason that sexual harassment on the job is a form of illegal discrimination, and they conclude that workers also have an important public interest in not being fired for resisting such harassment.

Example: Several women who worked at a catering company were subjected to the harassing behavior of their general manager. To their great consternation, he commented daily on their breasts, buttocks and physical appearance, intimated that they had better "show him a good time" and established a dress code for women employees, admitting that he required them to wear skirts, nylons and heels so he could admire their legs. Men had no dress restrictions.

When one woman complained to company supervisors about his behavior, he abruptly changed his tack toward her—constantly criticizing her work and cajoling her about her appearance. Shortly after she complained, he fired her. The court held that her wrongful discharge action was properly based on the evidence that she acted in an important public interest—eliminating sexual harassment in her workplace. (Dias v. Sky Chefs, Inc., *919 F. 2d 1370 (9th Cir. 1990).)*

THE BEST OF TORTS, THE WORST OF TORTS

Chapters 5, 6 and 7 discuss how the U.S. Civil Rights Act and state fair employment practices (FEP) laws ban most serious forms of sexual harassment.

And those laws as statements of public policy can also form the basis for a common law tort claim of wrongful discharge when an employee is fired for refusing to tolerate or attempting to put an end to sexual harassment. An employee who is fired as a result of sexual harassment will often have at least three claims that she can join together in one legal action: a claim for violating the Civil Rights Act, a claim for violating the FEP and a claim for wrongful discharge.

But beware: Courts in Hawaii, Illinois, Pennsylvania and Wisconsin have ruled that their FEP laws are the only remedy for wrongful discharge claims based on violations of public policy. It may be too strong to conclude that wrongful discharge lawsuits based on charges of sexual harassment in the workplace under federal law will be absolutely banned in these states. However, it seems likely that you will have a tougher task pleading and proving this legal action.

Also, your claim of wrongful discharge may be barred if you are a union employee and your collective bargaining agreement states that the Railway Labor Act or the National Labor Relations Act controls disputes. Other union employees, however, are not banned from filing this legal action.

7. Rape

The most outrageous and egregious form of workplace harassment is rape. Generally, rape requires that a man have sexual intercourse with a woman without her consent. But the specifics of the offense differ from state to state.

Until the mid 1970s, rape laws in most states covered only situations where a man forced a woman to have intercourse under the threat of bodily injury. Practically speaking, these cases were rarely proven unless the woman resisted strenuously—and there was outside corroboration for the attack. So most rapes went unprosecuted. For example, in the state of New York, which had this type of restrictive law in the early '70s, there was a paltry total of less than 20 rape convictions annually, although several thousand charges were filed. Of course, the poor likelihood of getting a conviction meant most women didn't bother filing charges.

Most laws still require proof that some force was used during a rape, but, fortunately, force is typically interpreted to include verbal threats in addition to physically overpowering a woman.

Today, most state laws include several degrees of rape charges under various names, such as sexual assault, which cover a broader range of situations. For example, the most serious charge under Florida's rape law prohibits sexual battery—which requires proof of penetration, nonconsent, use or display of a deadly weapon or use or threat of physical force likely to cause serious injury. A lesser charge, sexual assault, requires proof of physical force or violence not likely to cause physical injury.

And in some states, no force is required. For example, Wisconsin's law defines third degree sexual assault to include sexual intercourse with a women who has not agreed to it, even if she remained silent and he used no force.

Newer, tougher laws have meant that more cases of rape are filed and prosecuted. The most recent survey from the Justice Department's Bureau of Justice Statistics estimated that there are 500,000 sexual assaults annually on women in the United States—including 170,000 rapes and 140,000 attepted rapes. Experts estimate that in as many as 60% of all reported rape cases, the woman knows the offender. Since work is obviously a place where a lot of social contact takes place, rape in the workplace—which usually fits under the informal designation of acquaintance rape—is being prosecuted more often.

There are special circumstances to consider in workplace rape. Often, the rapist is a woman's supervisor who also uses threats of firing or demoting her if she resists. Many courts will view such threats as sufficient force or coercion to satisfy that demand in the law.

In addition, there has been a slow-to-emerge recognition that most women will not cry rape frivolously. Women's testimony about rape and assault is generally being given more credence—and an increasing number of women believe that the rape charges they file will be given proper consideration by the courts.

One issue that is still unsettled is whether an employer can be held liable when a co-worker or supervisor rapes an employee. The handful of courts that have considered this issue have differed.

8. Actions by those accused of harassment

Workers who feel the sting of being charged with sexual harassment are starting to bite back by suing their accusers. Their lawsuits typically allege they have been defamed by the charges or wrongfully discharged because of them—that they have become victims of reverse discrimination.

Few of these claims have succeeded so far. In one recent case, for example, a worker was found to have sexually harassed several of his co-workers. He was then put on a brief unpaid suspension before being transferred to another office. Shortly after arriving at his new workplace, he discovered that his new supervisor knew the skinny behind the transfer. This, he claimed, made him so ill that he was hospitalized—and he sued for defamation and intentional infliction of emotional distress. A Missouri court held that the former employee could not sue for defamation since the words were true: The initial workplace investigation had revealed that he had in fact harassed his co-workers. The court also noted that the supervisor and co-workers had an interest in knowing the company's policy on sexual harassment— even if that meant the worker had a tainted welcome to his new office. (*Rice v. Hodapp*, 919 S.W.2d 240 (Mo. 1996).)

But one such case succeeded with a vengeance recently, when a Wisconsin jury awarded a former brewery executive $26 million—apparently swayed that he was wrongly accused of sexual harassment and wrongly discharged because of it. Jerold MacKenzie worked at Miller Brewing Company 19 years before making the misstep of asking a female colleague, Patricia Best, about a racy episode of the

"Seinfeld" television show in which a lead character is prompted to remember the name of a woman by recalling that it rhymes with a female body part. The woman's name is ultimately revealed to be Dolores. Best was uncomfortable with the workplace conversation and reported it to management. MacKenzie was fired, but later sued Miller and Best for $9.2 million. At his trial, MacKenzie defended that he hadn't actually uttered the word "clitoris;" he only waved around a page copied from the dictionary with the word on it. Best testified that the conversation about the TV show was not the first episode of MacKenzie's unwanted behavior. He had disturbed her before with strange accounts of his dreams about her and untoward voicemail messages.

Jurors, who apparently were not swayed by evidence that MacKenzie had been reprimanded years earlier for sexually harassing his secretary, awarded him nearly three times what he asked for in damages. (*MacKenzie v. Miller Brewing Co.*, July, 1997.)

Much of the wind could be taken from the sails of such lawsuits if employers have policies for quick and confidential investigations in place—and they enforce them. Courts that have recently considered the issue support this view, concentrating on whether an employer that fires an employee accused of harassment believed that the charges were true—rather than requiring it to do what is sometimes impossible: prove that the harassment occurred.

Employers cowed by the prospect of being sued by an employee accused of harassment can take solace in knowing that good faith and reasonableness carry the day here, too. An employer defending itself against reverse discrimination and wrongful discharge actions will usually be found to have justly fired an employee accused of harassment if it can show:

- the charge was supported by substantial evidence—more, for example than gossip or rumor, and

- it reasonably believed the charge was true—based on a thorough investigation.

BACKLASH: BILL OF RIGHTS FOR THE ACCUSED

There are a growing number of cases in which those accused of sexual harassment claim the accusations are false or vengeful. In response, some workplace experts have proposed a Bill of Rights aimed at ensuring protections for those accused of sexual harassment on the job.

- No disciplinary action shall be taken until a neutral, independent source has conducted an investigation.

- The accused shall be allowed to review all materials gathered in the investigation and shall have the option, but not the obligation, to respond.

- The accused shall be entitled, before implementation of discipline, to a hearing, at which he or she may be represented by counsel. All evidence and witnesses shall be subject to examination during the proceeding.

- Management shall take such steps as are reasonable and necessary to assure maximum confidentiality in the disciplinary process, so as not to stigmatize the alleged perpetrator unfairly.

- The claimed harasser shall be entitled to appeal any disciplinary action to appropriate management personnel who are not associated with the disciplinary action.

Adapted from *The National Law Journal;* August 18, 1997

C. DISADVANTAGES OF TORT ACTIONS

Despite these encouraging words about tort actions you can file to fight back against sexual harassment, there are also a number of legal and practical reasons that may weigh against doing so.

1. Federal and state laws may be stronger

The 1990s were fraught with rapid changes in sexual harassment laws and their interpretations. In the late 1960s through the '70s, most harassment claims were filed with the EEOC under Title VII, as women hoped that the Civil Rights Act of 1964 would give them significant protection. The sands shifted drastically in the '80s. More women found Title VII and state discrimination laws came up short in curing the ills of sexual harassment on the job. As a result, state tort claims, especially those seeking lucrative damages for emotional distress, increasingly became the legal action of choice.

Today, we are at a new crossroad. Amendments to the Civil Rights Act passed in 1991 now make it possible for women filing Title VII actions to collect up to $300,000 in compensatory and punitive damages. (See Chapter 6, Section B.) This legal change allowing some damages, although limited ones—coupled with newfound public awareness that sexual harassment on the job is wrong—have led to an increase in these lawsuits. Also, the rights and remedies available to a harassed woman under many state FEP laws have been improved. It is unclear what effect that legal change will have on the number of common law tort actions filed against harassment.

2. Unpredictability

Another possible disadvantage of common law torts is that the rules and interpretations are much less well-defined and more open to subjective interpretation than actions for harassment filed under the Civil Rights Act or through state FEP agencies. For example, whether an employee has suffered mental distress or has been defamed requires a subjective evaluation of her mindset and reactions. Once you file one of these actions, you are at the mercy of the particular sensibilities and sensitivities of the judge or jury that will be evaluating your situation—mulling over whether the harassment you have suffered was sufficiently outrageous or sufficiently damaging to form the basis of a significant dollar judgment.

By contrast, when you file a sexual harassment claim with a state FEP agency or the EEOC, your proof problems are somewhat easier. The statutes not only define sexual harassment in fairly broad terms, they offer specific—albeit limited—types of relief. In addition, these investigations and subsequent hearings are less public and somewhat less prying than a lawsuit is likely to be.

3. Proving intent

For many women, there are additional practical drawbacks to bringing a lawsuit based on a common law tort charge as opposed to a claim under a state FEP law or the Civil Rights Act. To succeed in a tort case, you must typically prove the wrongdoer's bad intent. Proving intent can be difficult. It requires that you get inside the wrongdoer's mind.

An alarming number of male judges, for example, have reached the ludicrous conclusion that a man who repeatedly pinches, fondles or strokes a female co-worker did not intend to harass her.

4. Proving personal harm

Also, to win in most of the state court actions based on the torts discussed in this chapter, you must prove that you were harmed personally by the harassment. Typically, this means you must have suffered a fairly serious physical injury or illness that required extensive medical treatment. It is not enough that your job status suffered—that you were denied a promotion or fired.

This also means that you will likely need to speak up about painful personal history and intensely private facts of your life—your mental state, your physical health, your lifestyle, your feelings. And you may face hostile cross-examination on all of these issues.

For some women, that price is too high.

5. Getting a lawyer

Finally, to bring most state court common law cases, you will need to hire a lawyer to help—and that can be expensive, difficult and frustrating. The average legal costs of pursuing a sexual harassment case that goes to trial has been estimated at $80,000—with an additional $4,000 to $25,000 in fees for deposition transcripts and expert witnesses.

Few women can afford this, so almost all will have to find a lawyer to handle their case on a contingency fee basis—that is, taking a fee as a percentage of the final judgment (usually 33% to 40%), but not requiring the client to pay any money upfront. Since many more women hope to hire lawyers experienced in sexual harassment cases than there are lawyers, you will likely only find one to handle your case for a contingency fee if he or she is convinced that your case is sufficiently shocking to pay off big. (See Chapter 9, Section B.4.)

But by learning about your possible legal alternatives, you will be able to save great amounts in time and stress—not to mention legal fees. You may also be able to get a free or low-cost evaluation of whether your situation is likely to merit one of the legal actions described here by contacting a local law clinic or an attorney affiliated with women's special interest groups. (See the Appendix for contact information on many such groups.)

D. WORKERS' COMPENSATION: EMPLOYERS' DEFENSE

Workers' compensation is a system most states have established to deal with workers who are injured on the job. It works much like an insurance policy: Employers pay a certain amount per month into a general fund. Then, employees who are injured at work can file a claim and get some payment from the fund. Created partially in response to employers' fears of high-damage lawsuits by employees injured in industrial accidents, workers' compensation represents a compromise. Employees are paid quickly, but only a limited amount—and employers pay premiums to avoid other lawsuits.

Workers' compensation is a poor remedy in most sexual harassment cases, because it pays so little. You can recover only for physical injuries—not emotional injuries, and frequently not for stress-related injuries. And you can collect only your medical bills and some fraction of the wages you lost if your injury forced you to take time off work. That's all.

As a result, very few employees use workers' compensation in sexual harassment situations. But increasingly, employers seeking to avoid expensive tort judgments are arguing that sexual harassment claims should be handled exclusively under the workers' compensation system.

Unfortunately for some women, state tort actions may not be available to fill in the gap because courts in some states have absolutely ruled that their state's workers' compensation law is the sole remedy for sexual harassment—barring a harassed worker from bringing any other state tort legal action for the injury caused. This presents some harassed workers with a Catch-22: The only relief available to them is under the state's workers' compensation laws, which is inadequate for their injuries.

The trend is that most courts do not buy into this argument of workers' compensation as the exclusive remedy. In fact, courts in several states have taken the step of holding that injuries brought on by workplace sexual harassment are outside the scope of workers' compensation laws. These decisions advance the enlightened view that harassment is not a natural part of the workday and encourage employers not to tolerate it.

"The paramount destiny and mission of woman are to fulfill the noble and benign offices of wife and mother. This is the law of the Creator."
—*From* Bradwell v. Illinois, *83 U.S. 130 (1873)* ■

9

Lawyers and
Legal Research

I f you have read this far, you now have a solid understanding of what sexual harassment is—and what your options are for dealing with it. However, there may be situations when you will need to move beyond the information provided in this book. In this chapter, we give you some guidelines on when to consider mediation or arbitration to resolve your problem, how to select and work with a lawyer and how to do additional legal research on your own.

A. MEDIATION AND ARBITRATION

At least partly because of how the legal world is portrayed on television and in movies, some people think that a courtroom is the best—and only—place to resolve any legal dispute. In fact, mediation and arbitration can be faster, less expensive, more satisfying alternatives than going to court. Workplace experts are hailing these less confrontational methods of solving workplace disputes as the hallmark of forward-thinking companies. And many employers are jumping on the bandwagon by adding clauses to their written employment agreements and employee manuals requiring or suggesting that workplace disputes be resolved by arbitration or mediation.

Although mediation and arbitration are often lumped together under the general heading of alternative dispute resolution, there are significant differences between the two.

Mediation. Two or more people or groups get a third person—a mediator—to help them communicate. The mediator does not represent either side, or impose a decision, but helps the disagreeing parties formulate their own resolution of their dispute. Mediated claims have been resolved by requiring training, transfers, counseling—and often, a personal apology.

Arbitration. Both sides agree on the issue but cannot resolve it themselves. They agree to pick an arbitrator who will come up with a solution. Essentially, the arbitrator acts as an informal judge, but at far less cost and expense than most legal proceedings require. Arbitration is more formal, more like a court proceeding than mediation—and is less likely to result in a solution other than the traditional backpay award.

Mediation and arbitration are sometimes used to help work out the terms of an agreement to end a work relationship, but they are most effective where those involved have a continuing relationship and want to find a mutually acceptable way to work together.

IF YOU DON'T WANT TO, MAYBE YOU DON'T HAVE TO

Some disgruntled employees are surprised to find that when they read some fine print—in an employment contract or application signed long ago—it requires them to submit all workplace disputes to arbitration.

Some courts have ruled recently that many arbitration clauses do not really mean what they say. What is important is that employees know and understand that they have agreed to arbitration before signing up for it. And EEOC officials have declared recently that the agency will accept a complaint against a company even if an employee has signed a mandatory arbitration agreement.

But other recent cases have held that you can sign away your day in court. Courts that have upheld arbitration clauses have been swayed by employers' arguments that without mandated arbitration, too many employees would choose jury trials—a great expense for both sides.

While the legality of arbitration clauses shakes out in courts across the country, employees are likely to see more of them more often. According to a 1995 poll commissioned by Robert Half International, a headhunting firm, 30% of U.S. companies with 20 or more employees planned to increase the use of arbitration contracts; 17% indicated they would use them less.

---

1. When Mediation Works Best

Mediation can offer benefits to many employers and employees, since particular problems are usually resolved quickly and creatively. And because all involved feel they have a stake in fashioning the agreement, they are more likely to abide by the solution.

But mediation is not the best solution for all types of disputes, since success depends on both sides being willing to meet in the middle and deal directly with one another. However, many workplace experts have found that mediation may be particularly effective in resolving some workplace conflicts involving sexual harassment.

Many such problems involve an initial misperception about what is and what is not considered acceptable workplace behavior—and are made worse by an inability to discuss the differences openly. Mediation can open communication and help ease the hostility that may pollute a work environment. Mediation may be especially effective in resolving these types of claims, where the harassment alleged is not severe or long lasting and where it is in the best interests of the employer, accused and accuser to preserve the working relationship.

Note, however, that mediation is usually not a wise way to resolve a claim if:

- the sexual harassment alleged is violent or physically threatening, or

- either the accused or accuser strongly distrusts the process; the magic of the mediation solution is that it is voluntary and uncoerced.

2. Where to Get More Information

Leading sources of professional arbitrators and mediators and of information on how to use these approaches to resolve disputes are:

American Arbitration Association
140 West 51st Street
New York, NY 10020
212/484-4000

American Bar Association
Standing Committee on Dispute Resolution
1800 M Street, NW
Washington, DC 20036
202/331-2258

National Institute for Dispute Resolution
1726 Street, NW; Suite 500
Washington, DC 20036
202/466-4764

For more information on how to choose a mediator, prepare a case and go through the mediation process, see *How to Mediate Your Dispute,* by Peter Lovenheim (Nolo Press).

ARBITRATION IS NOT A PANACEA

A Dallas woman forced to arbitrate her sexual harassment claim sued recently, charging that the arbitrators were mostly white males, experienced in defending company management and biased in its favor.

J. Meg Olson recently filed a novel lawsuit against the American Arbitration Association (AAA), the nation's largest provider of alternatives to courtroom resolution. Olson claimed that she was forced to arbitrate her 1994 sexual harassment claim because her employer had earlier required her to sign a clause requiring it. But when she began to select the panel of three arbitrators to hear her claim, Olson claims she was given a pool of 15 possible arbitrators—only three of whom were women and nearly all of whom commonly represented management.

AAA defended that it provided Olson with more names after she complained, but acknowledged that of the 286 arbitrators it offers to hear employment disputes, 212 are men; 247 are lawyers—and 76 of them primarily represent employers.

Olson also asserts that contrary to AAA's claims that it is an inexpensive service, its help came with a hefty price: over $21,000 in fees.

Legal experts say that Olson's claim sounds the clarion to arbitration services, which may need to prove that their services are impartial if questions arise.

B. HIRING A LAWYER

Many readers who are subjected to sexual harassment on the job will need to hire a lawyer to get more information about laws and legal strategies. For example, you will likely need a lawyer's help if:

- You have used the formal procedures for filing a complaint against harassment in your workplace, but the company representatives do not seem willing to negotiate with you fairly or openly.

- You have filed a complaint with your state fair employment practices (FEP) agency or with the Equal Employment Opportunities Commission (EEOC), but you would like to find out more about your specific options. Lawyers on staff at the EEOC handle a few cases in court for harassed women, but very few—typically, only those that catch the mind of a particular investigator or are thought to be surefire wins. If you wish to pursue a claim for sexual harassment, you will most likely need to hire a lawyer to represent you.

- You have suffered serious injuries from the harassment, which make it appropriate for you to file a lawsuit.

1. Where to look for a lawyer

If you decide to hire a lawyer, the first task is to find one who best suits your needs. The legal field of sexual harassment is new and evolving very quickly, and you need a lawyer who has experience in handling the nuances and complications of a sexual harassment lawsuit. Out of the nearly 800,000 lawyers in the United States, only a few thousand have such training or experience.

Depending on your circumstances and location, there are a number of places to turn for a referral to a lawyer in this group. They include:

Your state fair employment practices agency or the federal EEOC office. Some, but not all, of these offices maintain lists of lawyers who are experienced in handling sexual harassment lawsuits. Frankly, the help you get from these agencies depends greatly on the knowledge and helpfulness of the person who answers the telephone. It will be worth your while to persist until you find the person in the agency with the willingness and moxy to really tell you which local lawyers know what they are doing.

Legal aid clinics. Many local legal aid clinics or legal services offices have sexual harassment lawyers on staff—a phenomenon that developed in the last few years. Most of these offices have income or geographical restrictions on the clients they can accept, but even if you don't qualify, someone there may be able to refer you to a competent attorney. Locate your community's legal aid clinics by looking in the telephone directory under Legal Aid Society or Legal Services—or check with the nearest law school.

Local women's organizations. Most larger cities have helplines established by women's groups—often affiliated with a local law school—that answer legal questions about sexual harassment. Many other women's groups maintain lists of attorneys with experience in handling sexual harassment and discrimination problems. Check the Yellow Pages of the telephone book under Women's Organizations & Services or Crisis Services.

National women's organizations. Several groups that concentrate on women's legal rights, such as NOW, the ACLU and National Women's Political Caucus, also maintain lists of experienced lawyers from which they'll make referrals. (See the Appendix for contact details.)

Employee groups. Specialized employees may have access to legal help offered by special interest groups. Union workers, for example, can contact the Coalition for Labor Union Women for legal guidance and referrals to experienced attorneys. (See the Appendix for additional specialized listings.)

BEWARE OF LAWYER REFERRAL SERVICES

Bar associations and other lawyer groups often maintain and advertise lawyer referral services. Usually, there is little or no screening before a lawyer can get listed in these services. While it is always possible you will find a good lawyer through one of these services, your chances are hit and miss.

---

2. Deciding on a particular lawyer

Once you have a referral to a lawyer—or even better, several referrals—you'll want to contact each and see whether he or she meets your needs. Come forearmed with some inside knowledge:

- Most lawyers are guided by the principle that Time Is Money. And time and money should also be your guiding concerns in deciding whether to hire a lawyer to help with your sexual harassment claim.

- Even the simplest problems can take a long time to be resolved through the legal system. And problems involving sexual harassment do not often present themselves in straightforward issues. Unless a case is settled—most cases are—a court proceeding can take from five to eight years before a final judgment is reached.

- A lawyer's help rarely comes cheap. Legal organizations estimate that harassment cases eat up an average of between $8,000 to $30,000 in lawyers' time and other legal costs such as court filings and witness interviews.

- Although the million dollar sexual harassment awards are the ones that get the most publicity, most workers who win their cases get only backpay and damages—riches of only tens of thousands of dollars. Because these limited awards often do not amount to enough to foot legal bills, many lawyers require a substantial retainer, or amount of money paid upfront, before they will consider taking on a case.

- Lawyers who agree to take your case for little or no money will depend on court-ordered fees and often a percentage of your recovery, or a contingency fee. (See Section B.4.) This option will probably be available only if you can convince a lawyer that your case will pay off.

Given these dire circumstances, you will want to be as certain as possible that any lawyer you hire will be doing the utmost to represent you fairly and efficiently—and that you are comfortable with his or her representation. Also, depending on your own interest and energy level, you may be able to help out on your case—by gathering documents and organizing information—which can go a long way toward saving time and money.

WHAT A LAWYER WANTS TO HEAR

From a lawyer's point of view, a good case has these attributes:

• Fairly serious harassment—usually either a few incidents of clearly bad conduct or a longstanding pattern of harassment that continues even after requests have been made that it stop.

• Personal injuries—the more serious, the better. If there are medical bills and loss of work time you can trace to sexual harassment, that will help get the lawyer's attention.

• A solvent defendant—large employers that are sensitive to maintaining a good public image may be the most willing to agree to a quick and sizeable settlement.

• A plaintiff with money to invest or lose—at least enough to cover legal fees and expenses, given that there are no surefire wins in court, especially in sexual harassment cases.

If your situation includes some or all of these elements, make sure the lawyer knows it.

---

3. The initial interview

Start by asking for an appointment. Some lawyers will try to screen you over the phone by asking you to discuss the basics of your case. A little of this can be appropriate—most experienced sexual harassment lawyers are inundated with potential clients these days, so he or she will want to be sure you need expert legal advice.

Many lawyers will agree not to charge you for an initial consultation to decide whether your situation requires legal action. But be prepared to pay a reasonable fee for legal advice. A charge of between $75 and $150 for a one-hour consultation is typical. If you organize the facts in your case well before going to your consultation, an hour should be more than enough to explain your case and obtain at least a basic opinion on how it might be approached and what it is likely to cost. If you find the right lawyer and can afford the charge, it can be money well spent. A good way to bring order to your case facts is to fill out a copy of the sexual harassment complaint form (Chapter 4, Section D.1) and bring it with you to the interview.

FEE ARRANGEMENTS—GET IT IN WRITING

Most disagreements between lawyers and clients involve fees, so be sure to get all the details involving money in writing—including the per hour billing rate or the contingency fee arrangement, the frequency of billing and how the attorney will handle any funds you're required to deposit in advance to cover expenses.

---

4. Paying your lawyer

Most sexual harassment cases are handled on some form of contingency fee arrangement. Under a contingency fee, a lawyer agrees to handle your case for a fixed percentage of the amount you finally recover in a lawsuit. If you win the case, the lawyer's fee comes out of the money awarded to you. If you lose, neither you nor the lawyer will get any money.

A lawyer's willingness to take your case on a contingency fee is a hopeful sign of faith in the strength of your claim. A lawyer who is not firmly convinced that your case is a winner is unlikely to take you on as a contingency fee client. Be very wary of a lawyer who wants to take your case on an hourly payment basis. That usually signals that he or she does not think your case is very strong in terms of the money you might be able to recover. It could also mean financial disaster for you, as your legal bills are likely to mount up with no useful results. At the very least, insist that the lawyer writes down some specific objectives to be accomplished in your case—and puts a limit on how high the fees can accumulate.

Although there is no set percentage for contingency fees in most types of cases, the standard amount demanded by lawyers in most areas is about 35% if the case is settled before a lawsuit is filed with the courts, and 40% if a case has to be tried. Keep in mind that the terms of a contingency fee agreement may be negotiable. You can try to get your lawyer to agree to a lower percentage—especially if the case is settled quickly—or to absorb some of the court costs.

Sometimes, a lawyer working for you under a contingency agreement will require that you pay all out-of-pocket expenses, such as filing fees charged by the courts and the cost of transcribing witness depositions. If this is so, the lawyer will want you to deposit a substantial amount of money—a thousand dollars or more—with the law firm to cover these expenses. From your standpoint, it is a much better arrangement for the lawyer to advance such costs and get repaid out of your recovery. A common sense arrangement might involve you advancing a little amount of money for some costs, with the attorney advancing the rest.

In Civil Rights Act and FEP cases, there is also the possibility of the court awarding you attorney's fees as part of final judgment. However, this award may not be large enough to cover the entire amount owed to your attorney under the legal fee contract. Therefore, the contingency fee contract should spell out what happens to a court award of attorney's fees. One approach is to have the fees paid to the attorney in their entirety—and subtract that amount from the contingency fee to which you have agreed.

5. Managing your lawyer

A great many complaints against lawyers have to do with their failure to communicate with their clients. Your lawyer may be the one with the legal expertise, but the rights that are being pursued are yours—and you are the most important person involved in your case. You have the right to demand that your lawyer be reasonably available to answer your questions and to keep you posted on your case.

You may need to put some energy into subtlely managing your lawyer.

Carefully check every statement. Each statement or bill should list costs that the lawyer has paid or that you are expected to pay. If any one lacks sufficient detail for you to verify that it complies with your written fee agreement, call your lawyer and politely demand that a new, more detailed version be sent before you pay it. Don't feel as though you're being too pushy by demanding more detail: The laws in many states actually require thorough detail in lawyers' statements.

Learn as much as you can about the laws and decisions involved in your case. By doing so, you'll be able to monitor your lawyer's work and may even be able to make a suggestion or provide information that will move your case along faster. Certainly if the other side offers a settlement, you will be in a better position to evaluate whether or not it makes sense to accept it.

Keep your own calendar of dates and deadlines. Note when papers and appearances are due in court. If you rely on your lawyer to keep your case on schedule, you may be unpleasantly surprised to find that an important deadline has been missed. Many a good case has been thrown out simply because of a lawyer's forgetfulness. Call or write to your lawyer at least a week before any important deadline in your case to inquire about plans to meet it.

Maintain your own file on your case. By having a well-organized file of your own, you'll be able to discuss your case with your lawyer intelligently and efficiently—even over the telephone. Being well-informed will help keep your lawyer's effectiveness up and your costs down. Be aware that if your lawyer is working on a hourly basis, you'll probably be charged for telephone consultations. But they're likely to be less expensive than office visits.

DISAGREEING ON A SETTLEMENT OFFER

In many case, your employer may offer a cash amount to settle the case. The problem is that you and your lawyer may have different interests at heart. If your lawyer is rushed or needs money, he or she may be ready to settle your case quickly for an inadequate amount. You, on the other hand, may want to hold out for what you consider to be more adequate. At this critical juncture, you may wish to get a second legal opinion as to whether the amount offered is realistic given the facts of your situation.

---

6. Firing a lawyer

Change lawyers if you feel that's necessary. If the relationship between you and the lawyer you chose doesn't seem to be working out, or if you feel that your case isn't progressing as it should, think about asking another lawyer to take over. Be clear with the first lawyer that you are taking your business elsewhere, and immediately put your decision in writing.

You could end up receiving bills from both lawyers—both of whom will claim they handled the lion's share of your case. Before you pay anything, be sure that the total amount of the bills does not amount to more than you agreed to pay. If you have a contingency fee arrangement, it is up to your new lawyer and former lawyer to work out how to split the fee.

Take prompt action against any behavior by a lawyer that appears to be deceptive, unethical or otherwise illegal. A call to the local bar association, listed in the telephone directory under Attorneys, should provide you with guidance on what types of lawyer behavior are prohibited and how to file a complaint. In most states, attorney regulatory bodies are biased toward lawyers. Unless the lawyer's conduct is plainly dishonest or he or she has abandoned your case, you will probably not get much satisfaction. However, sometimes the threat of filing a complaint can move your lawyer into action. And if worst comes to worst, filing a formal complaint will create a document that you'll need should you end up later filing a lawsuit against a lawyer for malpractice.

 For more information on what to do if you are unhappy with a lawyer's work, see *Mad at Your Lawyer,* by Tanya Starnes (Nolo Press).

C. LEGAL RESEARCH

Legal research is by no means necessary for everyone. This book gives more than enough details on sexual harassment law for most people. However, there are times when specific legal knowledge can give you additional control over your situation— and save you time and money. Think of legal knowledge as a form of power—the more you know, the more you can make informed choices, demand the treatment you're entitled to and plan an effective strategy for settlement and litigation. Some examples of when you might want to consider doing some legal research, either online or through more conventional library resources, include:

Presenting the facts of your case to a government agency. The first statement you make to an investigator for the EEOC or your state FEP agency is very important: It will form the basis for your claim and for any lawsuit you may want to bring later. Therefore, if your case involves particularly complex or unsettled legal issues—for example, whether local courts have been allowing more or fewer tort actions for sexual harassment since the U.S. Civil Rights Act was amended—it would probably be wise to do some hands-on research.

Getting more details on the law of your state. Sexual harassment law varies some-what in all 50 states. Chapter 7 gives you some details of each state's law. But to learn how state FEP policies have been applied by state courts, and to see how traditional common law torts have been used in sexual harassment cases in each state, you'll need to do some additional research.

Preparing for mediation or arbitration. Mediation and arbitration are increasingly popular avenues for handling many sexual harassment issues. Researching cases similar to your own may help provide you with a valuable reality check as to the options and results you can expect in your situation.

Choosing and working with a lawyer. If you decide to hire a lawyer, you will need to find one with some expertise in sexual harassment. Your own legal knowledge will help you determine whether your lawyer is well-qualified and will allow you to participate fully in your case.

DON'T START FROM SCRATCH

For more general information about sexual harassment, check the Appendix. You will find that many legal and special interest groups publish helpful bibliographies and pamphlets on the legal aspects of sexual harassment. Before you do extensive research on your own, first check on what others have done.

And don't overlook the most obvious source. The EEOC periodically publishes guidelines on the changing shape of how sexual harassment is defined by courts around the nation. Because EEOC office personnel are instructed to apply these guidelines in evaluating sexual harassment cases, they are a good barometer for how your own problem is likely to be analyzed.

And for those on the research trail, the guidelines are also a storehouse of information about recent cases. Pay particular attention to the footnotes, which generally list recent court decisions and explain legal embellishments on particular issues.

The EEOC also publishes regulations detailing how the U.S. Civil Rights Act is to be interpreted and enforced. Many law libraries will have copies of EEOC guidelines and regulations—or you can get copies from your state or the federal EEOC. Some of this information is also available at the EEOC's site: http://www.eeoc.gov/.

1. Library research

The reference sections in most larger public libraries contain a set of local and state laws, as well as a set of the federal statutes. The librarians there should be able to help you look up any laws—including your state fair employment practices law—that might affect your situation. However, if you want to look up a court case or a ruling by agencies such as the Equal Employment Opportunity Commission or your state's fair employment practices agency, you'll probably have to visit a law library.

In many states, county law libraries are free and open to the public. You can also try the library of the nearest law school, particularly if it's affiliated with a public university funded by tax dollars. Law school libraries offer one big advantage: They are usually open from early in the morning until late at night—even on weekends and some holidays. Whatever library you choose, you'll find that most librarians are not only well-versed in legal research techniques, but also are friendly and open to helping you through the mazes of legal citations.

If you are new to legal research, you may find that you need more guidance than we provide here. Excellent resources on legal research for the novice include *Legal Research Made Easy*—a 2½ hour video that explains how to do technical legal research and how to set priorities to get results in a reasonable time. Also, *Legal Research: How to Find and Understand the Law,* by Stephen Elias and Susan Levinkind, contains clear explanations and examples of legal research techniques. And *Legal Research Online and in the Library,* by Stephen Elias and Susan Levinkind, contains a searchable CD-ROM with access to over 4,000 law-related sites. All are published by Nolo Press.

There are several types of research materials concentrating on sexual harass-ment that you'll find useful: secondary sources such as books and law review articles, and also primary sources such as statutes and cases. These resources serve different purposes.

Secondary sources—books such as this one and articles—are primarily used to get an overview of a particular topic. If you find a good article or chapter on a topic you're interested in, it will give both an explanation of the law and citations to other materials—especially cases—that may prove helpful.

Primary sources—statutes (state and federal laws) and cases (published decisions of state and federal courts)—tell you the current status of the law. Very often, your goals in doing legal research are first to find the statutes that apply to you, and then to find the court cases that interpret the statutes in sexual harassment situations similar to yours. There may be cases with similar facts—for example, a supervisor who persistently asked a female employee to go out with him after she repeatedly said no. Or there may be a court case that raises a similar issue or legal question—for example, whether an employer is legally responsible for harassment by a co-worker or whether a state fair employment law covers a particular kind of employee. These court decisions may give you some indication of how a government agency or court is likely to decide your case.

With all this in mind, where should you begin your research? It depends on your situation. If you want some additional general information about sexual harassment, or an update on the law since this book was published, you will probably find a recent book or article more than adequate. However, if you want very specific legal information—for example, whether the common law tort of wrongful discharge is a valid legal theory in your state—you will probably need to look at both your state fair employment practice law and any judicial decisions dealing with the issue. The sections that follow describe several types of resources, how to find them and how to use them to learn about the law that applies to your situation.

"You do not conduct personal life at the office."
—Judith Martin, aka Miss Manners

THE TWO RESEARCH TRACKS: FEDERAL AND STATE

By now you know that there are two separate sets of laws on sexual harassment—federal law and state law. Each has separate statutes, regulations and court cases, so you must decide which law you are relying on before you start to research.

The U.S. Civil Rights Act is a federal law, and the court decisions which interpret it—including those involving the EEOC—are federal cases. However, not all federal decisions carry equal weight. The cases which will be most persuasive in federal court are those from the highest court in that jurisdiction: the United States Supreme Court. On the second level in the hierarchy are the federal courts of appeal. You should look first for cases in the same judicial circuit or geographical region as yours, since these will be more authoritative. And finally, on the lowest level are the federal district courts—again, look first for cases in your geographical area.

If you are researching your state's FEP law or common law tort theories, you will be looking at state court cases. Most state court systems are similar to the federal system, in that there are three hierarchical levels of courts. The most authoritative cases will be those from your state's highest court (usually called the supreme court), followed by decisions issued by your state appellate court, followed by decisions issued by your state trial court.

"Our supervisor tells us what kind of makeup to wear, what kind of lipstick to wear, if our hair is not the right style for us, if we're not smiling enough. They even tell us how to act when you're on a pass."

—*Terry Mason, 26, a flight attendant, in* Working, *by Studs Terkel (Avon, 1972)*

SEXUAL HARASSMENT LAW IS CHANGING FAST—WATCH FOR KEY DATES

A few important cases and legislative developments have substantially changed the legal complexion of sexual harassment—often wiping out all the decisions and developments that came before. When doing research on sexual harassment, some of the older resources may give you interesting historical perspectives, but check the following dates to be sure that the information they give on specific points has not become obsolete.

July 1964   Congress passes the Civil Rights Act outlawing sex discrimination in employment and creating the Equal Employment Opportunity Commission.

April 1976   A Washington, D.C., judge becomes the first to recognize sexual harassment as a form of sex discrimination—and allows a lawsuit by a Department of Justice employee who claims her supervisor harassed and fired her after she refused to have sex with him. *Williams v. Saxbe,* 413 F. Supp. 654 (1976).

September 1982   A federal judge in Wisconsin upholds a verdict in favor of a male social services worker who claims he was sexually harassed by his female supervisor. *Huebschen v. Dep't of Health and Social Services,* 547 F. Supp. 1168 (1982).

June 1986   The U.S. Supreme Court decides its first sexual harassment case, ruling that harassment is sex discrimination—and illegal under Title VII of the Civil Rights Act. *Meritor Sav. Bank v. Vinson,* 477 U.S. 57 (1986).

March 1990   The EEOC issues guidelines on how to define and prevent sexual harassment, updating the guidelines it issued in 1980.

January 1991   An appellate court in Florida rules that nude pin-ups in the workplace can be illegal sexual harassment. *Robinson v. Jacksonville Shipyards,* 760 F. Supp. 1486 (1991).

October 1991   The Civil Rights Act is amended to allow compensatory and punitive damages in sexual harassment cases.

November 1993   The U.S. Supreme Court rules unanimously that while psychological harm may be taken into account in evaluating whether sexual harassment has occurred, it is not a requirement in a claim. *Harris v. Forklift Sys., Inc.,* 114 S. Ct. 372 (1993).

1998   In a watershed year for sexual harassment, the U.S. Supreme Court decides four cases on the issue—one set in the school and three defining workplace standards. The Court's bottom line for both employers and employees: Act reasonably. Use common sense.

a. Statutes

When people refer to "the law," they are usually talking about statutes. Statutes are the written laws created by state and federal legislatures. The federal statute prohibiting sexual harassment is the Civil Rights Act of 1964. It can be found in title 42 of the U.S. Code, Section 2000.

Most states—although not all—also have their own laws prohibiting sexual harassment. To find your state's discrimination statute, locate the citation listed after your state in Chapter 7. Then ask the librarian where you can locate the state laws—often called codes—find the appropriate volume and read on. For example, if you live in California, look at the Fair Employment and Housing Act, found in the California Government Code beginning at Section 12900. If there is no citation listed for your state, that means there is no state statute prohibiting sexual harassment and you should probably concentrate your research on federal law.

b. Regulations

In some situations, you may also want to consult the regulations that pertain to a statute. Regulations are the rules created by administrative agencies for carrying out legislation. If, for example, a statute requires an agency to investigate sexual harassment complaints, there will probably be regulations that give more detail about what form the investigation will take, who will conduct it and how it will be done.

Federal regulations can be found in the Code of Federal Regulations—usually abbreviated as CFR. The EEOC regulations on sex discrimination can be found in volume 29 of the CFR, beginning at Section 1604.1. This set of books will be available in most law libraries, or you can request a copy of the regulations from the EEOC.

Most state fair employment agencies also publish regulations. Finding these regulations can be difficult. Often, all of the regulations for a given state will be gathered into an Administrative Code. Look in the index of the Code to determine if your state's fair employment agency regulations are published there. Other state agencies publish their regulations separately, in manuals. These may be available at the law library—ask the librarian for more information. Or contact your state FEP agency and ask it to send you a copy of the regulations, or at least to tell you where they can be found.

HOW TO READ STATUTE CITATIONS

Federal statutes are contained in the United States Code. For example, if you are looking for the Civil Rights Act, 42 U.S.C. 2000, locate title 42 of the United States Code and turn to Section 2000.

Finding state statutes is a bit trickier, because states use slightly different systems to number and organize their statutes. Most states use one of the following methods:

By topic. California uses this type of organization. To find Cal. Govt. Code §12900, locate the volumes that contain the state's government code and turn to Section 12900.

By number. Florida, for example, lists statutes numerically, without flagging the topics the laws cover. To find Fla. Stat. §760.01, turn to Section 760.01.

By title. Vermont, for example, divides its statutes into titles, similar to the federal citation system. To find 21 Vt. Stat. §495, locate Title 21 of the Vermont Statutes—and turn to Section 495.

Inside the back cover of the volume, you will find an unbound supplement called a "pocket part." This material will update the information in the main volume, telling you about any amendments or changes to the law that have happened since the main volume was published. It is organized just like the main volume, using the same numerical system. Be sure to consult this every time you use a statute: If you don't, you may be relying on law that is no longer valid.

DON'T FORGET LOCAL LAWS

Many major cities and some counties—especially those with larger populations—also have their own laws prohibiting sexual harassment, and regulations detailing how these laws should be carried out. Don't neglect these in your research. Sometimes a local law will contain the best protections against sexual harassment or provide the best remedies. Ask your law librarian how to find and use your city or county code.

c.   Cases

Sometimes, you will find all the information you need in the statutes and regulations. However, laws can be deceptively straightforward, impossibly complex—or somewhere in between. To be sure you get the point, it's wise to also look at court cases that involve the statute and see how the courts apply and interpret it. Courts have been known to take a law with an apparently obvious meaning and turn it on its head.

And sometimes, there will be no statute that applies to your situation. For example, when you are researching whether common law tort theories such as assault and battery or the intentional infliction of emotional distress apply to your situation, you will absolutely need to look at some court decisions, since these issues are decided on a case-by-case basis.

START WITH THE CASE CITATIONS IN THIS BOOK

Many court cases are cited throughout this book. Be sure to look at them as possible leads. If the discussion here makes a case seem similar in some way to your situation, you might want to look it up and read the court's ruling. For information on how to interpret case citations, see the explanation below.

Finding a case interpreting a statute. If you want to track down how a certain statute has been referred to by the courts in a case, your research task will be fairly simple: All you have to do is consult an annotated code. An annotated code is a version of the state or federal statutes that contains summaries of cases that have interpreted various provisions of a statute. There are two sets of federal annotated codes: the United States Code Service and the United States Code Annotated. Most states also have annotated codes. Ask the law librarian where you can find them.

To use an annotated code, first look up the U.S. Civil Rights Act or the FEP statute for your state. Then look for the numbered section of the statute that is relevant to your situation. If there have been any court cases interpreting that statute, they will be listed after the specific section of the statute, along with a sentence or two describing the case. If the summary of the case leaves you wanting to know more about it, you can track down the case and read it by following the citation given there.

Finding a case using secondary sources. In some situations, you will want to find court decisions on a particular topic without referring to a statute. For example, if you want to find out whether some uncomfortable situation at work might form the basis of a common law tort action in your state (discussed in Chapter 8), you should probably not begin your research with a statute. Common law tort actions were developed almost exclusively by case decisions. Sometimes these torts are also written into code, such as a state criminal statute defining and setting out the punishment for assault—but more likely, you will have to hunt down a few cases.

Quite often, a secondary source such as a law review article or book—including this one—will discuss key cases and give citations for them. If you find a source that analyzes an issue that is important in your case, you will likely get some good leads there.

Digests. Another good resource for finding cases is the West Digest System. These digests, published by the West Publishing Company, provide brief summaries of cases organized by topic. There are many sets of digests, divided by geographic region. If you are looking for cases interpreting the U.S. Civil Rights Act and regulations on sexual harassment, consult the federal practice digest—which contains all federal cases. If you are looking for cases about common law torts or cases involving your state's FEP agency, look at the state digests, which are published in nearly every state.

To use the digest system to find cases, first choose the relevant volumes—regional, state or federal. Next, look in the descriptive word index; most listings on sexual harassment can be found under the headings of Civil Rights or Discrimination. You will find a number of categories listed under each heading—such as Sex Discrimination, Remedies and Men/Women. Look in the digest under topics that are relevant to your search. Under each topic, there will be short summaries of cases, arranged chronologically. If a case interests you, you can find the complete decision in the state or regional reporter by using the case citation.

The digests have a handy feature: the key number system. All of the digests use the same headings to categorize cases. Topics are divided into subtopics; each subtopic is given a number. If you find a topic in the state digest that seems relevant, and want to find federal cases on the same point, look in the federal practice digest under the same key number.

HOW TO READ A CASE CITATION

There are several places where a case may be reported. If it is a case decided by the U.S. Supreme Court, you can find it in either the United States Reports (U.S.) or the Supreme Court Reporter (S.Ct.). If it is a federal case decided by a court other than the U.S. Supreme Court, it will be in either the Federal Reporter, Third Series (F.3d) or the Federal Supplement (F. Supp.).

Most states publish their own official state reports. All published state courts decisions are also included in the West Reporter System. West has divided the country into seven regions —and publishes all the decisions of the supreme and appellate state courts in the region together. These reporters are:

A. and A.2d. Atlantic Reporter (First and Second Series), which includes decisions from Connecticut, Delaware, the District of Columbia, Maine, Maryland, New Hampshire, New Jersey, Pennsylvania, Rhode Island and Vermont.

N.E. and N.E.2d. Northeastern Reporter (First and Second Series), which includes decisions from New York,* Illinois, Indiana, Massachusetts and Ohio.

N.W. and N.W.2d. Northwestern Reporter (First and Second Series), which includes decisions from Iowa, Michigan, Minnesota, Nebraska, North Dakota, South Dakota and Wisconsin.

P. and P.2d. Pacific Reporter (First and Second Series), which includes decisions from Alaska, Arizona, California,* Colorado, Hawaii, Idaho, Kansas, Montana, Nevada, New Mexico, Oklahoma, Oregon, Utah, Washington and Wyoming.

S.E. and S.E.2d. Southeastern Reporter (First and Second Series), which includes decisions from Georgia, North Carolina, South Carolina, Virginia and West Virginia.

So. and So.2d. Southern Reporter (First and Second Series), which includes decisions from Alabama, Florida, Louisiana and Mississippi.

S.W. and S.W.2d. Southwestern Reporter (First and Second Series), which includes decisions from Arkansas, Kentucky, Missouri, Tennessee and Texas.

A case citation will give you the names of the people or companies on each side of a case, the volume of the reporter in which the case can be found, the page number on which it begins and the year in which the case was decided. For example:

Thoreson v. Penthouse Int'l, 563 N.Y.S.2d 968 (1990)

Thoreson and Penthouse are the names of the parties having the legal dispute. The case is reported in volume 563 of the New York Supplement, Second Series, beginning on page 968; the court issued the decision in 1990.

---

* All California appellate decisions are published in a separate volume, the California Reporter (Cal. Rptr.) and all decisions from New York appellate courts are published in a separate volume, New York Supplement (N.Y.S.).

Employment law reporters. Perhaps the best way to find cases is through one of two specialized legal publications that gather both state and federal cases on employment law issues:

- Fair Employment Practices Cases (Fair Empl. Prac. Cas.) published by the Bureau of National Affairs, and

- Employment Practices Decisions (Empl. Prac. Dec.) published by Commerce Clearing House.

To use these publications, look in the index volumes under Sexual Harassment—and glance through for specific topics that interest you. You might try: Investigation, Retaliation, Employer Liability, State Law Claims. Then use the case citations listed to look for relevant court decisions in the reporter volumes.

Finding similar cases. Once you find a case that seems relevant to your situation, you can determine if there are more by using a publication called Shepard's Citations. Shepard's collects and lists every reference to a particular case. In other words, you can look up any case—state or federal—in the Shepard's volumes, and get a list of every case decided after it that has mentioned your case. This is very valuable for finding cases on the same subject, as well as for determining whether the original case you found has been influential or discredited.

d. Treatises

There are several books—sometimes called treatises—that cover sexual harassment. The drawbacks of most treatises is that nearly all of them are written by and for lawyers—with little effort made to translate legalese into English. Also, these books oftentimes devote many pages to lawyerly concerns, such as how to plead and prove picayune points of law. Still, these volumes will often provide you with helpful background information on sexual harassment—and will also often lead you to cases that pertain to your situation. When using a legal treatise, be sure to check the back inside cover; most publishers update the books periodically by issuing pocket parts, bound pamphlets noting changes and additions to the text.

Most libraries will have some legal treatises on sexual harassment or more general works on sex discrimination or employment discrimination that contain discussions of harassment issues.

Because legal books and publishers come and go at alarming rates these days, it is impossible to name the best and brightest titles available. Your best bet may be to plead for human intervention: Ask the law librarian for assistance in finding the most suitable tome.

e. Law review articles

There are also many law review articles on sexual harassment. Law reviews are periodicals containing articles written by lawyers, law professors and law students— usually covering a unique or evolving legal topic. Since sexual harassment is of great current interest, you'll find lots of articles about it. The inside joke about law review articles is that they're made up mostly of footnotes. While annoying to many readers, these footnotes—which contain references (citations) to other relevant cases, statutes and articles—can be goldmines for researchers. Look especially for articles that are published in law reviews from schools in your state, since these will be most likely to discuss your state's FEP law and court decisions.

There are two tools in every law library that can help you find law review articles on topics that interest you: the Current Law Index and the Index to Legal Periodicals. These volumes are published annually, except for the most recent listings, which are published every month. Both list articles by subject, by author and by the cases and statutes referred to in the article. If you don't have a case name or a specific statute in mind to guide you, turn to Sexual Harassment or Sex Discrimination in the index and peruse the listings of articles there.

HOW TO READ LAW REVIEW CITATIONS

Both the Current Law Index and the Index to Legal Periodicals will give you the author, title and citations of law review articles. The citations will give the title of the publication and the volume and page numbers of the articles you want to look at. For example, if you look under the main heading Sexual Harassment, you will see a listing for David Benjamin Oppenheimer's article "Exacerbating the Exasperating: Title VII Liability of Employers for Sexual Harassment Committed by Their Supervisors." The citation reads:

81 Cornell L. Rev. 66 (1995)

This article can be found in volume 81 of the Cornell Law Review, beginning on page 66; 1995 is the year of publication. If you have trouble deciphering the law review names, check the listing of abbreviations in the index—or ask a law librarian for help.

2. Online Resources

Many readers have discovered the wildly varied and rich resource known as the Internet, and it is only a matter of time before even the most stubborn technophobe will be drawn into its Web. There are many sites that can be useful to you in researching a sexual harassment question. These sites are not a substitute for a law library; nothing on the Internet is as complete and systematic as a library. But they may have just what you are looking for—and they certainly are convenient.

A passel of sites have sprung up that are maintained by lawyers attempting to snare clients. Approach them with the same caution that you approach other types of lawyer solicitations. (See Section B.) For now, your best use of a Web site may be a therapeutic one: it can provide a place for you to chat about your situation, and remain anonymous if you wish.

A few sites also offer interesting articles and studies on harassment, substantive information that may fill a void in your research. These are a few of the best:

- **Equal Employment Opportunity Commission**
  http://www.eeoc.gov/

  This site summarizes a few relevant topics: Facts About Employment Discrimination, Filing a Charge, Enforcement and Litigation. You will likely have to wade through a thicket of legalese to get the information you need here. But there's something reassuring about getting the word directly from the horse's mouth.

- **National Organization for Women**
  http://www.now.org/Issues/harass/

  This site contains NOW's Issue Report on Sexual Harassment in addition to a number of articles on current sexual harassment issues.

- **9to5. What Every Working Woman Needs to Know**
  http://www.cs.utk.edu/~bartley/other/9to5.html

  A pioneer in giving advice about an array of sexual harassment issues, this nonprofit group runs a site that also gives some substantive steering on what you can do about them—along with information on how to become a 9to5 member.

- **American Psychological Association. Sexual Harassment Myths and Realties**
  http://www.apa.org/pubinfo/harass.html

  Most interesting is this site's discussion of different types of sexual harassment—from gender harassment to sexual imposition. It includes a thorough explanation of the possible psychological effects harassment may have on workers.

- **Work Doctor—Employee Advocates**
  http://www.workdoctor.com

  Offers candid advice for dealing with bothersome workplace behavior that doesn't quite rise to the level of a legal infraction: bullying, power plays, other displays of insecurity. Includes an e-mail advice column and timely tips for bullybusting.

- **The Legal Information Institute at Cornell Law School**
  http://fatty.law.cornell.edu/topics/employment_discrimination.html

  Provides information about discrimination in the workplace, including relevant codes and regulations.

- **The Sexual Harassment Site**
  http://www.vix.com/pub/men/harass/harass.html

  Offers articles and other materials on sexual harassment, including relevant laws and perspectives on court opinions. ■

Appendix

Sexual Harassment Resources

HOW TO USE THESE LISTINGS

These organizations can give you additional information or assistance on sexual harassment. Some groups offer a wide variety of services, and others are more limited. To help you use these listings most effectively, we have organized them in two ways. First, there is a chart that shows which groups provide particular services. These services are divided into five categories:

1. Publications and written materials. Call first for price and order information, as these materials are rarely free.

2. Sexual harassment telephone counseling and hotlines for advice on your particular situation.

3. Support groups or in-person counseling for women who have been sexually harassed.

4. Attorney referrals—if you want to consult a lawyer, these groups will give you names of attorneys in your area. Note that a referral is not necessarily a recommendation. Some referral services are really just like advertising—if the attorney pays, he or she will be listed. Be sure to ask how attorneys are chosen for referrals, and whether they have experience in sexual harassment cases.

5. Workplace training resources, including on-site training programs and written and video training materials. These can be very expensive. Ask first for a catalog and price list.

We have also included an alphabetical listing of organizations on the chart, including their addresses and telephone numbers, and a brief description of their work. A few groups listed here are not included in our chart because their services are not easily reduced to a chart format.

Some organizations restrict their services to their members or to a limited geographic area, and we have indicated these limitations in our listings. However, some groups may have additional restrictions that don't appear here, so be sure to ask whether you're eligible to use their services.

Unions

Many unions and groups for union members are especially active in the fight against sexual harassment. We have listed several larger unions and union organizations here, but this list is by no means exhaustive. Contact your local to find out if they offer any special services or guidance. Also, the Coalition for Labor Union Women, listed below, is an excellent resource.

Other Sources of Help

Don't forget the Equal Employment Opportunity Commission (EEOC) and your state or local Fair Employment Practices (FEP) agency. Many will send you written materials on sexual harassment, and can provide information on local training programs, support groups and attorneys. For the address and telephone number of the EEOC office nearest you, see Chapter 6. For the address and telephone number of your state FEP office, see Chapter 7.

Some states and larger cities also have a Commission on the Status of Women, or a state or local agency dealing specifically with women's issues. The services these groups provide range from referrals to local women's rights groups, to advice and counseling, to legal referrals. Check your phone book to see if there is such a group in your area.

Finally, some law schools have clinics that deal with women's rights or employment law. These clinics are usually staffed by students, who are assisted by experienced attorneys. Many provide in-person or telephone counseling and legal advice, and some will even represent you in court. Their services are low-cost, often free. A few of these clinics are listed here. Call law schools in your area and ask if they have such a clinic.

SPECIAL MENTION: 9TO5

One group is doing so much to end sexual harassment that it deserves special mention. Be sure to see the writeup for 9to5, National Association for Working Women, which has been fighting to end sexual harassment since the early 1970s.

Resources at a Glance

	publications	telephone counseling	support groups	attorney referrals	training
AFL-CIO: Union Privilege				•	
Alexander Hamilton Institute	•				•
American Bar Association (ABA)	•			•	
American Civil Liberties Union (ACLU)		•		•	
American Federation of State, County and Municipal Employees (AFSCME)	•				•
American Federation of Teachers (AFT)	•				
American Psychological Association	•				
American Society for Training and Development					•
Asian-American Legal Defense and Education Fund		•		•	
Association for Union Democracy	•	•	•	•	
Bureau of National Affairs (BNA) Communications	•				•
Business and Legal Reports	•				•
Business and Professional Women/USA	•				
Center for Women Policy Studies	•				
Center for Working Life			•		•
Coalition of Labor Union Women (CLUW)	•			•	
College and University Personnel Association	•				•
Commerce Clearing House	•				•
Communications Workers of America	•				•
Coronet MTI Film and Video					•
Equal Rights Advocates		•		•	

	publications	telephone counseling	support groups	attorney referrals	training
Federally Employed Women (FEW)	•				
Feminist Majority Foundation	•	•			
Institute for Women and Work	•				•
National Association for Women in Education	•				
National Council for Research on Women	•				
National Education Association (NEA)	•				•
National Employment Lawyers Association				•	
National Lawyers Guild				•	
National Resource Center for Consumers of Legal Services		•			•
9to5, National Association of Working Women	•	•	•	•	•
NOW Legal Defense and Education Fund	•			•	
Pacific Resource Development Group	•				•
Society for Human Resource Management	•				•
Tele-Lawyer		•			
United Auto Workers Union (UAW)	•				•
U.S. Department of Labor, Women's Bureau	•				
Wider Opportunities for Women (WOW)	•				•
Women Employed Institute	•	•		•	•
Women's Alliance for Job Equity (WAJE)			•	•	•
Women's Legal Defense Fund	•				
Women's Rights Litigation Clinic	•	•			
Workers' Rights Clinic		•			

List of Organizations

AFL-CIO: Union Privilege

1444 I Street, NW, 8th Floor
Washington, DC 20005
(202) 293-5330
Nationwide legal services plan free to most
members of AFL-CIO. Initial consultation
and follow-up are free, and other attorney's
fees are discounted 30%. Many locals also
have their own legal services plan.

Alexander Hamilton Institute

70 Hilltop Road
Ramsey, NJ 07446
(800) 879-2441
Institute specializing in human resource
management issues, publishes booklet for
managers on how to prevent sexual
harassment, and materials on personnel
training.

American Arbitration Association

140 West 51st Street
New York, NY 10020
(212) 484-4000
National nonprofit organization offering
mediation and arbitration services through
local offices across the country. Also
provides fact-finding teams for neutral
investigations of workplace disputes,
including sexual harassment.

American Association of University Women Legal Advocacy Fund

1111 16th Street, NW
Washington, DC 20036
(202) 785-7700
TDD (202) 785-7777
Fax (202) 872-1425
Internet: http://www.aauw.org
Fund sexual harassment cases brought by
university women students, faculty and staff
against institutions of higher education.

American Bar Association (ABA)

750 North Lakeshore Drive
Chicago, IL 60611
(312) 988-5555
Booklet listing local lawyer referral services
by state and county. Many state bar associations will also give legal referrals.

American Civil Liberties Union (ACLU)

Internet: http://aclu.org
Legal advice and counseling, as well as
attorney referrals provided by local offices
throughout the country. Contact your state
ACLU office.

American Federation of State, County and Municipal Employees (AFSCME)

1625 L Street, NW
Washington, DC 20036
(202) 429-1000
Fax (202) 429-1293
Booklet available to state and local union
members of AFSCME on how to stop sexual
harassment. Training workshops for
AFSCME members.

American Federation of Teachers (AFT)

Human Rights Department
555 New Jersey Avenue, NW
Washington, DC 20001
(202) 879-4400
Fax (202) 879-4545
Internet: http://www.aft.org
Booklet on sexual harassment, available
for $5

American Psychological Association

750 1st Street, NE
Washington, DC 20002
(202) 336-5500
Fax (202) 336-6-69
Internet: http://apa.org
Referrals to state and local associations that
provide names of specialists who deal with
the psychological problems associated with
sexual harassment. Also pamphlets on how
to choose a therapist.

American Society for Training and Development

1640 King Street
Alexandria, VA 22313
(703) 683-8100
Fax (703) 683-8103
Internet: http://www.astd.org
National organization of professional
workplace trainers, provides information
and referral services on sexual harassment
training.

Asian-American Legal Defense and Education Fund

99 Hudson Street, 12th Floor
New York, NY 10013
(212) 966-5932
Legal advice and attorney referrals for
Asians and Asian-Americans.

Association for Union Democracy

Women's Project
500 State Street
Brooklyn, NY 11217
(718) 855-6650
Nationwide attorney referrals, legal advice,
counseling and organizational assistance for
women in unions. Also training, workshops
and educational programs on sexual
harassment. Also publishes "Manual for
Survival for Women in Nontraditional
Employment" and "Model Sexual Harassment Policy and Procedures for Unions."

Bureau of National Affairs (BNA) Communications

9439 Key West Avenue
Rockville, MD 20850
(800) 233-6067
Books, special reports, audio-video materials
and training programs on sexual harassment.

Business and Legal Reports

39 Academy Street
Madison, CT 06443
(203) 245-7448
Handbooks, video and other training
materials on sexual harassment.

Business and Professional Women/USA

2012 Massachusetts Avenue, NW
Washington, DC 20036
(202) 293-1100
Fax (202) 861-0298
National membership organization of working
women in over 3,000 local chapters, publishes
position paper on sexual harassment.

Center for Women Policy Studies

1211 Connecticut Avenue. NW, Suite 312
Washington, DC 20036
(202) 872-1770
Fax (202) 296-8962
E-mail: HN4066@handsnet.org
Written materials on sexual harassment.

Center for Working Life

3814 SE Martins Street
Portland, OR 97202
(503) 788-6016
National nonprofit organization providing
workshops and sexual harassment training
in the workplace. Support groups for
women who have been sexually harassed,
including a group specifically for blue-collar
women workers. Short-term counseling for
women who have been sexually harassed.

Coalition of Labor Union Women (CLUW)

1126 16th Street, NW, #104
Washington, DC 20036
(202) 446-4610
Fax (202) 776-0537
National organization with 75 local chapters,
provides education on sexual harassment,
organizes conferences and workshops,
testifies and lobbies for legislation, supports
strikes and boycotts, and publishes a
bimonthly newsletter and other written
materials for union women. Referrals to
attorneys and legal rights groups for union
workers. Sample contract language, resolutions and policies on sexual harassment.

College and University Personnel Association

1233 20th Street, NW
Washington, DC 20036
(202) 429-0311
Book on sexual harassment in business,
industry and education, and a video on
sexual harassment in higher education.

Commerce Clearing House

4025 West Peterson Avenue
Chicago, IL 60646
(312) 866-6000
(800) 835-5224
Training manual for managers and supervisors.

Communications Workers of America

501 3rd Street, NW
Washington, DC 20001
(202) 434-1100
Fax (202) 434-1279
Internal training for union members and staff.
Written materials on sexual harassment.

Equal Rights Advocates

1663 Mission Street, Suite 550
San Francisco, CA 94103
(415) 621-0672 (General information)
(415) 621-0505 (Advice and counseling
hotline)
Legal advice and counseling, in both English
and Spanish. Referrals to women's groups
nationwide.

Federally Employed Women (FEW)

1400 Eye Street, NW, Suite 425
Washington, DC 20005
(202) 898-0994
Fax (202) 898-0998
Internet: Http://few.org
National nonprofit membership organization
of federally employed women with chapters
throughout the United States. Written
materials on how federal workers can stop
sexual harassment, find and select an EEO
attorney and go to court.

Feminist Majority Foundation

1600 Wilson Boulevard
Arlington, VA 22209
(703) 522-2214 (General information)
(703) 522-2501 (Sexual harassment hotline)
Hotline gives feminist strategies for dealing with sexual harassment and advice on how to file a claim and deal with the EEOC. Free special report on sexual harassment also available.

Institute for Women and Work

School of Industrial and Labor Relations
Cornell University
15 East 26th Street, 4th Floor
New York, NY 10010
(212) 340-2812
Bibliography of sexual harassment resource materials. Occasional training seminars on sexual harassment, primarily for union members.

9to5, National Association of Working Women

614 Superior Avenue, NW,
Cleveland, OH 44113
(216) 566-9308 (General information)
(800) 522-0925 (Hotline)
National nonprofit membership organization for American office workers with local chapters throughout the country. Toll-free confidential telephone hotline, staffed by trained job counselors, provides information and referrals on how to deal with sexual harassment and other problems on the job. Books and reports on sexual harassment, available at a discount to members. Members also get legal referrals to attorneys specializing in sexual harassment. Newsletter published five times a year. Some 9to5 local chapters offer sexual harassment support groups and referrals to training resources.

National Association for Women in Education

1325 18th Street, NW, Suite 210
Washington, DC 20036
(202) 659-9330
Fax (202) 457-0946
E-mail: nawe@clark.net
Written materials on sexual harassment on college campuses.

National Council for Research on Women

Sexual Harassment Information Project
530 Broadway, 10th Floor
New York, NY 10012
(212) 274-0730
Coalition of 75 centers and organizations that support and conduct feminist research, policy analysis and educational programs.

National Education Association (NEA)

Human and Civil Rights Department
1201 16th Street, NW
Washington, DC 20036
(202) 833-4000
Fax (202) 822-7292
Training, videos and brochures on sexual harassment, available to union members only. Contact local or state NEA office for more information.

National Employment Lawyers Association

600 Harrison Street, Suite 535
San Francisco, CA 94107
(415) 227-4655
National directory of 1,100 employment law attorneys, including brief descriptions of their practices. Send self-addressed stamped envelope for more information.

National Lawyers Guild

Anti-Sexism Committee
131 George Street
San Jose, CA 95110
(408) 292-0174
Referrals to experienced attorneys who are members of the Guild, an association of progressive attorneys.

NOW Legal Defense and Education Fund

99 Hudson Street, 12th Floor
New York, NY 10013
(212) 925-6635
Legal resource kit on sexual harassment that is specifically geared towards attorneys, plus other publications on sexual harassment.

National Resource Center for Consumers of Legal Services

P.O. Box 340
Gloucester, VA 23061
(804) 693-9330
Nationwide legal referrals to attorneys experienced in sexual harassment cases. Publishes materials on how to choose a lawyer.

National Women's Law Center

11 Dupont Circle, NW, Suite 800
Washington, DC 20036
(202) 588 5100
Fax (202) 588-5185
National nonprofit organization focuses on policy areas important to women including sexual harassment. Research and testimony on sexual harassment.

National Women's Political Caucus

1211 Connecticut Avenue, NW, #425
Washington, DC 20036
(202) 898-1100
Fax (202) 785-3605
Internet: http://www.feminist.com.nwpc
Model sexual harassment policy for congressional members, and honor roll of members of Congress who have adopted sexual harassment policies.

Pacific Resource Development Group

4044 NE 58th
Seattle, WA 98105
(206) 782-7015
(800) 767-3062
Employee handbooks and videotape training package on sexual harassment, monthly newsletter and training manuals for managers. In-house training workshops and presentations.

Society for Human Resource Management

606 North Washington Street
Alexandria, VA 22314
(703) 548-3440
Membership organization for human resources managers. Written information for members, including advice on developing sexual harassment policy. Video training program.

Tele-Lawyer

P.O. Box 110
Huntington Beach, CA 92648
(800) 835-3529
Legal advice over the phone at a reasonable per-minute charge. Staff lawyers may also review documents, such as employment contracts and do legal research.

United Auto Workers Union (UAW)

8000 East Jefferson
Detroit, MI 48214
(313) 926-5212
Internet: http://uaw.org
Written and video training materials and
workshops for UAW and other union
members.

U.S. Department of Labor, Women's Bureau

200 Constitution Avenue, NW
Washington, DC 20210
(202) 219-6659
Fax (202) 219-5529
Internet: http://www.dol/wb/welcome
Detailed list of sexual harassment resources,
including organizations, training materials,
court cases and articles.

Wider Opportunities for Women (WOW)

815 15th Street NW, Suite 916
Washington, DC 20005
(202) 638-3143
Fax (202) 638-4885
National nonprofit organization, primarily
focusing on women in nontraditional
employment. Reports and materials on
sexual harassment. Consulting and training
services for employers.

Women's Alliance for Job Equity (WAJE)

1422 Chestnut Street, Suite 1100
Philadelphia, PA 19102
(215) 561-1873
Information and public education seminars
in Philadelphia area. Regular job problem
meetings, peer support program and legal
referrals for WAJE members, primarily
women working in nonmanagement jobs.
On-site training program for local
employers.

Women Employed Institute

22 West Monroe, Suite 1400
Chicago, IL 60603
(312) 782-3902
Membership organization providing telephone counseling on sexual harassment in
Chicago area. Local attorney referrals.
Factsheet on sexual harassment. Sexual
harassment prevention training for area
employers.

Women's Legal Defense Fund

1875 Connecticut Ave., NW, Suite 710
Washington, DC 20009
(202) 986-2600
Fax (202) 986-2539
E-mail: info@wldf.org
National nonprofit membership organization
providing public education, written information, advocacy and targeted litigation on
sexual harassment.

Women's Rights Litigation Clinic

Rutgers University Law School
15 Washington Street
Newark, NJ 07102
(973) 353-5637
Legal advice and counseling, written
materials on sexual harassment, and
technical legal support in some cases.

Workers' Rights Clinic

Rotates among several locations. Call for
more information.
(415) 864-8208
Legal clinic for low income workers in the
San Francisco Bay Area with employment
problems, including sexual harassment.
Telephone and in-person legal advice and
counseling. ■

Index